China Briefing, 1990

中国

China Briefing, 1990

edited by
Anthony J. Kane

Published in cooperation with the
China Council of The Asia Society

Westview Press
Boulder, San Francisco, & Oxford

Published in 1990 in the United States of America by Westview Press, Inc., 5500 Central Avenue, Boulder, Colorado 80301, and in the United Kingdom by Westview Press, Inc., 36 Lonsdale Road, Summertown, Oxford OX2 7EW

Library of Congress ISSN: 0740-8005
ISBN 0-8133-8011-1
ISBN 0-8133-8012-X (pbk.)

Printed and bound in the United States of America

The paper used in this publication meets the requirements of the American National Standard for Permanence of Paper for Printed Library Materials Z39.48-1984.

10 9 8 7 6 5 4 3 2 1

Contents

Preface vii
Map of the People's Republic of China ix

Introduction: Reunderstanding China 1
ANTHONY J. KANE

1. **A Year of Great Significance** 9
KENNETH LIEBERTHAL

2. **The Prospects for China's Economic Reforms** 25
DWIGHT H. PERKINS

3. **The Social Sources of the Student Demonstrations** 47
MARTIN KING WHYTE

4. **China's Foreign Relations after 40 Years** 65
ALLEN S. WHITING

5. **The Crisis of Culture** 83
LEO OU-FAN LEE

6. **One Country, Two Systems: The Future of Hong Kong** 107
FRANK CHING

7. **The Dragon and the Snow Lion: The Tibet Question** 129
MELVYN C. GOLDSTEIN

1989: A Chronology 169
Glossary 189
Appendix A: Changes in the Chinese Leadership 196
Appendix B: Books and Articles on Tiananmen 198
Suggestions for Further Reading 201
About the Contributors 205
Index 207

Preface

When the tanks rolled into Tiananmen Square early in the morning of June 4, 1989, they crushed an unknown number of demonstrators and the once-vibrant student movement for which they stood. They also crushed the career of Chinese Communist Party General Secretary Zhao Ziyang and the hopes of innumerable reform-minded workers in public agencies and private think tanks whom Zhao had charged with restructuring China's political and economic system. More tragic still, they crushed the hopes of Chinese everywhere who believed in the leadership's commitment to replacing the rule of men with the rule of law. The excitement of events in Eastern Europe in the fall, which made all things seem possible, made the taste of China's increasingly repressive authoritarianism more bitter still.

There is an old saw in the China field: if you visit China for a week you can write a book; after a month you can write an article; and after a year you cannot write anything at all. The contributors to *China Briefing, 1990* have spent many years studying China and have written many books, but 1989 was the kind of year that puts the most discerning analyst to the test. For many professional and amateur China watchers the crackdown that began June 4th crushed a growing hope that in the wake of the inexplicable madness of the Cultural Revolution, China was once again embarked on the kind of stable modernization process its leaders claimed to prefer. It is the task of this book to explain what went wrong and provide some understanding of what might come next.

China Briefing, 1990 continues the tradition of its predecessors by analyzing the key events and trends in Chinese affairs over the course of the previous year. However, many people will be chronicling and analyzing the dramatic events of 1989; a partial listing of those efforts already in print appears at the end of this volume. We have taken a somewhat different approach, asking the authors of our annual chapters on politics, economics, culture, and foreign relations to answer a broader question than simply "what happened" in 1989. We have asked each author to ponder how the events of the past year fit into the longer history of the People's Republic of China, which observed the 40th anniversary of its founding on October 1, 1989. Was 1989 a watershed year, whose events sharply reversed China's course, or will those events prove to have been relatively minor disruptions of longer-term trends? What broader systemic issues were raised or brought into sharper focus in the course of that less-than-celebratory anniversary year?

To help round out the picture, we have also addressed these questions in a chapter on society. And we have added special chapters on Hong Kong, which was dramatically affected by the year's events, and Tibet, which continues to cause problems for Beijing both domestically and in its relations with the rest of the world.

China Briefing is prepared annually by the China Council, a program of The Asia Society's Education and Contemporary Affairs Division. The division also produces an annual *India Briefing*, and, for the first time this year, a *Korea Briefing*. The Asia Society is a nonprofit, nonpartisan educational organization committed to increasing understanding of Asia and of U.S.–Asian relations through a nationwide program of cultural and informational events and publications.

The editor wishes to thank the staff of the Education and Contemporary Affairs Division who work so hard to bring this series to press on a very tight schedule: particularly Senior Editor Deborah Field Washburn and Publications Assistant Andrea Sokerka. Ellen Lenson prepared the chronology, the glossary, and the appendix, with help from Dorothy Grant. Salma Hasan Ali and Puneet Talwar provided excellent research assistance and editorial suggestions. Patricia Farr was extremely helpful in the final copyediting of the manuscript.

Anthony J. Kane

Source: U.S. Department of State, "Background Notes: China," December 1983.

Introduction: Reunderstanding China

Anthony J. Kane

Tiananmen Square was created to witness history, and it has witnessed a lot. It spreads out before the Gate of Heavenly Peace, entrance to the ancient Forbidden City and the platform from which Mao Zedong proclaimed the founding of the People's Republic of China on October 1, 1949. In 1966 Chairman Mao used the square to rally millions of Red Guards and launch his Great Proletarian Cultural Revolution. And it was there nearly ten years later, on April 5, 1976, that demonstrators mourned the death of Premier Zhou Enlai and initiated a movement that brought the Cultural Revolution to an end.

For many years to come, however, Tiananmen will be associated with the tragic events of June 4, 1989, when six weeks of often joyous demonstrations for democracy came to a brutal and bloody end. Now it is not just millions of Chinese but hundreds of millions of people around the world who think of Tiananmen and mourn.

A year later, many of those who were there and many more who watched from afar are still struggling to understand how things could have gone so terribly wrong. The painful scars left by the chaos and madness of the Cultural Revolution were thought to be healing after a decade of reform, reform that was supposed to bring peace and prosperity back to China and to the world around it. Now many of the old wounds have opened once again, and no one seems to know how to stop the bleeding.

It is difficult to remember what the world was like when 1989 began. China was undergoing a difficult economic retrenchment program following a serious bout with inflation and other problems produced by an overheated economy. Nevertheless, the spirit of reform was pervasive in free markets and tiny independent enterprises around the nation. Soviet leader Mikhail Gorbachev was scheduled to make a pilgrimage to Beijing, hat in hand it seemed at the time, after giving in on all of the "three obstacles" (as defined by the Chinese) to improved Sino-Soviet relations: troops on the Sino-Soviet border, the

Soviet presence in Afghanistan, and Soviet support for the Vietnamese in Cambodia. U.S. President George Bush rushed to get to Beijing first, and when the Chinese blocked dissident astrophysicist Fang Lizhi from attending an American-hosted banquet the president refused to let it upset his relationship with his good friend Deng Xiaoping.

This is not to say that trouble was not expected, but even when expected, trouble came in unexpected ways. Plans to commemorate the 70th anniversary of the May Fourth Movement were short-circuited by the unexpected death of former Chinese Communist Party (CCP) general secretary Hu Yaobang on April 15. In spontaneous tribute to the man who had been forced from office for not suppressing the pro-democracy demonstrations of December 1986, tens of thousands of people, mostly students, came to Tiananmen Square to mourn both the man and the movement.

When the government threatened to drive the mourners from the square, the students organized, and then the unthinkable happened. Reacting to rumors that troops were about to suppress the demonstrations, people took to the streets in even greater numbers (more than 100,000 on April 21), and the troops backed away. An angry editorial in the April 26 edition of the CCP organ *People's Daily* virtually accusing the students of sedition merely served to fan the flames of resistance among growing numbers of students and others now flush with the taste of victory.

By the time Gorbachev arrived in Beijing the demonstrators numbered in the millions, and they included people from all walks of life. Demonstrations of some kind were reported in at least 80 other cities and towns. When Gorbachev left the capital the authorities declared martial law, but it was more than two weeks before the order was enforced. Then it was enforced with a brutality that shocked the nation; concerns were raised by party members and even some in the army itself. We may never know how many died: there are no official figures for military, much less civilian, casualties.

It has been said that the leadership's brutality on June 4 and its repressiveness since that time offer proof that nothing has really changed in China. It is the consensus of the authors in this volume that, on the whole, quite a bit has changed. True, Kenneth Lieberthal remarks in his chapter on politics that "the frequently used phrase 'the evolution of China' is somewhat misleading" because the changes that have occurred "do not appear to have brought the country significantly closer to establishing the essential conditions for stable national government." But he also acknowledges that China has changed a great deal in other respects: "demographically, economically, socially, and in other ways." Dwight Perkins notes that in economic terms, at least, China has changed beyond the recognition of its aging leadership, many of whom see a country "rooted in conditions of a backward, near subsistence rural economy" that simply no longer exists.

Where these two analyses, and others in the book, converge is in their description of a nation changing much faster than the people who rule it. What Lieberthal sees as a failure to establish the conditions for stable government is a failure of leadership, and that failure comes precisely from the inability of the octogenarians who seized power on June 4 to acknowledge that China needs new leaders whose vision is focused on the nation's future needs, not its past revolutionary glories.

One might well ask how a leadership so out of touch with the needs and desires of its own people survived the crisis of 1989 and continues to maintain its grip in 1990. The simple answer to that question lies in the leadership's willingness to use brute force and intimidation, but there are other factors as well, factors well analyzed in the pages of this book. Martin Whyte, for example, makes it clear that while the impulse for reform was powerful, a large majority of the Chinese population was either satisfied with the pace of reform or felt the reforms had already gone too far. In the countryside, especially, China's conservative leadership had a base of support that had been strengthened by the success of the reform movement in improving people's lives.

This analysis is underscored by Perkins in his answer to the question, Did reform cause Tiananmen? He argues that while reform produced many new problems, it also solved important problems and thereby ensured the support of those who benefited from it.

If this is true, then one might turn around and ask whether Zhao Ziyang and his reformist minions were in fact even more isolated than the octogenarians who removed them from power. If their constituency was a small minority, those who felt that reform had not gone far enough, then is the current leadership not justified in claiming to have ousted a few troublemakers in the name of the Chinese masses?

The answer suggested in the pages of *China Briefing, 1990* is that, however isolated the reformers had become and whatever doubts had been raised in people's minds about the continued viability of the reform economy, there is nothing in the record of the post-June 4 leadership to suggest that the conservatives are either more popular or more able to solve the many problems that remain. As Whyte argues, the struggle of last spring was not essentially between those who believed that reform had gone too far and those who thought it had not gone far enough. Rather it was a crisis precipitated by a forced alliance between these two groups against a leadership that seemed to be increasingly unable to satisfy either constituency. Retrenchment policies introduced in September 1988 may well have been necessary in the face of rapidly rising prices, but by the spring of 1989 it was clear that other fundamental problems remained unsolved. Premier Li Peng proved to be no more effective than Zhao Ziyang had been in eliminating corruption or addressing other inequities in the system, and the slow growth brought on by the conservatives' retrenchment policies had not won fans for the leadership.

For better or for worse, the events of 1989 seem to have helped crystallize the differences between the more adventurist reform policies represented by Zhao Ziyang and the more conservative approach represented by Li Peng. (Although Deng Xiaoping has designated new CCP General Secretary Jiang Zemin the "core" of the leadership, nobody inside or outside of China seems to believe that Jiang is truly in charge.) While Zhao was a frequent target of the demonstrators in late April and early May, by the time martial law was declared on May 20 he had become their hero. Just as Hu Yaobang became increasingly popular after his fall from power and was idealized as a hero of the Democracy Movement following his death, Zhao's tearful farewell to the demonstrators on May 19 served to galvanize support behind him. Thus the current leadership, while stripping Zhao of his party posts and keeping him from public view, has been unable to expel him from the party or to bring charges against him (despite an official ongoing "investigation"). To the extent that the events of last spring became an accelerated struggle between would-be successors to Deng Xiaoping, that struggle is far from over, even if it has moved once again behind the scenes.

If the only leaders in China who are popular are those who have fallen from official grace, is it possible for anyone to succeed? What will it take to modernize China and to restore it to the status its people expect, that of a great world power? These are the questions facing all Chinese, both leaders and led, in the wake of last year's tragic events. But they are not new questions; they have been asked repeatedly in the course of China's many 20th-century revolutions. As Leo Lee's chapter reveals, they are questions that were raised 70 years ago in China's original "cultural revolution," the May Fourth Movement, and they are questions many of China's more courageous intellectuals were raising again in the 1980s. In the process of "cultural self-reflection" that Lee describes, China's intellectuals are asking now, as they did in 1919, whether the political crisis China faces might not have deep cultural roots requiring a massive rethinking of past experience, current practice, and future needs.

The difference between 1919 and 1989, however, is that whereas 70 years ago Marxism provided radical new answers to China's problems, now it is part of the tradition being questioned. Perhaps the greatest weakness of the current leadership is not its inability to solve the many problems China faces today, but its unwillingness to allow these probing questions to be asked. It is in this respect that the leadership most closely resembles the leftists who were in power during the Cultural Revolution. Mao Zedong's fear of losing control of the revolution led him to destroy its strongest institution, the Chinese Communist Party. Deng Xiaoping fell prey to the same fear when he joined other retired rulers in overriding the established political structure to resolve the crisis created by the Tiananmen Square demonstrations. In destroying a process of institutionalization he had nurtured over ten years of reform, Deng also destroyed what might well have been his greatest legacy.

In Lieberthal's analysis, failure to replace personalized rule with enduring political institutions is half of the core agenda of issues on which China has failed to progress in its struggle for modernization. The other half of that agenda pertains to "the quest to shape a national consensus on China's posture toward the world." Allen Whiting sees cause for pride in China's record on foreign relations, noting that "China had never been more secure in this century" than it was in 1989. But although China had never been less vulnerable to foreign *attack*, Whiting agrees with Lieberthal that its leaders seemed to feel increasingly (one might almost say irrationally) afraid of foreign *influence*, claiming the need for "a fine mesh screen to keep out the 'worms, flies, and mosquitoes' whose dangerous infections had poisoned the body politic."

One major source of these "foreign" influences, of course, is not the West but a part of China itself: Hong Kong. Set to be returned by the British to Chinese control in 1997, Hong Kong is a modern society that the leadership both covets for its wealth and fears for what it suggests about China's future. In attempting to reassert its control over the British colony, Beijing hopes to avoid destroying one of the most vibrant of East Asia's newly industrializing economies, an economy that could potentially be a boon to China's own. But China's communist leaders have always been concerned about the noneconomic impact this paragon of capitalism would have on the People's Republic, and in 1989 that concern turned to outright fear. Freelance journalist and Hong Kong resident Frank Ching details the three-way dance between Hong Kong, Beijing, and London as the leaders of all three societies try to figure out how to make the "one country, two systems" formula work.

China's leaders now admonish Hong Kong not to spread capitalism to the mainland, but they continue to offer some degree of autonomy by allowing the territory to remain a "special administrative region" after 1997. However, Beijing's record for tolerating autonomy within China's borders has not been good, as demonstrated by anthropologist Melvyn Goldstein in his chapter on Tibet. Believing it had righted the wrongs Tibetans suffered in the Cultural Revolution, when thousands of temples were destroyed by Red Guards, China's reformist leadership reacted angrily when demonstrations erupted demanding more autonomy from China in the name of preserving the Tibetan way of life. Martial law was declared in March 1989 in Lhasa, the Tibetan capital, after another outbreak of violence in a chain of disruptions that began in 1987.

Tibet has in fact been a particularly intractable problem for the leadership in Beijing since 1959, when the Dalai Lama, Tibet's traditional spiritual and political leader, fled to exile in Dharamsala, India. It has also been a focus of attention for human rights activists, U.S. congressmen, and others suspicious of the rapidly warming relations between Beijing and Washington. The drama of Tiananmen Square seems to have temporarily swept from many people's minds the ongoing and in many ways even more painful drama being played out in Lhasa, but the two became connected in people's minds in October when the Dalai Lama was awarded the Nobel Peace Prize. Without progress on Tibet, many critics feel, the relationship between the United States and China should never be allowed to progress too far.

As of mid-1990, those on both sides of the Pacific who have been critical of the Sino-American rapprochement of the 1970s and 1980s are getting the reassessment they had hoped for. In the fall of 1990 and again in 1992 George Bush's China policy will almost certainly be an issue. Democrats and Republicans alike have criticized the president's "softness" in response to the 1989 crackdown. Relations between Congress and the administration deteriorated through the fall of 1989 and turned to confrontation after the visit of National Security Adviser Brent Scowcroft and Deputy Secretary of State Lawrence S. Eagleburger to Beijing in December. The president won a crucial showdown in January 1990 when Congress failed to override his veto of a bill protecting the status of Chinese students in the United States, but the victory may have been a Pyrrhic one. Even Republicans who supported the president made it clear that their support stopped short of approval for his policies.

The national media have trumpeted the outrage of the American public in its reaction to events in China and to the debate in Washington. Deng Xiaoping, who had twice been named "Man of the Year" by *Time* magazine for his reformist policies, quickly turned from hero to villain, and opinion polls registered unprecedented swings from positive to negative feelings toward China. And just like in the 1950s, China scholars who dared to defend the relationship with the communist leaders have come under attack (see, for example, a March 9, 1990, column by Anthony Lewis in the *New York Times* titled "Trahison Des Clercs").

The question critics seem to be asking is why the United States could not save the Democracy Movement in China, and this is disturbingly close to that earlier question, why we "lost" China in 1949. Sino-American relations in the 1990s are likely to look a lot more like those of the '50s than those of the '80s, and that is not good news for either side. Mutual anger and recrimination across the Pacific and deep dissension in both capitals over what to do about it will not bring democracy to China. Nor will they hasten China's integration into an increasingly interdependent world as we try to work globally to save the environment, conserve resources, and limit populations.

Ironically, one place in which the chill in Sino-American relations seems to be welcome is Beijing, where the conservative leadership accuses the United States of trying to change China through a policy of "peaceful evolution." When Richard Nixon visited China in the fall of 1989, Deng Xiaoping told the former president, "Frankly speaking, the United States was involved too deeply in the turmoil and counterrevolutionary rebellion that occurred in Beijing not long ago. China was the real victim, and it is unjust to reprove China for it" (*New York Times*, November 1, 1989). One can only wonder what Deng meant his reform program to do, if it was not to transform China from the inside by a process of peaceful, evolutionary change.

Of course when Deng and others complain of an American policy that advocates "peaceful evolution," their complaints stem from a fear that China is being changed not from internal necessity but rather in response to external pressure. As *China Briefing* authors have pointed out repeatedly, Chinese leaders have been trying for over a century to preserve the essence of what it means to be Chinese while adopting some of the more useful advances introduced by the barbarians from across the seas. It is a strategy based on resisting change as much as possible, a variation on the time-honored Chinese adage that one must use the barbarians to fight the barbarians.

One problem with that strategy is that technology does not come "value free," as several authors in this volume point out. An even greater problem is that in reality China had begun to change in important ways long before the Chinese were startled into an awareness of their technological backwardness in the Opium Wars (1840–42). By 1800 change was already occurring at speeds that tested the capacity of the country's conservative leaders, both Han and Manchu, to adjust. It is for that reason that historians no longer mark the birth of modern China as 1840; the roots go far deeper. (*The Search for Modern China*, a comprehensive history by Jonathan Spence [New York: W. W. Norton, 1990] begins in 1600.) Thus the problem with attempting to preserve the Chinese essence while adopting Western methods is not just that those methods come with an essence all their own, it is that the essence of China itself has already changed dramatically. China was in some ways becoming more and more like the rest of the world—less agrarian and more commercialized, for example—even before its rulers began to equate that kind of change with Westernization. It was becoming modern. As Leo Lee indicates, even those who claim to be Westernizers in China (both historically and today) often have little real idea what the West is like. They advocate change in the name of Westernization for much the same reason that those who oppose change do so in the name of protecting China from "spiritual pollution." The West is for both sides a symbol of change itself, whether or not the content of any particular change resembles something that actually exists in the West.

One thing seems clear: whether conservatives or liberals are in power in Beijing and whether United States policy favors engagement or disengagement, China will continue to change. The current leadership in Beijing has learned this in its failed attempt to reestablish an atmosphere of fear in which neighbors inform on one another and orders are obeyed without question. That kind of passive cooperation in repression made the Cultural Revolution possible, and the Chinese people, by not cooperating this time around, are silently making it clear that China cannot go back in that direction.

Americans angry at the suppression of the Democracy Movement can take solace in the Chinese people's reaction to the repression that has followed the bloody crackdown. But our reactions must be tempered by the knowledge that while American values have had an impact on China, we are not the ones who will shape China's future. President Bush learned that lesson the hard way when he tried to soften the repression with promises of rapid reengagement. Change will come in China, but it will come at its own pace, and, most likely, in continually unexpected ways.

1
A Year of Great Significance

Kenneth Lieberthal

Many Chinese and China specialists wondered at the end of the 1970s whether the reform effort recently begun by the Deng Xiaoping leadership would survive for more than a decade. They pondered this question because the history of the People's Republic of China (PRC) had provided startling evidence of policy reversals or large-scale political instability roughly every ten years. Significantly, the events of 1989 demonstrated that ten years of reform policies and of opening the country to the outside world, while bringing dramatic changes, nevertheless had not created institutions or policy consensus that would enable the PRC to break out of this destructive decennial cycle.

Each period of disruption has resulted from two broad phenomena: first, the policies being pursued create increasingly acute problems, thus generating considerable tension; and second, the political system's long-term failure to make progress toward resolving two underlying issues, identified below, leaves the system susceptible to major political storms. The strains of the first set of problems create disputes that combine with the underlying stresses on the political system to produce dramatic consequences, including major substantive policy shifts. Thus, in the late 1950s strains created by the First Five-Year Plan combined with political flaws in the system to produce the disastrous Great Leap Forward, while the late 1960s witnessed violent political conflict among the elite as the country moved against the radical mobilization policies of the Cultural Revolution. In the late 1970s the political crisis that occurred in the wake of Mao Zedong's death produced the far-reaching reforms of the Deng era. And in 1989 the unresolved issues erupted yet again as new policies ran their course and produced new strains.

This framework of analysis suggests that the events of 1989 should be viewed through two prisms. First, the immediate problems that precipitated the mass movement that began in April 1989 and went on for seven weeks and the leadership's policy responses throughout the remainder of the year warrant scrutiny. And second, the events of the year require analysis for evidence of China's progress (or lack of progress) toward resolving the two core problems that have rankled and weakened the system over a much longer period: the investment of political power in officials rather than in offices and the lack of a national consensus on China's posture toward the world.

Substantive Policy Runs Its Course: Reform and Its Discontents

The reforms begun in 1978 sought to ignite the initiative of a disillusioned populace and channel that initiative into efforts that would serve the development of the country's economy. Broadly speaking, the reforms reduced the role of politics in people's lives, increased the role of the market in shaping economic decisions, and broadened China's exposure to the international arena. Combining appeals to individual self-interest with a retreat from active state management of the economy, the Deng leadership tried to spark an explosion of creative and efficient effort that would lift China into the ranks of the rapidly developing countries around its eastern periphery.

Deng Xiaoping's early reform policies released many of the bonds that had kept talented Chinese from working effectively. In 1979 the Chinese Communist Party (CCP) declared that it would dismantle the castelike system of class categorization that held roughly 50 million citizens in a state of permanent discrimination. Subsequent policies essentially declared that individual Chinese should have far greater personal freedom in matters of daily life—hobbies, clothing, hairstyles, recreational preferences, and so forth.

Of more fundamental importance, during 1979–84 the collective system in agriculture gave way to family-based farming, and a massive exodus of farmers from the land was not only tolerated but encouraged. New freedoms for private enterprise created a situation in which by 1988 fully 25 percent of the country's industrial production occurred outside the state sector. At the same time, the reformist leadership turned abroad to acquire foreign technology, capital, managerial skills, and worldwide market expertise.

The results of these and related initiatives were, overall, impressive. Chinese GNP and foreign trade grew rapidly, while the PRC during the early 1980s absorbed more foreign capital than did any other Third World country. Real per capita income grew at a tremendous pace, a remarkable feat for a country whose population encompasses more than 22 percent of humankind. While the actual number of foreigners in China—and of Chinese living abroad—did not reach the level of earlier periods in the 20th century, the impact of foreign ideas and styles greatly exceeded that of any previous period due to the explosion of access to television throughout China.[1]

The net effects of these changes were profound. Urbanization proceeded at remarkable speed, with some 100 million individuals shifting from rural- to urban-based remuneration between 1984 and 1986. Consumer mania gripped large segments of the Chinese population, rapid regional differentiation of wealth became evident, and large portions of the population became aware of living standards elsewhere in the country, around Asia, and in the West. All these developments produced changes in popular sentiment that, on balance, increased expectations concerning living standards, heightened the sense of individualism among many, and exacerbated jealousies over inequality and fears of unemployment.

The initial reforms focused on agriculture and on opening China to the outside world. The early rural reforms paid off handsomely, with unprecedented gains in grain production and rapidly increasing rural living standards. But the output of grain peaked at roughly 410 million metric tons in 1984. Until that time, production gains had reflected in part the removal of disincentives and structural inefficiencies in the agricultural system, but these generally were one-time gains. Since 1984, insufficient new investment for agriculture and other problems have caused output to level off, even as the population has continued to grow.

Between 1979 and 1984 the reformers trod lightly in the most complex arena—the urban industrial economy. But beginning in 1984, with a great deal of momentum having been created by the initial successes of the rural reforms, the top leaders turned their attention to making serious changes in the way the urban economy functioned. Since 1986, however, the urban reforms have, on balance, run into trouble. Components such as the dual-price system[2] have created an environment in which corruption has flourished, while other anomalies in the reform effort produced increased local protectionism and rapidly accelerating rates of inflation from 1987 to early 1989.

As a result, mass-level grievances grew substantially during the years leading up to 1989. Inflation created widespread fears and, especially in the summer of 1988, panic buying. Top-level indecision nurtured popular unease about future policies. And, perhaps most se-

[1] James Townsend, "Reflections on the Opening of China," in *Proceedings of the Four Anniversaries Conference* (Armonk, NY: M. E. Sharpe, forthcoming).

[2] This system stipulates that goods produced "on the plan" sell for a fixed (generally low) price, while those produced above plan targets sell for a higher, market-driven price.

rious, popular awareness of the abuse of power by officials and their relatives grew dramatically.

In the popular mind, a "new class" was forming in a richer society, comprising those with political connections who used their official power to capture fortunes and to monopolize prized opportunities such as travel abroad. Thus, growing numbers of Chinese viewed the once-popular reforms as having created financial and job uncertainty for themselves while nurturing opportunities for unjustified enrichment by an increasingly corrupt elite. The fact that the reformers never developed a cogent rationale for their efforts added to the sense of disquiet.

Among the various sectors of the population, university students and faculty felt especially aggrieved for several reasons. They more than most were exposed to the international arena and thus were more likely to measure China against the standards prevailing abroad. They more than most felt the reforms had undercut their prestige, for in the new social environment where income equaled success many street vendors made more money than did university professors, who were on fixed, low salaries. And they more than most felt a historical obligation to serve as the conscience of society. By 1989, therefore, the universities were set to explode, and the potential for unrest elsewhere in the population had grown ominously.

The dissatisfaction of intellectuals became evident early in the year, as unprecedented petitions and open letters calling for increased human rights and the release of political prisoners garnered signatures and attention. Some intellectuals formed discussion groups to thrash out the need for political reforms. In this effort, the increasing ties between intellectuals in China and Chinese intellectuals living abroad played a role. Astrophysicist Fang Lizhi exemplified the crosscurrents that fed this activity. Fang had spent a year at Princeton University in the mid-1980s, and upon his return to China he became an outspoken advocate of democratic reform and human rights.

The Chinese government was aware of the enormous popular concern about inflation and corruption, but it reacted hesitantly and ineffectively. In autumn 1988 the government tightened credit as a means to reduce the demand-driven inflation, but this produced increased popular disaffection. The Agricultural Bank found itself without sufficient funds to honor its procurement obligations for the 1988 fall harvest, and thus many peasants were paid with IOUs.[3]

The credit crunch also caused severe distress to many small-scale private and collective enterprises. And the credit squeeze produced

[3] FBIS, *China Daily Report*, August 4, 1989, pp. 38–40; *Nongmin ribao*, July 17, 1989.

widespread unemployment in the urban construction industry, as many new projects lost their financial underpinning. As a result, disgruntled peasants who had recently moved from rural areas into the urban construction trades became potential sources of social instability in major cities. Moreover, efforts by the political leaders to stem corruption proved so ineffective that they merely served to highlight to the population the extent to which politically powerful families in the country had become untouchable.

During the winter of 1988–89 popular support for the political leadership collapsed. Moreover, the leadership showed every sign of disagreeing about how to deal with the inflation that contributed so strongly to popular discontent. Some felt the situation required greater use of state administrative controls to tighten up on credit, reduce the growth in the money supply, and bring inflation under control. Others viewed the fundamental problem as being insufficient reform, where partial movement toward the use of market forces had created a situation in which the country benefited from neither the discipline of the plan nor the discipline of the market.

Advocates of tightening up included the octogenarian Chen Yun and two members of the Standing Committee of the Politburo, State Planning Commission Chairman Yao Yilin and Premier Li Peng. Advocates of accelerated reliance on the market included CCP General Secretary Zhao Ziyang, along with Tian Jiyun and other leaders closely associated with Zhao. Deng Xiaoping in the late spring of 1988 had supported Zhao's position, but as inflation worsened during 1988 Deng essentially left Zhao and his market-oriented reformers to take the blame and increasingly sided with those who sought greater administrative controls.

The Chinese leadership thus was gripped by unease and division as it grappled with serious economic and political challenges in the spring of 1989. Indeed, many political observers believed that Zhao Ziyang had lost Deng's confidence to the extent that Zhao himself would be edged out of power soon after Soviet party leader Mikhail Gorbachev visited Beijing for a summit in mid-May. These factors provided the immediate background for the leadership's handling of the growing agitation by democracy and human rights activists from January through March and the tidal wave of protest that began in April.

This widespread popular discontent and the tension within the elite combined with specific, unanticipated events to produce the mass movement and temporary disarray of China's leaders that gripped the capital and the country in the spring of 1989.

First, former CCP general secretary Hu Yaobang's sudden death on April 15 created an opportunity for students to challenge the political leadership by mourning Hu as an individual who had been wronged by being purged in 1987 for supporting greater freedom in China. Hu acquired greater stature (and liberalism) in death than he had enjoyed in life, and students in Beijing astutely utilized mourning rituals (banners, wreaths, eulogies, elegiac poetry, processions) to make their political point.

Second, Deng Xiaoping and most of the top party leadership adopted tactics for handling the student demonstrations that proved counterproductive. They enraged the students by stating in an April 26 *People's Daily* editorial (such editorials are a major vehicle for communicating authoritative views to the population) that the students were merely troublemakers and that they had been hoodwinked by those who sought to destroy the socialist system in China. The editorial made it clear that the demonstrators must be stopped. But the authorities then failed to use force to back up their words and, indeed, virtually yielded control over Beijing during the ensuing weeks to the demonstrators.

Another tactical blunder occurred on May 20 when the leaders declared martial law in parts of Beijing but ordered the troops not to cause bloodshed in securing key points around the city. This order proved to be a contradiction in terms, given popular resistance to the troops. Finally, the leaders applied massive and deadly force in early June to bring the movement to an end. This series of misjudgments and inconsistent signals from the top played an important role in sustaining the movement during its seven-week life.

Third, several events in May boosted the energy behind the movement. The 70th anniversary of the May Fourth Movement produced marches and speeches that stressed the continuity of goals between students of that earlier generation and those of 1989. The visit in mid-May of Soviet leader Mikhail Gorbachev further inflamed the situation. Chinese students saw Gorbachev as a communist leader who dared to promote political reform, and thus his presence encouraged calls for comparable changes in the PRC. Beyond this, major television networks around the world had months earlier identified the Sino-Soviet summit as the news event of the year, and thus the world's media converged on Beijing. The popular movement proved ideal for worldwide TV coverage—something that the movement's leaders (with their close ties to students abroad) quickly grasped but that the country's leaders handled poorly.

Finally, the student leaders of the movement proved as tactically adept as the top party leaders proved tactically inept. The students maintained extraordinary discipline in their ranks, thus avoiding the violence and hooliganism that could have alienated the populace. Some 3,000 students in mid-May began a hunger strike that touched the souls of the populace as a whole. The hunger strike also provided a rationale for other citizens to join the protests safely—they could argue that the country's leaders should meet the student demands in order to save the lives of the hunger strikers. In this way, people cloaked their demands for political change in humanitarian garb. At the end of May, the students gave new life to the movement by erecting what became known as the Goddess of Democracy statue in the northern part of Tiananmen Square, thus drawing crowds back into the square. In these and other ways, the students maintained the momentum of the movement through seven long weeks.

In sum, the major political earthquake that struck China during the spring of 1989 grew directly out of problems, most notably inflation and corruption, that had become closely identified with the reform effort. Disagreements among the elite over how to cope with these problems had produced tensions that made it more difficult for the leaders to control the popular movement once it began. A series of occurrences, such as Hu Yaobang's death and the Gorbachev visit, added fuel to the fires and exacerbated the disagreements within the elite.

When the leadership finally did respond decisively on June 3 and 4, it chose to use massive military repression as its vehicle for reestablishing its control over the capital and its image of decisiveness throughout the country. The bloodletting that resulted from the introduction of troops produced sharp reactions around the world, and for a period of time many countries curtailed their dealings with the Chinese leaders.

Domestically, one important result of the popular movement was leadership change at the top. The hard-line Premier Li Peng won in the power struggle with reform-minded CCP General Secretary Zhao Ziyang, and the latter was purged. Zhao was last seen in public on May 19, and he formally lost his position at a party Central Committee meeting in late June. Although it appears that Li Peng and others sought to put Zhao on trial later in the year as part of their effort to discredit the reformers, no such trial occurred, and Zhao continued living under house arrest for the remainder of the year.

Deng Xiaoping sought to prevent a total victory by hard-liners who wished to throw the reform baby out with the pro-democracy bath water. While Deng himself firmly believes that CCP dominance is vital to China's stability and development, he also wants to see economic reform and the opening to the outside world continue. He therefore brought two individuals who seemed to share his priorities—Jiang Zemin and Li Ruihuan—into the Standing Committee of the Politburo in the wake of Zhao's ouster. The Politburo Standing Committee is a small group (five to seven people) who formally direct the activities of the CCP and thus of the country.

Jiang Zemin had served as the political leader of Shanghai, and Li Ruihuan had filled the same role in Tianjin. Both men had gained considerable exposure to foreign businesspeople, and both recognized the dangers and inefficiencies of an administratively controlled economy. Deng made Jiang the head of the party and, a few months later, of the powerful party body that commands the military, the Central Military Commission. Li Ruihuan assumed responsibility for the propaganda portfolio. Both men were careful to doff their hats to hard-line principles through the remainder of the year, but each also projected an image of commitment to long-term reform and openness to the international arena.

With the ouster of Zhao and the removal or weakening of many of his colleagues, greater administrative control over the economy was stressed in government policy. The leadership tackled inflation with renewed vigor, producing a severe credit squeeze. The harsh medicine showed clear signs of taking effect by the fourth quarter, as industrial production slowed, inflation eased off, unemployment increased, and inventories of unsold goods piled up.

Corruption proved more difficult to tackle. The new leadership quickly acknowledged that corruption had become a major factor in causing popular discontent, but it made only marginally effective efforts to correct the problem. New rules prohibited a few of the top leaders and their relatives from engaging in commerce and business, but there is little evidence that these subsequently were applied with vigor. Much-heralded audits of major state corporations, such as the China International Trust and Investment Corporation, for example, produced minor slaps on the wrist at best. As often happens, a few individuals at lower levels in the system suffered harsh punishments while the upper crust continued to pursue its activities unscathed by the anti-corruption efforts. The net result of these efforts was further evidence of the existence of a new class above the law.

The months of June through December witnessed a concerted effort by the government and party to discredit the spring 1989 popular movement as an attempt at "turmoil" designed to "overthrow the party and the state and produce chaos." Constant propaganda depicted the movement as secretly led by a few elitist elements who wanted to establish a nonsocialist system. Massive efforts were made to determine the identities of those who were active in the demonstrations. As of the end of 1989, however, relatively few of the students and other intellectuals and officials who had participated had been arrested, and none of those arrested was known to have been executed. Workers, the unemployed, peasants, and vagrants who were rounded up, however, suffered more severe punishment, with many executed and others sentenced to long prison terms.

The quite limited information available about China toward the end of 1989 suggested that the top leadership had restored calm but had not regained a substantial measure of popularity or legitimacy. The national media produced a drumbeat of criticism and harsh rhetoric, but resistance in many pockets throughout the political system greatly reduced the real effects of the pronouncements from Beijing.

The political earthquake that overturned communist dictatorships throughout Eastern Europe in the last months of 1989 highlighted a dramatic fact: China at the beginning of that year had been widely regarded as the socialist system most committed to reform and most advanced in moving along a market-oriented path; but China as of the end of the year was equally widely seen as one of the most hard-line, even retrograde, socialist societies, a country whose ideological brethren now included the likes of Albania and North Korea.

In sum, the contradictions inherent in reform fully caught up with China in 1989, and the country paid a heavy price for its inability to manage these matters effectively. But there was also a deeper set of political issues at stake, and China's overall progress must be measured against this core agenda, too.

The Core Agenda

China has experienced two revolutions in this century, but still its political system has not resolved two fundamental issues that extend back into Chinese history: the extent to which power resides in institutions versus in individuals and the relationship China should seek with the international community of nations. Many believed that the major reforms starting in the late 1970s signaled at last an emerging consensus on these fundamentals, but the events of 1989 call that judgment sharply into question.

Where Does Power Reside?

There is tension in every political system over the relationship between offices and the individuals who hold them. The power of an official inevitably reflects both that person's own qualities and background and the formal characteristics of the office itself. Chinese history abounds with examples of conflict between a highly personalistic system and a highly articulated bureaucratic environment.[4]

There has been great uncertainty since 1949 concerning the integrity of the bureaucratic institutions established to govern the PRC. The lack of institutional integrity was manifested in three ways during the Mao Zedong era:

1. *The power of the incumbent was not distinguished from the power of the office.* Mao Zedong never felt bound by formal rules and procedures, and to support this attidude he was able to draw from a strand of traditional Chinese political thought that argues that people gain the right to rule because of their virtue rather than because they have been chosen to hold a particular position.[5] Indeed, he rebelled against the constraints of bureaucratic office. He also repeatedly encouraged officials high and low to break out of normal organizational routines and seize the initiative to grapple with problems in new and more effective ways. Mao's proclivity toward anti-bureaucratism meant that China suffered periodically from considerable disruption as the chairman's own concerns and energies changed over time. While this phenomenon was the most visible and destructive at the very top of the Chinese system, it in fact extended down through all levels and produced, ultimately, a ruling apparatus that was unconstrained either by law or by a conservative bureaucratic ethos.

2. *The scope of authority of the major ruling bureaucracies (the party, the government, and the military) changed substantially.* Essentially, as Mao became dissatisfied with the results being achieved by the efforts under way, he sought to shift the initiative to other major bureaucratic hierarchies, which in turn expanded the scope of their activities until they had overreached themselves and engendered Mao's displeasure. Thus, the government dominated the First Five-Year Plan (1953–57), the party dominated the Great Leap Forward (1958–61), and the military dominated the Cultural Revolution (1966–71). This history left major questions about the legitimate scope of activities of any of China's major bureaucratic behemoths.

3. *The process of transferring power at the highest levels lacked any procedural basis of legitimacy.* Constant demonstrations that top leaders stood above the system meant that formal rules did not become a ba-

---

[4] See, for example, Alexander Woodside, "Emperors and the Chinese Political System," in *Proceedings of the Four Anniversaries Conference* (Armonk, NY: M. E. Sharpe, forthcoming).

[5] It is also true, of course, that many non-Chinese autocrats have ignored formal rules and procedures in order to maximize their power. While Mao may have drawn from traditional Chinese thought, the explanation of his behavior should not rely wholly on cultural factors.

sis for conferring or transferring legitimate power. With the power of assignment concentrated in the hands of Mao personally for the very top appointments, the succession to Mao would become a potentially disruptive element in the political system—one that could not be resolved in any secure way while the chairman lived and that the system lacked a legitimate means of resolving once he died. In the event, "succession politics" played a very significant role in the political development of the PRC from 1959 until Mao's death in 1976 and beyond.

Deng Xiaoping fully understood the deleterious effects of the lack of institutional integrity during Mao's reign. He felt that this approach had robbed China of the use of many of its talented people, caused tremendous waste of resources, and sapped the confidence of both Chinese and foreigners in the political stability of the PRC. This last factor, he believed, could stand as a major obstacle to eliciting foreign cooperation in building the modern Chinese economy of which he dreamed.

Deng undertook numerous initiatives during the decade of reforms to enhance the institutional integrity of the political system. He made major efforts to regularize meetings of the party and government, to reduce the role of politics in the policy process, to lay the groundwork for a career civil service, to clarify the division of tasks between the party and the government, to limit the civilian activities for which the military assumed responsibility, and to make a sharp break with the former style of "campaign politics" that had so often swept aside normal procedures and institutions in order to mobilize people to achieve high-priority goals. In addition, Deng encouraged a spate of law-making and frequently stressed the importance of regularity and integrity in China's institutions.

Deng's attack on the cult of personality was an integral part of these efforts. He carefully guided the party's dissociation from the megalomania of Mao's later years, and he insisted that nobody view himself as standing above the party. In this regard, Deng himself never assumed the titular leadership of the party or the state, and in 1981 he had the CCP abolish the position of chairman, thereby making the highest position in the party that of general secretary. Previously, China alone among ruling communist parties had had both a general secretary and a chairman, and this situation had highlighted the notion that the chairman was above the party organization. Deng, in short, made greater institutionalization a high priority of his administration.

No system works at its best in a crisis. Still, the performance of the Chinese system of government from late April through early June highlighted the very limited extent to which Deng's tremendous efforts over the years had succeeded in creating greater institutional integrity. Throughout this critical period key decisions were made almost exclusively by an octet of octogenarian officials such as Chen Yun, Peng Zhen, and Bo Yibo, who almost to a man had formally retired from politics during the previous few years. These elderly leaders at times caucused separately and at other times sat in on regular decision-making bodies. The leaders who held the highest party and state offices, themselves men in their sixties and seventies, played at best staff and advisory roles to the powerful octogenarians during this period. During the entire seven weeks, as far as is known, there were either no meetings or only "expanded" meetings (which means that key nonmembers such as the octogenarians participated) of the country's various governing bodies (the CCP Politburo or its Standing Committee, the Central Committee, the National People's Congress or its Standing Committee, the State Council, the party Secretariat, and the Central Military Commission). Yet during this period decisions were made to oust the general secretary of the party and to replace him with a provincial party leader, to declare martial law in Beijing, and to order the People's Liberation Army to use deadly force to restore control over Beijing.[6]

In short, when critical decisions about top offices and key activities were made, no legitimate decision-making body and no formally designated official made them. After years of creating a facade of institutions and of procedural regularity, Deng and his elderly colleagues demonstrated that ultimate power in China does not yet adhere at all to formal offices.

The fact that these decisions included the ouster of Zhao Ziyang exacerbated the damage done to Deng's earlier attempt to build up institutional integrity. Given the highly personal way in which Zhao's removal was decided by the group of party elders in violation of party rules, it appears that no procedural formality will suffice to confer legitimacy on Deng's successor as party leader. Thus succession politics is again a prominent feature of the Chinese political system.

The resurgence of the party elders further sharpens this issue. Having octogenarians dominate a political system makes succession a matter of ongoing salience. That they ignored formal rules throughout the crisis has robbed future decisions of procedural legitimacy. The highly personal nature of political power means, moreover, that the order of departure of the octogenarians from the political stage will

---

[6] An excellent sense of the personalistic style of decision making during this period can be obtained from reading Deng's comments to Li Peng and Yao Yilin on May 31, in which Deng informs the other two that Zhao Ziyang should be replaced by Jiang Zemin: "Key Points of Deng Xiaoping's Talk with Li Peng and Yao Yilin," *Huaqiao ribao* (Overseas Chinese Daily), July 24, 1989.

probably strongly influence the prospects of various potential successors. Under these conditions, there is a high probability of future debilitating factionalism and power struggles.

In addition, the CCP fundamentally collapsed as a disciplined organization during the popular movement in the spring of 1989. Ultimately, the party elders had to turn to the army to reestablish their control over the country. In the wake of the June crackdown, the top leaders tried throughout the remainder of 1989 to rally the party forces to resume responsibility for a wide range of activities, including many they had essentially yielded to the government during the previous decade of reform. As of the end of 1989, the distribution of authority among the party, the government, and the military was uncertain, as it had so often been in the earlier history of the PRC. The events of 1989 demonstrated that, earlier appearances notwithstanding, power in China still resides overwhelmingly in individuals rather than in official positions and that, on the issue of institutional integrity, the progress made since 1979 has been uncertain, at best.

How to Relate to the Outside World?

In many different ways, the Chinese revolution grew out of China's encounter with an industrializing, expansionist West and Japan. Even before the turn of the century, core tensions had developed within the country over the basic posture that China should assume in order to manage effectively its relationship with this new external environment. While this situation has been extremely complex and is still not fully understood, several general observations may clarify the deep divisions over this issue throughout the 20th century.

Representatives of three basic positions have competed on the Chinese political stage over the past nine decades:

1. *Nativists* have sought to ensure China's security and tranquillity by uniting the people through ideological indoctrination and shutting out divisive influences from the outside world. In their view, all outside influences are corrupting and weaken China. Nativists have included individuals from the radical right and the radical left, for each of these extremes has been represented by xenophobic ideologues in modern China.

2. *Selective modernizers* seek to utilize the technology that makes the West strong while retaining the values that make China special. "Chinese learning for the essence and Western learning for practical use," a distinction first raised in the 19th century self-strengthening movement, remains their basic philosophy. These individuals believe that technology can come value-free, and they seek to provide an opening

to the outside world that carefully limits the penetration of foreign ideas.

3. *Total modernizers* are the true iconoclasts. They feel that China must become a society that can itself produce the technological dynamism that is the basis for wealth and power in the 20th century. Nothing in Chinese tradition is sacred to total modernizers. At the same time, few of them seek to remake China in the image of the West. It is Western technological dynamism—not Western society itself—that total modernizers seek to emulate in China.

The above descriptions somewhat artificially posit three points on what is in fact a continuum from absolute xenophobes to those who wish China to be completely open. A glance at the history of China since 1900 suggests two noteworthy phenomena with regard to this continuum. First, each national leader has at the peak of his career been a selective modernizer, but each has occupied a place on our imaginary continuum farther in the direction of the all-out modernizer than did his predecessor. Second, each has eventually been confounded by the inherent contradictions in this position (technology does in fact have values) and has moved in a more nativist direction as those contradictions have forced difficult choices late in life. In sum, there has been a secular trend toward a China that is increasingly open to the outside world, but no top leader has been a total modernizer, and each has finished his career in some degree of retreat from a posture of openness.[7]

Deng Xiaoping's career fits well into the above scheme. Deng during most of the decade of reform carried China to greater openness to the outside world than any Chinese leader had previously willingly permitted.[8] But Deng and many of his colleagues became increasingly concerned by the values that crept into China as a result of this open posture—values that they derisively characterized as "bourgeois liberalism" that could produce "spiritual pollution."

China's stance of openness to the international arena in the Deng era certainly provided many shocks to the Chinese system. Foreign firms sought to encourage change in the Chinese economy toward more market forms, with substantial repercussions for the distribution of power and resources in the state. Opening combined with other

[7] This analysis is presented in greater detail in Kenneth Lieberthal, "Domestic Politics and Foreign Policy," in Harry Harding, ed., *China's Foreign Policy in the 1980s* (New Haven: Yale University Press, 1984), pp. 43–70.

[8] This degree of openness was rivaled only by that of China to the Soviet Union at the height of the Sino-Soviet alliance in the mid-1950s. See Townsend, *op. cit.* Earlier periods of great openness of China to the outside world resulted from the forced encroachment on China by foreign powers.

policies to accelerate growth in many coastal areas at a rate that widened the gap between coast and interior. Sending students and others abroad helped to create a restless generation, impatient with the ideas of its elders and yet not fully familiar with the realities of China's interior. And the advent of modern telecommunications simply widened and deepened the impact of all of this throughout China.

In the wake of the June 1989 crackdown in Tiananmen Square the Chinese media again showed evidence of nativist perspectives. The important point about the events of 1989 is not their demonstration that disagreements still exist regarding the specific stance that China should adopt toward the international arena. That is certainly not remarkable. The major lesson of 1989, rather, is that these disagreements are so fundamental and far-reaching that they constitute a highly volatile ingredient in the politics of the country. Ten years of substantial exposure to the international arena have left some people longing to move abroad and others highly agitated that the West should hold any allure for the country's citizens. Overall, zigs and zags in China's domestic policies over many years have created tremendous confusion in basic values among the Chinese population. The "open" policy introduced in 1978 seems to have deepened and exacerbated that national malaise and left China fundamentally uncertain of how it should relate to the rest of the world.

The traumatic events of 1989 demonstrated the continuing lack of consensus in China on the basis for institutionalized political power and on the relationship of the country to the outside world. In this regard, the frequently used phrase "the evolution of China" is somewhat misleading. A great deal is changing in China demographically, economically, socially, and in other ways. But these changes do not appear to have brought the country significantly closer to establishing the essential conditions for stable national government: a reasonable degree of institutional integrity and a moderately stable consensus on the basic posture the country should assume toward the international arena. Given that these two issues remain unresolved at the end of ten years of rigorous reform efforts, it will be a very long time before anyone can say with confidence that China has begun to address successfully its core agenda. It was the revelation of the continuing depth and dimensions of this situation that made 1989 a year of great significance.

2
The Prospects for China's Economic Reforms

Dwight H. Perkins

At the end of 1989 China was in an East Asian–style economic recession. It was a recession because growth of industrial output was well below the levels of previous years of the decade; toward the end of the year, in October, industrial output actually fell slightly. It was an East Asian–style recession because real growth for the year as a whole was still positive, with an increase of just under 4 percent in gross national product (GNP), which is a rate many developing countries would be happy to achieve.

The decline in the growth rate in 1989 was not caused by bad weather, the regular rhythm of the Chinese business cycle, or even the events of June 3 and 4 in Tiananmen Square. This decline was deliberately engineered by China's economic policymakers. The immediate reason was the desire to bring down a rate of inflation that they deemed excessive by tightly controlling credit to enterprises. But inflation was just the most overt manifestation of an economy that some of China's leaders felt was beginning to careen out of control. Although the leadership claimed that putting brakes on economic growth was not intended to reverse the decade-long process of economic reform, many Western observers view the new policy of economic austerity as sounding reform's death knell.

Whether the economic reforms of the past ten years were the cause of the rapid growth that worried economic policymakers and whether the reforms carried with them political seeds that in the end undermined them are questions this chapter will address. To that end, it examines not only the events of 1988 and 1989 but also the reform efforts that led up to them.

First, however, it is important to note that the tightening of credit, which began in 1988, was almost inevitable given the acceleration in price rises in that year. One did not have to believe that the reforms in general were in trouble to conclude that something needed to be done about inflation. The official 1988 cost-of-living index for workers was 20.7 percent above that of 1987, and the inflation rate at the end of the year was even higher.[1] There is also reason to believe that the official indexes understate the full magnitude of the price rise that actually occurred.

An inflation rate of 20 or 30 percent is not unusual for a developing country. But the acceleration in the rate would have been worrisome to any policymaker. Would the rate of increase level off at 30 percent or would it keep on rising until the country was in a hyperinflation? Even at 20 percent China's urban residents were alarmed that inflation might wipe out the gains in income that they had made over the past decade. Older residents remembered the hyperinflation of the 1940s that had helped bring down the rule of the Nationalist Party, and everyone had gotten used to the virtually zero price increases of the 1960s and 1970s. Government officials (especially the honest ones) and intellectuals were particularly unhappy because they were, for the most part, on fixed incomes. Taxi drivers and other entrepreneurs, in contrast, could often benefit from inflation.

This near consensus over the need to bring down inflation, however, masked fundamental differences over a wide variety of other economic reform issues. These differences were being fought out in 1988 and early 1989 before the events of Tiananmen. After June 3 and 4 the debate was muted or stopped altogether, but the issues were not in any way resolved. The political "victors" or "survivors" of Tiananmen were preponderantly on one side of the argument, but there were exceptions. To understand the influence of inflation and Tiananmen on economic reform, therefore, one must have a clearer picture of what the debate between the opposing forces was all about. With the issues in contention clarified, it will be possible to define with more precision just what has happened to the economic reforms to date and what may happen to them in the future.

The History of the Economic Reforms

There is a tendency to treat all events since the Third Plenum of the Eleventh Central Committee of the Chinese Communist Party (CCP) in December 1978 as an undifferentiated period of steadily accelerating reform. In a crude way this view has an important element of truth, but at a more refined level there have been major shifts in the

---

[1] State Statistical Bureau, *Zhongguo tongji zhaiyao, 1989* (Beijing: China Statistics Press, 1989), p. 89.

balance of reform forces during the past decade, and some important reforms predated December 1978.

In two key respects, the economic reform effort began almost immediately after the death of Mao Zedong in 1976 and the arrest of his wife and her Shanghai colleagues a few months later. During the previous Cultural Revolution decade (1966–76), economic policy had carried self-reliance and moral incentives (exhortations designed to get people to work for the good of society instead of for direct material benefits such as bonuses) to an extreme. Self-reliance came to mean rejecting most of what the outside world had to offer, including modern science and technology. Those who suggested that it might make more sense to import a modern chemical plant from abroad rather than to build an inefficient one at home were subject to harsh political criticism even on the rare occasions when their view prevailed. As to material incentives for workers, wages and promotions were frozen throughout the decade and bonuses and wages for piecework were eliminated. Farmers who were organized into collective units called production teams received incomes that bore only a vague relationship to the effort expended.

In 1977 and 1978 these two features of the Cultural Revolution period were decisively rejected by China's new leaders. Industrial enterprises were told that going abroad for better technology was a good thing, not something to be condemned, and these enterprises responded immediately. In fact, the response was so overwhelming that China's foreign exchange earnings could not possibly pay for the hundreds of billions of dollars' worth of imports that these enterprises wanted to purchase. As a result, there was a tightening of central control over the use of foreign exchange, but the basic view that foreign technology imports were needed did not change. Material incentives for workers were reintroduced in the form of general wage increases, a return to bonuses and piece rates, and renewed promotions.

The December 1978 plenum marked a substantial change in reform efforts, but the post-1976 emphasis on turning outward and relying on material incentives was reinforced. What was new in 1978 was the de-emphasis of heavy industry and the concerted effort to solve the problem of slow agricultural growth by vigorously restoring incentives for farmers to produce and market their product. Instead, the emphasis was to be on a slower rate of overall growth based more on consumer industries and agriculture. The emphasis on consumer goods was due in part simply to the recognition that China did not have the energy resources to continue an all-out drive to build up heavy industry. The offshore oil bonanza that some had hoped for had not materialized, and heavy industry is a major consumer of energy. But there was also a recognition that more consumer goods were essential if material incentives were to mean anything. Wage increases that cannot be used to purchase more goods, a common phenomenon in centrally planned economies, may do more harm than good.

Chen Yun, who had had a major influence on the effort to restore order in the economy in the early 1960s after the chaos of the Great Leap Forward (1958–60), was once again a dominant figure.[2] The new emphasis on slower growth probably reflected his view that too-rapid growth leads to inefficiency and economic chaos. It is likely that he feared that the policies of 1977 and 1978, although far less extreme than those of the Great Leap, were heading the country in a similar direction. By restricting the growth of heavy industry, one could rein in the pace of economic growth in general and ensure balanced planned development. In the industrial sphere this goal was in fact realized. Heavy industry grew slowly in 1979 and 1980, and output in that sector actually fell in 1981.

The cautious slow-growth policy of the 1979–81 period began to give way even before the period was completed, however. The reason had less to do with the specific objectives of the third plenum than with the changes in rural China that were acquiring a momentum of their own. The first step toward reform in the rural areas had been to remove many of the restrictions on rural markets. The impact was immediate and readily visible by mid-1979. Farmers' markets blossomed everywhere, stimulating production of the household subsidiary products that were the main items sold in such markets.

The effort to increase farmer incentives vis-à-vis the major grain and cash crops led to experimentation with a variety of systems designed to tie income earned to effort expended. Initially, these changes retained the collective form of organization. However, by 1981 experiments with household-based agriculture were under way and had begun to spread, often spontaneously. In many areas, rural cadres (low-level officials) tried to resist this trend toward household agriculture, but high CCP officials stepped in at critical times to make sure the process continued. Major actors in this drama included provincial leaders such as Wan Li, then in Anhui province, and Deng Xiaoping himself.

The combined impact of these various rural reforms was an extraordinary acceleration in agricultural output. Agricultural value added (net output after subtracting intermediate inputs) grew by 7.7 percent a year

[2] Those interested in a fuller exposition of Chen Yun's views in this earlier period are referred to a collection of his writings: Nicholas R. Lardy and Kenneth Lieberthal, eds., *Chen Yun's Strategy for China's Development: A Non-Marxist Alternative* (Armonk, NY: M. E. Sharpe, 1983).

from the end of 1978 through 1984. Part of this increase was due to farmers shifting to higher-valued cash crops and subsidiary products, but grain output over this same period also grew at 5 percent a year, reaching a peak output of 407 million tons in 1984. The supply of grain temporarily outstripped demand and China became a net exporter of grain, something that had not been true since the 1950s.

It is difficult to overstate the importance of this agricultural performance in general and grain performance in particular for what followed from late 1984 on. Economic policymakers who shared Chen Yun's views placed great stress on the need to maintain adequate supplies of grain. The Chinese crop failures of 1959 to 1961, which had killed tens of millions of people and deeply split the CCP, strongly reinforced this opinion. By 1984, though, radical reform through decollectivization and unleashing of market forces had seemingly eliminated China's slow agricultural growth problem. With this success attributed to a willingness to carry out radical reform, the conservative reformers were no longer in a position to resist the ideas of the more radical reformers grouped around Premier Zhao Ziyang.

Agricultural success laid the groundwork for an all-out effort to achieve a similar transformation of industry beginning at the Third Plenum of the Twelfth Central Committee in October 1984. The principal document of this plenum dealt with reforms of the urban industrial economy. The document itself does not make the intentions of the government clear. There is much talk in it about the importance of "guidance planning" instead of the compulsory plan targets that had characterized planning up to that point. But the meaning of the term "guidance planning" was not clear even to many who were in charge of implementing the new practices. This lack of clarity probably reflected the fact that the reformers themselves were entering uncharted territory. The Yugoslavs, the Hungarians, and the Poles had all introduced important changes in their industrial systems, and the Chinese reformers studied these changes, but there was no East European blueprint showing how to reform an urban industrial system. Neither the Chinese nor the East Europeans had a well-developed idea of where they hoped the reform process would eventually lead. Few at the beginning were willing to come out forthrightly for a socialist market economy. Even fewer saw much of a role for a private capitalist sector.

What followed over the next four years was a wide range of experiments, some of which appeared to work and were expanded, and others of which performed poorly and were abandoned. Most of these efforts built on earlier pilot reform programs started in the early 1980s. Those actively pushing the urban reforms under the leadership of Zhao Ziyang did not present a united front. Debate was the order of the day, with some wanting to go faster than others. There were also considerable differences over which aspect of the urban reforms ought to receive primary emphasis.

These changes in China's economic system were accompanied by a very rapid rate of increase in GNP—over 10 percent a year according to the official estimates. Because some of the effects of inflation on these figures may not have been properly accounted for, the real growth rate may have been a little below 10 percent a year, but by any standard China was growing very rapidly.[3] From the beginning of the economic reforms, whether one uses 1977 or 1979 as the base year, per capita national product had more than doubled. For a full decade, China had managed to nearly match the kind of economic performance experienced by its East Asian neighbors in the 1960s and 1970s.

There is little doubt that the agricultural reforms contributed to the spurt in farm output through 1984.[4] But did the urban reforms account for the more than 17 percent growth rate in industry between the end of 1984 and the end of 1988? Research by economists to date does not allow one to draw a causal connection between the two phenomena. There is not even any agreement as yet over whether industrial productivity rose or fell in this period.[5] Until the issue of productivity growth is settled, it is not really possible to decide whether the reforms increased productivity and hence growth or whether the growth was caused by factors unrelated to the reforms. It is likely, however, that the opening up to foreign trade with the rapid expansion of both exports and imports accounted for at least part of the acceleration in industrial growth. It is also possible that the greater role of market forces in the urban industrial system fostered competition that created pressures to raise enterprise efficiency. All we know for sure is that for four years there was both a great deal of reform and a great deal of growth.

---

[3] A major problem with the official figures is that collective industry appears to be included in the totals for real growth at current rather than fixed prices. If this turns out to be the case generally, the industrial output component of real GNP growth would be inflated by a significant amount.

[4] One recent econometric study suggests that reforms accounted for nearly half of the 42 percent increase in crop output. Justin Yifu Lin, "Rural Reforms and Agricultural Productivity Growth in China," UCLA Working Paper No. 576, December 1989.

[5] Work on this subject is under way at present both in the Chinese Academy of Social Sciences and in the United States, but more remains to be done before a consensus on whether productivity rose or not can be achieved.

The Agricultural Issues in the Reform Debates

The issues connected with the reform of the agricultural sector are easier to explain than those related to the urban industrial sector. Once it was agreed that material incentives were critical to raising agricultural productivity, the main issue left with respect to incentives was whether to retain some degree of collectivization or to go all the way to private household agriculture. This issue was settled in favor of a household-based system, but that system created problems of its own. Farmers, for example, in theory had the right to use the land allotted to them for 15 years, but they were unsure whether they would really be able to keep it for that long. If they were uncertain of their rights (and who wouldn't be, given the shifts and turns in Chinese policies over the years), these farmers would be unwilling to invest in the land or in irrigation systems. Poorly defined property rights created another problem. Individuals who wished to leave the land to work in the city received no compensation if they surrendered their right to use the land allotted to them. One solution was to get a relative to farm it, even if only part-time, but that often meant that the land was underutilized.

There are two paths out of these dilemmas. One is to strengthen individual ownership of the land and the right to sell it, and there have been experiments along this line. The other path, which appears to be favored by those in power in late 1989, is to return to collective efforts in some areas. At present crops may still be farmed on a household basis, but it appears that labor for land and irrigation improvements is being mobilized by rural cadres—or at least that there are people advocating this.[6] Whether the quantity and quality of land investment has really fallen and whether collective labor effort is capable of reversing this trend are questions open to debate. In the past, the benefits of such labor mobilization were badly oversold, and there is little recent evidence that future efforts of this kind will do better.

Another area of debate is the importance of China's maintaining self-sufficiency in grain. The logic of the grain self-sufficiency argument is straightforward. Grain, consumed directly or indirectly in the form of grain-fed meat, is the main source of calories in the Chinese diet. A failure in the grain supply, such as those which occurred in China between 1959 and 1961 and periodically throughout Chinese history, leads to the death of millions of people and shakes the foun-

[6] The State Council in October 1989, for example, called on local areas to launch capital construction projects by amassing materials and labor forces. Willy Wo-lap Lam, "Major Step Taken toward Re-collectivization," FBIS, *China Daily Report*, November 1, 1989, p. 45; *South China Morning Post*, October 31, 1989, p. 13.

dations of any government that happens to be in power at the time. The more astute emperors understood this and hence paid special attention to grain prices as a way of monitoring the quality of the grain harvest in various parts of the country.

Historically, China had to produce its own grain because the world grain market was small and transport costs were high. By the 20th century the world grain market was no longer small, but China's foreign exchange earnings were modest and hence the nation's ability to pay for grain imports was limited. Even in the 1960s it was a strain on China's balance of payments to import 5 or 6 million tons of grain a year at a cost of several hundred million U.S. dollars when total foreign exchange earnings came to only US$2 billion annually. And 5 or 6 million tons accounted for only 3 percent of China's total grain supply. If China had tried to import 20 percent of its grain requirements in the 1960s, its entire foreign exchange earnings would barely have been enough. Nothing would have been left over for the purchase of other essential imports. Little wonder, therefore, that not only Chen Yun but most Chinese economic policymakers in the early 1960s felt that China had to rely mainly on its own efforts when it came to the supply of grain.

The late 1980s are not the 1960s, yet much of the analysis of China's grain problem by those currently in charge of Chinese economic policy does not recognize the difference. Two conditions relevant to the state of the Chinese grain supply have changed. First, even after five years of stagnant grain output since 1984, Chinese domestic grain production in 1989 was 20 percent higher on a per capita basis than at any time prior to the reform decade. Even if grain output were to stagnate at current levels for another ten years, China would at worst be back to the per capita supply levels of the 1950s or the early 1970s.[7] There is, therefore, no serious danger of a repeat of the failure of 1959–61.

The problem for the 1990s is a quite different one. How does one meet the demands of an increasingly prosperous population that wants to consume more and more of its calories in the form of meat when it takes several kilograms of grain to produce one kilogram of meat, ranging from a ratio of 8:1 for beef to 2:1 for chicken? Either the supply of grain must grow much faster than the population in order to make this possible, or the government will have to reintroduce ra-

[7] Per capita grain output in China in 1978 was essentially the same as in 1955–57. From 1979 through 1984, grain output rose by 33.6 percent while population rose only by 7.9 percent. Between the end of 1984 and the end of 1989 population rose another 7.1 percent for a total rise since 1978 of 15.6 percent.

tioning of grain and meat and tighten the rations (and/or raise prices) year after year. The impact of the latter measures on worker incentive and on political support for the government could be devastating.

If China must meet its domestic grain supply requirements solely with domestic production, then major steps must be taken to ensure that grain output resumes a growth of at least 3 percent a year.[8] Some in the current Chinese leadership appear to believe that this can be accomplished by ordering the farmers to plant more land in grain. But it was precisely the removal of interference of this kind that made possible the large spurt in grain output between 1978 and 1984, although good weather and increasing supplies of chemical fertilizer also helped. A return to administrative controls over farmer decisions is likely to dampen incentive and lower overall performance in the long run. Only through major investments in new high-yielding grain varieties, improved farmer incentives, and more investment in rural infrastructure is a 3 percent or greater increase in grain production likely to be feasible.[9]

But does China really have to be nearly self-sufficient in grain when the world grain market regularly supplies deficit nations with several hundred million tons of grain (or meat from grain-fed animals) each year? That brings one to the second major difference between the late 1980s and early 1990s in China and the 1960s. Since 1978 China's foreign exchange earnings have grown dramatically. From a figure of US$9.75 billion in 1978, export earnings had risen to US$52.5 billion by 1989, a nominal annual increase of 17 percent. Additional foreign exchange is available from tourism and foreign investment, although exports are by far its main source. Even if China in 1990 were compelled to import 40 or 50 million tons of grain in order to meet domestic requirements, the foreign exchange required would be substantially less than 20 percent of foreign exchange earnings in that year. If exports continue to grow even at a rate of, say, 7 percent a year, an import of 40 to 50 million tons of grain in the year 2000 would account for less than 10 percent of total foreign exchange earnings.[10]

---

[8] This 3 percent figure is based on the assumption that per capita incomes wil grow by 3 or 4 percent a year and that the income elasticity of demand for grain consumed directly and indirectly is 0.6. Both of these assumptions are conservative. China's demand for grain is more likely to grow at a rate above 3 percent than below 3 percent.

[9] Yao Yilin's "Report on the Draft 1989 Plan for National Economic and Social Development," *Beijing Review*, March 1–7, 1989, p. vi, for example, calls for a variety of measures to promote agriculture, including some mentioned in this chapter, but nowhere does the author discuss how farmers are to be motivated to play their critical role. The emphasis in the plan is on what the state will do.

[10] If China imported 40–50 million tons of grain in the year 2000, the world price of grain might rise to as much as US$200 per ton and China would have to use US$8–10

Thus there is no grain crisis in China in 1990 unless one assumes that World War III or some devastating climatic change will destroy the world grain market. China's grain problem is solvable over the next decade or two by a combination of investment in agricultural research, continued maintenance of farmer incentives, and the promotion of manufactured exports to pay in part for increased grain imports. There are agricultural economists in China who understand this argument and make it themselves. There are also senior policymakers such as Du Rensheng who understand what is required, but Du is now apparently involuntarily retired. The real danger to China's grain supply is that those who believe that there is a crisis in 1990 will take steps that will slow farm output growth further and manufacture the very crisis that is feared.

The Industrial Reform Debates

The issues in the debates over industrial reform are considerably more complex than those relating to the agricultural sector. These debates are about the proper role for government planning and whether one should or should not aim to establish a market-oriented economy. Discussion of market forces versus planning goes to the heart of numerous related issues such as how to control inflation or limit corruption.

The one area where there do not appear to be major differences of opinion among policymakers is China's decision to promote exports in order to be able to increase imports. Even foreign investment and the Special Economic Zones (free-trade areas designed to attract export-oriented investment), potentially much more sensitive topics, do not seem to be under serious pressure for fundamental change. There is an effort by the central authorities in Beijing to get greater control over the foreign exchange that is earned, but that is part of a general effort by the center to gain more authority over the localities in setting basic investment priorities.

The major debate, with many different dimensions, is over the proper role of the market. No one, even among the most radical reformers, expected China to establish a full market system with no interference from the bureaucracy. This kind of market system exists almost nowhere in the world outside Hong Kong. But the reform groups around Zhao Ziyang (and some critics of Zhao as well) were advocates of giving market forces the dominant role in the urban industrial sector. There were no doubt many differences of opinion

---

billion in foreign exchange to make these purchases. But Chinese exports, if they grew at 7 percent a year, would have approached US$100 billion by that time.

even among the radical reformers over how far market-oriented reforms should go. The main issues publicly debated, however, had to do with how to implement a greater role for market forces.

For market forces to work properly, four key elements must be in place. First, goods must be available to be sold in the market rather than allocated by central planners. Second, prices must reflect the relative scarcities in the economy so that goods will go to the right places. Third, enterprise managers must behave in accordance with the rules of the market. And fourth, there must be competition among enterprises.

Distribution through the Market

Consumer goods were freed up from administrative allocation early in the reform process, but by 1988 capital goods were also distributed to a large degree through market and other noncentral planning channels. By 1988, for example, the kinds of goods subject to distribution by the state's monopoly system had fallen to 27 from 256 in 1979. In 1988, 71.5 percent of the means of production supplied to the nation's enterprises were obtained through the market or by other means outside the state distribution system. Even for such strategic goods as steel and coal, state-controlled allocation amounted to only 47 and 44 percent respectively of total allocation.[11]

This decline in central administrative control over the allocation of industrial inputs was a critical element in the boom that occurred in the collective industrial sector. Collective industry nominally includes all firms where income and production decisions are shared by workers themselves. In state enterprises, by contrast, the workers are paid wages and managers are appointed by central or provincial government authorities. In practice what distinguishes collective industry is its relatively small scale and the fact that it is not under any substantial degree of control by the central planners in Beijing. Accounting for 21 percent of total gross industrial output in 1980, collective industry rose to 36 percent of the total by 1988. Provincial and county governments were among the most enthusiastic supporters of these changes. The growth of local enterprises put resources in the hands of local authorities who could carry out any number of governmental and industrial development tasks. In regions of the country where local enterprises congregated, such as Guangdong and southern Jiangsu, everyone shared in the prosperity that was generated.

[11] "China's Capital Goods Market," *Beijing Review*, November 13–19, 1989, p. 20.

But the very success of industrialization created a problem for the central planners, and over time these planners became increasingly vocal. In essence, the central planners' argument was and is that local enterprises were diverting investment funds and critical material inputs from such high-priority sectors as energy and transport. If energy and transport continued to be neglected, eventually they would create bottlenecks that would bring the entire economic system to a halt. As it was, many factories throughout the country were operating with electricity for as few as six hours a day and for less than five days a week. The railroads and roads were being utilized at well above 100 percent of their rated capacity.

The differences between local and central interests were also one part of the cause of inflation. Local authorities generally do not see themselves as being responsible for controlling the money supply. If one province restricts credit in order to curtail investment and excessive wage increases by enterprises, that will not affect the other 29 provinces. Only the center can take the steps necessary to get everyone to rein in excessive credit expansion. In principle, the center had this authority throughout the 1980s, but for a variety of political and economic reasons it was reluctant to exercise that authority.

Pricing

The second element essential to making markets work properly is prices. Chinese prices had been frozen by 1979, in many cases for over two decades, and as a result China's price structure did not begin to reflect true relative scarcities in the economy. Price reform was essential, but how was it to be implemented? One way was to create committees to investigate the supply and demand conditions of each market and to recommend specific changes to the government. This method, tried in the early and mid-1980s, has one big disadvantage. Every price change becomes a political battle between those who would receive higher prices and those who would have to pay more. Because it is difficult and time-consuming to change even a few prices, the distortions remain.

The solution to this problem devised by the reformers around Zhao was to create a dual-price system. Goods allocated through central planning channels would still carry state-set prices, but goods sold outside those channels would be priced to bring demand and supply into balance. The government would have little or no direct involvement in this second market, and hence price changes would happen automatically and not be subject to political debate and pressure.

As a temporary solution the dual-price system worked as planned and freed up most prices. Freer prices under conditions of excess demand, as is generally the case in socialist economies, often led to sharp price increases, thereby contributing to inflation. Dual prices, however, also contributed in a major way to another increasingly serious problem, growing corruption in government.

When goods are sold at two different prices, one much higher than the other, there is a large potential profit for those who can get goods allocated to them at low state-set prices and then turn around and sell those goods at high market prices. The problem is not so serious if the low-priced goods are actually used as inputs in high-priority industries. The low prices will inflate the profits of those industries, but the state can tax away those profits if it deems them excessive. True corruption occurs when individuals or firms are able to divert low-priced goods away from priority sectors to themselves and then reap a large profit by selling them back to whoever will pay the going price. By the late 1980s there was apparently a great deal of diversion of this kind going on, although data are not publicly available that would allow one to measure its extent.

There are really only two solutions to this kind of corruption, and both solutions have their advocates in China. One solution is to mount vigorous anti-corruption campaigns and severely penalize the offenders. That is the path chosen by the government since June of 1989. But this path is not likely to be effective unless the moral quality of the political leadership rises sharply across the board, or unless the Chinese go back to the ways of Maoist days when individuals could not spend large amounts of money on themselves without becoming subject to severe criticism from Red Guards and the like. Put differently, in the atmosphere prevailing in China in 1989 and 1990, anti-corruption campaigns are likely to increase the sense of political repression without eliminating much corruption.

The other method of reducing corruption is to remove the easy opportunities for making corrupt incomes. One way to do this is to eliminate the dual-price system and replace it with a one-price system. A central committee document of November 1989 apparently calls for the elimination of two-tier prices, although the document itself has not been made public.[12] If this does in fact occur, the next question will be whether the new single price is a market price or a price set by the state at a level below that which the market would have determined. Given the control-oriented atmosphere of late 1989,

[12] Daniel Southerland, "China Sets Sharp Turn for Economic Policies," *Washington Post*, November 30, 1989. I am indebted to Nancy Hearst for this citation.

the latter is more likely, which means that the role of the market in the allocation of inputs will be cut back. Either the state will have to return to centralized allocation of these inputs or, more likely, inputs will be allocated through thousands of informal deals between enterprises. Neither method is likely to do much for enterprise efficiency.

Eliminating the dual-tier price system will remove only one source of corruption. Many other opportunities will remain. Any time a state official has some discretionary authority to issue permits or licenses or to allocate key inputs, there is an opportunity for a payoff. A system of central planning is riddled with such opportunities, and in fact central planning would not work if it weren't for the numerous informal deals, many illegal, that help get around the rigidities and mistakes of the planners. If one really wants to reduce corruption, the only effective way of doing so is to reduce the need for these informal arrangements by allowing the impersonal forces of the market to govern most enterprise decisions concerning the allocation of inputs and outputs.

Management Goals

For markets to work, enterprise managers must maximize profits by cutting their costs and raising their sales. In a Soviet-style command economy, in contrast, the goal of managers is to raise the gross value of output. There is little concern for profits or for control over the excessive use of inputs.

In the latter half of the 1980s, enterprise reforms in China did succeed in turning the attention of managers away from output goals and toward profits. The profits earned, however, depended on whether the enterprise succeeded in negotiating for a low tax rate or for the allocation of larger amounts of inputs at low state prices. Rather than relying on their own efforts to cut costs or raise sales, managers made high profits by maintaining close ties to superiors in the government bureaucracy who were in a position to hand out low tax rates and goods at low prices.

To force managers to behave according to market rather than bureaucratic rules, some way had to be found to break the ties between enterprises and higher levels of the government to make the enterprises truly independent. Among Chinese economic reformers, some saw this as the central task of reform. Others did not. Still others were bothered by the kinds of steps that might be required to make enterprises independent.

One way to make enterprises independent is to allow them to go bankrupt. If the managers of a firm know they will never be allowed to go bankrupt, they don't have to worry about such issues as costs because they can always go back to the government for a bail out. Bankruptcy, however, means that workers will become unemployed, at least temporarily, and socialist systems are very uneasy about allowing unemployment. Still, the Chinese have continued experiments with a bankruptcy law even after June 1989. A large collective-enterprise bankruptcy actually occurred toward the end of 1989.

Even more controversial than bankruptcy is the question of the appropriate role for private ownership in a socialist system. In Eastern Europe the reformers have virtually given up on trying to break the ties between government and enterprises in the context of public ownership. Privatization in some form is seen as essential. Few if any Chinese reformers were prepared to go this far. They were prepared, however, to talk about forms of stock ownership in which one public firm might own shares in another. Such measures, it was believed, would help raise capital and make possible an enterprise board of directors that was independent of the central ministries. Outright private ownership was confined to the small-scale sector, although it was not always easy to differentiate between collective and private ownership.

Since June of 1989, the government's attitude toward privately owned firms has become more restrictive, but there is also recognition of the role that these small firms play in providing many people with employment. Experiments in share ownership continue, but it is unlikely that they will become a major element in the way industry is organized anytime soon, and they could be abolished altogether.

Competition

The fourth element in a well-functioning market system is competition among enterprises. One of the principal advantages of a market system is that it fosters vigorous competition, which in turn raises productivity. Central planning, in contrast, favors monopolies, because monopoly control of particular markets makes planning easier. Efforts to introduce competition into the urban industrial system began in the early 1980s. In the service sector, in areas such as retail sales for example, the impact of competition was immediate and positive. Department stores, facing challenges from small collective retailers, often stayed open longer and became more customer-oriented. In industries, such as those producing clocks and watches, where supply exceeded demand, the breakup of regional monopolies forced the more inefficient producers to cut costs and raise quality.[13] Many Chinese industries, however, were faced with ex-

[13] William Byrd *et al.*, *Recent Chinese Economic Reforms: Studies of Two Industrial Enterprises*, World Bank Staff Working Papers, No. 653, 1984.

cess demand for their products rather than excess supply. When excess demand is present, competition has little impact because firms can easily sell whatever they produce.

For markets to work as they are supposed to, all four elements must be in place. Reformers do not need to achieve perfection, but substantial progress is required along all four fronts. In China in the 1984–88 period, there was controversy over how fast and by what methods to proceed along each of these four fronts, and there was debate over the ultimate goals of the reform efforts. The spectrum of opinion ranged from those who felt progress toward full-blown market socialism was too slow, through those who supported a more moderate pace toward the same end, all the way to those who wanted to restore planning and bureaucratic commands to a more central role.

Did Economic Reform Cause Tiananmen?

Was it inevitable that reform would lead to the kind of social pressures that blew up in April through June of 1989? If the blowup was not an inevitable result, did the reforms nevertheless make possible what happened or would something similar have happened in the absence of reform?

One point is clear. The decision to turn the economy outward and to accelerate the introduction of advanced technology from Japan and the West brought into the country much more than just better machinery. By 1989 several hundred thousand of the most influential people in China had seen the advanced industrial countries with their own eyes. Millions of overseas Chinese and other tourists and visitors had traveled throughout China, bringing ideas as well as cash. The flow of information from the outside world could not be confined to certifiably "reliable" cadres. Television and radio helped ensure that the audience for this new information numbered in the hundreds of millions.

If China had retained a closed economy, had severely limited travel abroad, had confined television to pictures of Chinese factories and Chinese operas, and had similarly restricted information in other areas, the events of April to June 1989 would be difficult to imagine. China is not Romania, a small country surrounded by rapidly changing societies. Mao demonstrated that it was possible to keep the minds of most Chinese closed to what was going on in the world beyond China's borders. But it is no longer possible in China to open up the economy by taking only selectively from the outside, with that selection made by only a few leaders. It has been the goal of Chinese leaders since the late 19th century to limit Western imports to technology narrowly defined, and it doesn't work. Restrictions on foreign contact overly limit the availability of technology, but from the point of view of the leadership, easing restrictions results in too many undesirable ideas.

Did the specific reforms initiated in the urban industrial areas in October 1984 cause Tiananmen? In some ways the reforms contributed to the tensions that exploded in the spring of 1989. In other ways the reforms helped alleviate potential sources of tension. Certainly inflation and rising corruption contributed to urban discontent, which, when combined with the student demonstrations, caused those demonstrations to take on much greater significance. Student demonstrations carried out in isolation seldom threaten political systems, but when they tap into sources of discontent in society at large, governments tremble. That was what happened in the spring of 1989.

Inflation was certainly a result of the economic reforms. Excess demand, the ultimate source of inflationary pressure, is a characteristic of central planning. It was the reforms, however, that made it possible for inflationary forces to become overt in the form of price increases rather than suppressed and transformed into long lines for scarce goods. Some forms of corruption were the result of the urban reforms, notably the dual-price system. But corruption is most of all a fundamental characteristic of any system that operates through discretionary bureaucratic commands. A pure market system has fewer opportunities for corruption. In a bureaucratic command system, the only ways to avoid corruption are to ensure that all bureaucrats are selfless and dedicated or to have a police state that is intrusive in the extreme, backed up by leaders who are determined that bureaucrats will not be allowed any material benefits. In the 1950s China's bureaucrats were the recent products of a civil war in which they had fought selflessly for the greater good. In the 1960s and 1970s Mao saw to it that it was almost impossible for most people to enjoy any luxuries, even good haircuts. Luxuries were an invitation for a visit by the Red Guards.

In the 1980s China's leaders no longer led a selfless revolutionary cadre and they no longer wanted to deny themselves the amenities of a higher standard of living. Given the value systems of all levels of the party and the bureaucracy, corruption on a large scale was probably inevitable as long as the system created so many opportunities. The developing world is full of examples, and in the socialist world one has to look no farther than the Soviet Union to see that it is bureaucratic power, not markets, that creates opportunities for illegal gain.

Finally, it is important to note that in two fundamental ways, the reforms substantially reduced the pressure on the political system. First, the rural reforms, leading as they did to a dramatic rise in farm incomes, created a peasantry that was not at all disaffected from the government. Second, between 1978 and 1988 China's labor force increased by 141 million people. Of that number, 41 million found employment in state enterprises and urban collectives, 61 million found employment in township and village enterprises and other nonagricultural occupations, and only 39 million in agriculture and fishing.[14] By way of contrast, between 1965 and 1978 the labor force rose by 115 million persons and more than half that number worked in agriculture, where there was already a large labor surplus and incomes were stagnant. If the prereform economic policies of the 1970s had been continued through the 1980s, it is quite possible that increasing repression would have been required to contain the rising discontent of a rural labor force with no prospects for advancement in the countryside and with nowhere else to go.

Economic Policy after Tiananmen

As indicated at the beginning of this chapter, even before June 1989 and continuing thereafter there was a near consensus in China that something had to be done to bring down inflation. Much of the activity of the central government in the economic sphere has been directed to that end. At the center of this effort has been an attempt to restrict bank credit to enterprises in general and new investment in particular except for investment in the energy and transport sectors. The cutback in investment is real and substantial, and the rate of increase in prices in the latter part of 1989 appears to have fallen below 7 percent, down from well over 20 percent in the latter half of 1988.[15] The cutback in credit and money supply may mainly be responsible for this drop in inflation, but the government's decision to freeze some prices at below-market levels may also have played a role.

---

[14] The agricultural labor force data and the total labor force figures are from State Statistical Bureau, *Zhongguo tongji zhaiyao, 1989*, pp. 15–16, and State Statistical Bureau, *Zhongguo tongji nianjian, 1988*, p. 154. The nonurban nonagricultural figure was derived as a residual.

[15] The Chinese government in 1989 generally reported the price increase in one month over the same month in the previous year, which in this period greatly exaggerates the actual rate of inflation in 1989. The end-of-December 1988 to October 1989 rate of price increase was around 7 percent on an annual basis if Chinese official statements are reliable.

The credit crunch has clearly had a substantial impact on industrial production and overall GNP growth. GNP in 1989, however, was still up 3.9 percent over 1988. Industrial output was up 8.3 percent for the year as a whole but was virtually stagnant during the last three months of the year.[16] Agriculture may have achieved a bumper harvest and helped carry the economy during an otherwise difficult time. The summer grain crop was 2.5 million tons over 1988's harvest; state grain purchases were up, and the fall harvest was good enough so that grain output for the year as a whole, at 407.5 million tons, just surpassed the peak level of 1984.[17]

In many ways the most critical economic figures have to do with foreign exchange earnings. China began 1989 with foreign exchange reserves of US$17.55 billion, the highest end-of-year figure on record, up from US$2.26 billion in 1980, so there was a considerable reserve to fall back on. China also had an external debt of US$40 billion, but the ratio of debt-service to exports was well below a level that would cause repayment problems.

Most of the attention of outside observers in the area of foreign exchange has focused on foreign investment and tourism. Both were clearly hurt by the events of June 1989. But the amounts of foreign exchange involved in these two categories are not large relative to China's total foreign exchange earnings. In 1988 foreign exchange receipts from tourism were approximately US$2 billion, and foreign direct investment actually used was US$3.7 billion out of total foreign exchange receipts of about US$60 billion.[18] If tourism and foreign direct investment in the latter half of 1989 and the first half of 1990 fell to half the level of 1988, that would still only be a fall of US$3 billion, or 5 percent of total foreign exchange received in 1988.

More critical in terms of foreign exchange earnings is China's 1989 export performance. For the year as a whole the increase in exports was 10.5 percent. While this was a slower rate of growth than in many recent years, China's balance of payments may have improved,

---

[16] *Xinhua*, November 15, 1989, as reported in BBC, *Summary of World Broadcasts*, November 29, 1989, and "Statistics Show Economic Growth," *Beijing Review*, November 13–19, 1989, p. 12. State Statistical Bureau, *Communiqué on the Statistics of 1989 Economic and Social Development* (Beijing: February 20, 1990).

[17] Sheryl WuDunn, "China Says Grain Harvest Hit a Record Level in 1989," *New York Times*, January 22, 1990. State Statistical Bureau, *Communiqué on the Statistics of 1989 Economic and Social Development* (Beijing: February 20, 1990).

[18] Exports in 1988 were US$47.54 billion and loan receipts were US$6.5 billion, to which one can add US$2 billion in tourist revenues and US$3.7 billion in direct investment to reach US$59.7 billion. Additional sources of foreign exchange earnings include such items as remittances.

because imports in 1989 only grew by 7 percent due to the tight control over credit that restricted enterprise demands.[19]

Have foreign economic sanctions made a difference? The European foreign aid programs that were suspended were tiny in this context. Japanese and World Bank loan cutoffs would have a larger impact if exports were also stagnant in 1990 and 1991, but the Japanese banks were already beginning to lend again in late 1989, under the technicality that they were honoring existing contracts. If the world's industrial nations were to impose sharp restrictions on Chinese exports, the impact on the economy in the short run could be substantial. Such embargoes, however, are usually imposed in wartime, which hardly describes China's current relations with the industrial world. Over the longer run such embargoes would force China back toward a more autarkic development policy. How such a turn inward would help human rights or other desirable political goals is unclear. All this suggests that drastic sanctions are not likely to be imposed.

Overall, therefore, the political crisis of 1989 did not create a comparable economic crisis, although there were some negative repercussions. The more important question is how the political crisis and lesser economic problems will lead to changes in the direction of reform efforts in the immediate future. The outward orientation of trade and foreign investment policy, as already indicated, remained in force throughout 1989. The foreign investors not already committed to China were shying away, but that reflected uncertainty about the political future in China, not basic changes in the policies toward such investors.

Does the current political leadership have a well-developed plan for the future of reforms? Part of the answer to this question will come as the 39 points of the November 1989 plenum are fleshed out and implemented. The backbone of those 39 points includes calls for increasing central control over the allocation of investment and key industrial inputs, a generally slower rate of growth, and more emphasis on large state enterprises and less on small township, village, and especially private enterprises. All this will be accomplished in part by an increase in government controls at the expense of market forces. Some of these bureaucratic controls will be imposed deliberately. Others will happen unintentionally as prices are frozen well below levels that equate supply and demand.

---

[19] These data are based on customs statistics as reported in State Statistical Bureau, *Communique on the Statistics of 1989 Economic and Social Development* (Beijing: February 20, 1990).

Will the central government really be able to implement such a policy, and will it like the results if it does? The provincial and county governments that have benefited from the more liberal policies of the reform period, particularly those along the coast, are already resisting any large-scale curtailment of their independence in economic affairs. Even the center is reluctant to close down many smaller enterprises for fear of the consequences that could occur in the form of rising unemployment. Private businesses are to be more closely supervised, but no one advocates closing them all down, not least because they employed 23 million people by the end of 1988.[20] Township and village enterprises number nearly 1.6 million units with 49 million employees. There is no conceivable way that the inputs and outputs of these numerous small businesses can be controlled and coordinated efficiently from Beijing through the use of bureaucratic commands. It is even harder to imagine how the state can efficiently direct 209 million farm households through the use of such direct orders.

The current slogan used to describe the kind of economic system China wants is "planned commodity economy," which means a mixture of central planning and market forces. The reality is that the bureaucratic interventions are more ad hoc than planned, and, partly as a result, the markets don't function very well. Will such a system lead to sustained and rapid growth sufficient to employ a labor force that is growing by 15 million people each year? Perhaps, but the experience of Eastern Europe, which has had this kind of bureaucratic/market hybrid for some time, is not encouraging. It is not that bureaucratic/market hybrids cannot be made to work. South Korea did very well with such a hybrid in the 1960s and 1970s, but South Korea left far more to market forces than is the case in present-day China, and what it did plan, it planned more systematically than China is doing today.

Between 1978 and 1989, China traveled down a path for which there were no clear guideposts. During the course of that period, many Chinese economists began to understand what moving toward a system that gave a major role to market forces involved. Many of those economists and others knowledgeable about reforming economic systems are still in China and still occasionally state their views. Whether anyone is listening to them, however, is difficult to say. That might not matter if those opposed to many of the earlier reforms and now in power had a clear vision of their own. But to the extent that there is such a vision, it appears to be rooted in conditions

[20] "Private Businesses Need Protection," *Beijing Review*, November 6–12, 1989, pp. 11–12.

of a backward, near-subsistence rural economy, and China is not really that kind of an economy any longer.

All of this adds up to considerable uncertainty over where economic policy is likely to go over the next two or three years, uncertainty that is compounded by the even greater questions surrounding China's political future. Over the longer run, it is likely that China will have to return to a more vigorous effort to expand the role of market forces within the economy. This is not likely to be triggered by an economic crash such as occurred in 1959–61. China's economy will grow faster than those of Eastern Europe even without further reform. But China's standard of living is far behind that of its East Asian neighbors or Eastern Europe, and it is unlikely that the people of China will tolerate for long a system in which living conditions improve at a snail's pace and a majority of the new entrants to the labor force have to eke out their existence by plowing increasingly small plots of land. The last decade, if nothing else, has demonstrated that there is an alternative.

3
The Social Sources of the Student Demonstrations

Martin King Whyte

As 1989 began, China could boast a population that was much better clothed, fed, and housed than it had been a decade earlier, when a program of sweeping economic and political reform was introduced. One testimonial to the magnitude of the country's transformation came from Chinese who had the opportunity to travel to the Soviet Union and Eastern Europe at the end of the 1980s. They reported back incredulously that frustrated East European consumers were trying to buy the clothing off their backs, as well as any food items and consumer durables they had happened to bring along. It was almost as if they were visitors from the rich and capitalist West. This was quite a turnabout from the 1950s, when China had taken lessons from her socialist elder brothers. Deng Xiaoping's version of "goulash communism" appeared to be outpacing the original East European version.

The reforms not only improved economic conditions; they also increased cultural diversity. The rigid political restrictions of the Mao era governing acceptable proletarian literature, art, and popular ideas were relaxed, and an increasing variety of cultural forms became available to the Chinese. The "open" policy produced a proliferation of Western cultural products, ranging from politically "rehabilitated" classics (for example, Shakespeare and Beethoven) to newly "liberated" foreign radio broadcasts and translations of the likes of Sigmund Freud, Henry Kissinger, Herman Wouk, and Sidney Sheldon. New imports even included such choice examples of Western proletarian culture as motor-cross racing, Rambo movies, and bodybuilding. With foreign tourists, teachers, and businesspeople streaming into China and with increasing numbers of Chinese going abroad, contact with Western individuals, ideas, and institutions began to reach beyond the small circle of the Chinese political elite.

The relaxation of restrictions based on ideology extended to China's own cultural heritage as well. Temples were restored and monasteries reopened, Confucius and his ideas were reexamined, and in general an effort was made to retrieve artistic, musical, and literary products of the past. This revival of tradition was not confined to high culture. The restoration of family farming helped to fuel revivals of ancestor worship, wedding feasts, elaborate funerals, geomancy, and other customs the authorities had earlier branded "feudal remnants." Peasants appreciated the new opportunities these changes offered to pursue family goals and participate in culturally meaningful rituals. The restoration of temples and sacred sites and the new tolerance for religious activity also resulted in revivals of temple worship, religious pilgrimages, and the manufacture of ritual items (for example, spirit incense, sacred charms, coffins), all of which had been banned during the Mao era.

The general relaxation of control in the political sphere, combined with growing incomes and increased leisure, led to a boom in domestic tourism. Foreign travelers accustomed to having a near monopoly on sites such as the Great Wall found themselves increasingly bumped and jostled by throngs of Chinese, who were able to enjoy the sights of their native land.

Better economic conditions and greater cultural diversity were accompanied by social healing. Large numbers of people who had been condemned to political purgatory during the many struggle campaigns of the Mao era were rehabilitated and allowed to resume normal lives. The system of class labels used to stigmatize individuals and families and to foster class struggle in the Mao era was formally dismantled. Millions of urban youths who had been sent to the countryside were allowed to return to the cities, there to resume interrupted educations, careers, and spouse searches. Many couples separated by arbitrary job assignments or by reeducation campaigns were able to arrange transfers so that they could live together for the first time in decades. Such developments made it possible for individuals to retreat from the scars and battles of public life without apology and devote more time and attention to affairs of the home and family. In general, the frazzled nerves produced by the tumult of the late Mao era began to be soothed.

Given these considerable improvements in the quality of people's lives, one would have expected the reforms, and the post-Mao leadership responsible for them, to be hugely popular. Since no popular elections or referendums on the reforms were held, and since the public opinion polls that began to be carried out during the 1980s were for the most part officially sponsored and rather unscientific, readings of popular opinion can only be impressionistic. Many observers would argue that had a referendum on the reforms been conducted in, say, 1984 or 1985, the result would have been overwhelming approval. Yet by the close of the decade the rule of Deng Xiaoping and his cronies had to be maintained by massive force of arms against widespread public disapproval. To reform-minded Chinese, at least, Eastern Europe seemed to have leapt ahead of China once again.

The Social Roots of Popular Discontent

Why was popular discontent increasing despite the apparent success of the reforms? In addressing this question I shall distinguish three separate groups within the population: those who felt the reforms had not gone far enough, those who thought that they had gone too far, and those who were generally satisfied. For the sake of simplicity, I shall call these groups the "not far enoughs," the "too fars," and the "satisfieds."

China's post-Mao reforms introduced dramatic changes in society initially; however, increasingly after the mid-1980s the reform momentum stalled, leaving a partial transformation of the system that made nobody very happy. The reasons for rising disaffection in the late 1980s, though, differed sharply between the "not far enoughs" and the "too fars." The social dynamite that exploded in the spring of 1989 was formed by a combination of circumstances that made it possible for social groups holding quite contrary views to overcome their differences and unite in their common hostility to the leadership.

Too Little Reform

The Beijing Spring demonstrations were spearheaded by those who believed that the reforms had not gone far enough. These included not only students but also many intellectuals and a newly emerging group, urban entrepreneurs.[1] In part the "not far enough" reaction of these groups involved frustration that political reforms had been repeatedly placed on the national agenda and just as often taken off without producing any concrete results. For example, Deng Xiaoping's August 1980 speech calling for fundamental changes in China's

---

[1] This combination is symbolized by the leadership-in-exile that emerged in Paris after the June crackdown, composed of student Wuer Kaixi, intellectual/reformer Yan Jiaqi, and the founder of the Stone Computer Company, Wan Runnan.

political structure was republished on three separate occasions in the 1980s, each time stimulating discussion that led nowhere.[2]

Students and their allies found the economic reforms insufficient as well. The slogans and goals of the reformers implied that intellectuals and experts would have a leading role in plotting China's future and that intellectual talent and expertise would play the central role in China's modernization drive. Improved treatment of intellectuals and future intellectuals (that is, students) became a standard slogan voiced by officialdom, and reforms were launched aimed at giving such individuals greater autonomy, more comfortable working conditions, greater rewards, and increased freedom to select where and on what they would work. The idea that the leadership would increasingly rely on the advice of the experts in formulating national policies held enormous appeal for most students and their allies, for whom this notion resonated with ancient ideas about the active incorporation of intellectuals into state service.

When students looked at the society around them, however, they perceived that not much had changed. State investment in education was pitifully low, even compared with many other Third World countries, and the material conditions and prospects of most students remained bleak. Most could look forward to lives earning modest and largely fixed salaries in jobs not of their choosing, under less well-educated supervisors who often did not appreciate their talents and aspirations, and with only limited chances to cash in on the new opportunities created by the reforms. Student optimism about the future was further dampened by a spate of articles published during the mid-1980s claiming that middle-aged intellectuals were not only poorly paid but also had greater health problems and shorter life spans than people in other occupations.

Intellectuals similarly saw a large gap between reform goals and present realities under reform. Instead of being able to work unob-

---

[2] This important speech was not openly published until 1983, when it was included in Deng's *Selected Works*. In the wake of the campaign against "spiritual pollution" that began later in the same year, discussion of political reform and of this speech disappeared from the media. However, the same speech was republished in 1986, was ignored again after the student demonstrations at the end of that year and during the ensuing campaign against "bourgeois liberalization," but reappeared in print for a third time later in 1987. Since June 1989 one may assume that Deng Xiaoping would like to disown his bold 1980 speech, which inspired great hopes among radical political reformers. For the initial publication of Deng's speech, see *Beijing Review*, October 3, 1983, p. 18. On the debate over the effort to alter China's Leninist political system, see my article, "Who Hates Bureaucracy? A Chinese Puzzle," in Victor Nee and David Stark, eds., *Remaking the Economic Institutions of Socialism* (Stanford: Stanford University Press, 1989).

structed and contribute to China's future, many found themselves locked into the same jobs as before. Bureaucratic overseers and constant shifts in the national political atmosphere presented repeated reminders of the Mao era, when intellectuals were presumed to be infected with bourgeois tendencies. Successful and aspiring entrepreneurs faced blatant hypocrisy as well. Instead of competing in a fully developed market, they had to make their way through a mine field of changing regulations and petty regulators. Access to the resources and opportunities they needed to run their businesses was never fully secure. As one bitter description put it, "A 'visible foot' is stepping on the 'invisible hand.' "[3]

Although the specific ways in which the "not far enough" sentiment was felt by these groups varied, they were united in their anger at the hypocrisy involved in the meritocratic vision of the reforms. Although the reforms were supposed to produce a society in which the educated, the skilled, the hardworking, and the innovative would receive the most rewards and prestige, the reality often looked quite different. A few individuals were benefiting disproportionately, even though they had done relatively little to merit such benefits. These included suburban peasants and children of high-ranking officials who happened to be situated favorably in relation to new market opportunities and who had personal access to scarce resources and foreign contacts.

Those groups angered by these inequities found they had little opportunity to vent their grievances or effect change. Their resulting frustration produced increased pressure for political reforms whose general goal would be to create a more equitable society. It is well to keep in mind the distinction between equity and equality. In political terms the "not far enough" groups wanted to reduce the power of the party/state bureaucracy, but their preferred alternative was not in most cases some sort of mass egalitarian democracy. Rather, they were concerned with gaining their own deserved places in the political sun. Many would have been horrified at the idea that an intellectual should have no more say in society than a worker or a peasant. Equity was thus seen as demanding not equality but rather a society in which the educated and technically skilled would increasingly take over from the politically loyal. This frankly elitist picture of the good society is expressed most clearly in the speeches and writings of astrophysicist Fang Lizhi, "China's Sakharov," whose views aroused such indignation within the CCP leadership that he was ousted from

---

[3] FBIS, *China Daily Report*, February 10, 1989, p. 33; *Guangming ribao*, January 28, 1989, p. 3.

the party in 1987 and had to seek refuge in the American embassy during the June 1989 crackdown.

It would be a mistake, however, to see all the discontent of the Deng era in economic or political terms. Perhaps equally important in undermining support for the regime were critiques stressing the loss of cultural and moral cohesion in post-Mao China. China's leaders were seen as jettisoning the cultural and ideological orthodoxy of the Mao era without providing a coherent alternative. A long period during which individuals knew precisely what was good and bad and how they should behave gave way in the Deng era to a confusing variety of cultural practices and moral arguments. Official slogans such as "socialism with Chinese characteristics" provided only the vaguest of guidance.

In this arena of moral confusion, most of those who shared the "not far enough" view came to the conclusion that the institutional reform agenda of the May Fourth Movement (China's other great student-led, Western-oriented reform movement, launched in 1919) should be resumed. They felt that the failures of Maoist socialism represented, in large part, the continuing influence of China's long feudal legacy, and that only a thorough critique of both Marxism-Leninism and the traditional legacy, combined with institutional renewal drawing on modern Western models, could save China. Throughout the 1980s these sentiments led to increasingly sharp and systematic critiques of both China's traditional legacy and its bureaucratic socialism.

Too Much Reform

The sentiment that the reforms had not gone far enough in dismantling the bureaucratic system of state socialism was by no means the dominant view in society at large. In terms of sheer numbers, more people probably leaned toward the opposite view that the reforms had already gone too far. It is one of the persistent dilemmas of reforms in China, and elsewhere, that changes that are not sufficient to satisfy critics threaten and alienate other previously satisfied groups. This tendency makes the task of building popular support for further reform problematic. In China those who were increasingly worried that the reforms were going too far included industrial workers, low-level bureaucrats and party officials, the army, and the police. The members of these groups are much more numerous than intellectuals, students, and entrepreneurs, even if they are not as articulate.

China's workers had seen job and income security as among the greatest achievements of the revolution. Lives that before 1949 were characterized by constant fear of unemployment, inflation, and impoverishment were transformed by the socialist system. Those on the state payroll were provided with permanent employment, compensated with secure wages, and protected by a range of health care and other benefits that were unusually broad for a developing society. Even though opportunities for advancement and wage increases were limited, and were terminated almost entirely in the last decade or so of Mao's rule, the enhanced security provided by state employment made it possible for workers to plan their lives and build families in a more secure environment.[4] The efforts by the reformers to destroy the "iron rice bowl" system of job security in favor of limited-term employment contracts, the right of managers to demote and fire workers, and newly promulgated bankruptcy legislation threatened this proud victory of socialism. Even though these reforms were not fully implemented, the Chinese media came to be filled with accounts of disgruntled workers who retaliated with threats or even violence against those pushing such reforms locally.

Women workers were particularly upset that, as a consequence of the industrial reforms, many enterprises began to selectively lay off female employees or to refuse to hire any but males, using the justification that male workers were less troublesome and more productive.[5] Although advocates of these changes argued that returning women to the home would open up more employment opportunities for young males and provide more nurturance and discipline within families, women employees, accustomed to slogans of the Mao era that said that women "hold up half of heaven," were often hard to convince. The normally sluggish Women's Federation took up this issue and denounced the increasing discrimination against female workers that the reforms spawned.

When in 1988 and 1989 the government experimented with contracting out the management rights over failing state firms to private entrepreneurs, not only many workers but also bureaucrats and even

[4] Of course, greater economic security was combined with increased political insecurity in the Mao period, and individuals who got into political trouble forfeited all claims to the security provided by Chinese socialism.

[5] Generally, factories and other work organizations fund their own sick leave, maternity leave, and pension funds, rather than having these supported by general state funds. In the Mao era, when enterprises had no power to retain their own profits and could request funds freely to cover any deficits, there was no incentive to economize on either labor costs or fringe benefits. Under the reforms, enterprises can retain a share of their profits for reinvestment or for spending on employees, and this change produces increased incentive to minimize labor costs and fringe-benefit expenditures. Employers claim that women are more costly due to higher absenteeism, maternity leave, and earlier retirement, and on this basis they may resist hiring and retaining female employees.

some intellectuals were outraged. Although the justification for this measure was that it would turn failing enterprises around and preserve jobs, it was widely seen by workers as representing a sellout of socialism and a return to dependence upon exploitative capitalists. (Not surprisingly, such experiments were repudiated after the crackdown, despite the claims of China's gerontocrats that the reforms would proceed.)

Workers at least could see that the reforms provided them with new opportunities to increase their salaries and bonus payments. Most other groups in the "too far" camp were not in this situation. Low-level bureaucrats, party officials, soldiers, and police shared with intellectuals the complaint that their modest and mostly fixed incomes prevented them from benefiting as much as others from the reforms. In addition, they perceived that the reforms threatened their power and prestige within their local bailiwicks as well as within society generally. Indeed, in many cases they were being blamed for the abuses and inefficiencies of the Mao era. Subordinates, colleagues, and neighbors who had formerly paid them deference now treated them with disrespect or even hostility. For individuals in these groups who felt that they had followed the call of Mao and devoted their lives to the revolution, the perception that others regarded them as political Neanderthals or worse was particularly galling. In rural areas such sentiments often led grass-roots cadres to resign in order to free themselves to concentrate on getting rich, but this was not an option readily available to their urban counterparts. The changes introduced by the reforms created morale problems in organizations such as the army and the police and complicated recruitment of young people into careers in these organizations, careers that had once commanded great respect.

The "too far" groups' vision of the good society was decidedly not one in which party bureaucrats would be replaced at the top of the social pyramid by meritocratic experts. While some of the members of these groups may have yearned for a more ideal socialist society in which the actual producers would be the masters of the state, most were more realistic and assumed that Chinese society would remain sharply hierarchical. However, they were generally more comfortable with "reds" than "experts" in charge at the top. For many this preference resulted in nostalgia for the perceived benevolent concern of Mao Zedong for the problems of workers, peasants, and soldiers. They saw precious little of such benevolence in the policies and pronouncements of the reform-era leadership, and many feared the elitism and arrogance of China's intellectuals. (These groups found the slogans about favoritism toward experts convincing, even if the experts themselves did not.)

The resentments generated in such "too far" groups were aimed at a variety of targets. For some the villains to be blamed for their loss of privileges and prestige were the new entrepreneurs and the well-educated experts and managers who were taking over leadership at the grass roots. However, equally likely to receive blame were the higher-level leaders who were pushing through the changes that left grass-roots cadres and party officials feeling scapegoated and powerless. One of the weak points of a Leninist system is that it substitutes the very visible hand of the state (or the "foot" alluded to earlier) for the invisible hand of the market. When groups feel that they are being treated unfairly, they are not likely to blame fate, their own imperfections, the market, or even rival groups. Their angry glances are quite likely to be directed upward at those who command the entire system.

The increased alienation of the "too fars," like that of the "not far enoughs," had cultural and moral dimensions beyond the economic one. The "too fars" saw the preferred remedy of the "not far enoughs" for China's cultural malaise, Westernization, as precisely the wrong solution. Indeed, when they looked around and saw such things as the revival of open prostitution, an upsurge in Christianity, and a fever among the young for foreign ideas and culture, they could agree with the claim of party conservatives that China was being "spiritually polluted" as a result of the "open" policy. For example, the 1988 documentary television series "River Elegy," with its highly unfavorable comparisons between China's bureaucratic lethargy and the dynamic West, deeply offended many "too fars" on patriotic grounds. But within this group ideas about the preferred alternative to Western culture varied. Some felt the solution to China's problems was to be found in a return to China's Confucian tradition. Such critics of complete Westernization began to produce laudatory evaluations of how Confucian values had contributed to economic development in Taiwan, South Korea, and Japan. Other opponents of the new infusions of Western culture tried to resurrect the democratic spirit of original Marxism from under the distortions introduced by Lenin, Stalin, and Mao, or even yearned for the perceived moral purity of the Mao era.

The "not far enoughs" and the "too fars" saw the world in very different terms. However, they agreed that the economic situation in the late 1980s was unacceptable and that China in the Deng era had become an unsatisfying mixture of cultural confusion and moral decay. Two factors acted together to make the economic frustrations experienced by many particularly severe. First, there were the long years of enforced spartan living of the Mao period, which left every group in society feeling that its just demands for material improvement urgently needed to be met. One effect of this backlog of unmet material aspirations was to make the early post-Mao grass-roots discussions of pay increases particularly angry and tearful. This phenomenon helps to explain why so many raises and bonus payments that were supposed to be distributed to the most worthy ended up being doled out equally to all. The second aggravating factor was inflation, which became increasingly serious after the mid-1980s. Many groups found their hard-won gains in buying power undermined and reversed; for some the fight to stay on top of the inflation treadmill brought back memories of the (much more serious) inflationary spiral of the late 1940s.

Sufficient Reform

The reader may wonder whether there were any groups at all in China who perceived that they were benefiting from the reforms. The answer is yes. Within both the "not far enough" and the "too far" groups there was, of course, diversity of views, and some students, intellectuals, workers, soldiers, and others were quite content with their lot in life. But in addition, there were two groups with particular cause for satisfaction, who felt gratitude rather than hostility toward the reformers.

One such group was the peasantry. Many if not most peasants felt that the reforms had rescued them from years of state-enforced poverty. Rural incomes initially increased more rapidly than did urban incomes, and peasants created a boom in construction of new housing and competed with urbanites for the televisions, washing machines, and other new symbols of reform-era prosperity. As noted earlier, the new rural prosperity also found more traditional outlets—in elaborate weddings and funerals, in restoration of local temples and lineage halls, and in pilgrimages and tourism. No doubt the renewed ability of families to escape from the day-to-day supervision of rural cadres and plan their own lives and work activities was also a source of considerable satisfaction. However, satisfaction on this score was tempered by one increasingly severe and unpopular way in which the lives of peasant families were regulated by the state in the Deng era—the mandatory birth-control program which culminated in the one-child policy after 1979. Even among the peasants, of course, views varied widely. In many disadvantaged regions, and among disadvantaged peasant families within every region, there were strong reasons for feeling that the benefits of the reforms were not trickling down the way they were supposed to. Even peasants who prospered under the reforms often felt anger at the shifts in rules and regulations and the demands for "contributions" and bribes that kept them from enjoying their economic success. In addition, localities and families that had prospered in the Mao era often felt threatened by official demands that they disband organizational forms painfully developed over the years in order to revive competition in the marketplace. Both "not far enoughs" and "too fars" could be found in the Chinese countryside, although they were in the minority.

Because peasants make up the single largest group in Chinese society, constituting between 70 and 80 percent of the total, one might have thought that their general satisfaction with the reforms would have provided the leadership with a powerful source of support. However, those peasants who had prospered under the reforms and who felt they could now operate successfully under them did not form a well-organized group that could make its influence felt effectively in support of the leadership. The difficulty of mobilizing peasants, short of revolution, combined with their concentration on local horizons and activities, made them a negligible factor in the political battles that erupted in the late 1980s.[6]

The other major group with cause to be satisfied with the reforms as they were was, of course, the high-ranking bureaucrats and their friends and families. The stalled nature of the reforms made available many opportunities for gaining new riches and prestige without providing a level playing field that would enable all groups to compete for those new opportunities. The continued substantial bureaucratic obstacles that restricted access to resources, information, and opportunities worked to the advantage of those who had the personal connections to take advantage of them, and the official slogans about the desirability of getting rich provided legitimation for their pursuit of gain. Since this small and privileged group was increasingly seen by both the "too far" and the "not far enough" groups as the cause of the problem, its satisfaction with the situation in 1989 was not an effective barrier against growing popular discontent.

[6] Trends such as stagnation in grain production after 1984, continued state niggardliness in investing in agriculture, and budget deficits that required some peasants to be paid for their grain in IOUs rather than cash had, by 1989, eroded support for Deng and his colleagues even in the countryside. Toward the end of the decade, outbursts of anger directed at the state agents became increasingly common in rural areas.

From Discontent to Mass Demonstrations

The existence of widespread popular discontent in the reform era is not a sufficient explanation for either the student demonstrations or the mass response to them. Widespread popular discontent has existed in many societies, and it certainly existed during a number of periods in the Mao era, without producing anything comparable to the events of the Beijing Spring. A number of other developments were required in combination to produce those events.

One such element was the relaxation of political controls that occurred in the reform era. Political study and mutual criticism sessions in schools and work units were less intense and less frequently held than in the Mao era. As noted earlier, large numbers of individuals and groups were "rehabilitated," and although many of those who lost their negative labels concentrated on lying low and enjoying their restored lives, others began to seek out audiences for the critiques of the system that their years in political oblivion had nurtured. Similarly, former Red Guards who had survived factional battles, years in rural exile, and university entrance exams took their place as teachers of the young and found enthusiastic disciples for their unconventional analyses of the ills of Chinese society. Exposure to China's cultural legacy and to the growing flood of ideas and models from the outside world provided a new awareness of political and cultural alternatives. Images of "people power" sweeping aside Marcos in the Philippines and of the legalization of alternative parties in Taiwan also provided examples of how to organize to bring about desired changes. These concrete models were probably more influential than accounts of the separation of powers in the American political system.

Over the years, as people could see public declarations of formerly heterodox views being raised without those raising them getting into political trouble, the feeling began to grow that dissent and efforts to change the system were safe. By the mid-1980s, avowedly autonomous clubs and associations began to emerge all over China. Even though most of these were apolitical and cautious, they provided a venue within which growing numbers of individuals (mostly urbanites, and disproportionately educated ones) could acquire a sense of being able to organize activities without CCP guidance and control. Although no major changes in the structure of the political system were carried out during the 1980s, the loosening of the political atmosphere created increased opportunities for critical views to be shared beyond the boundaries of family and close friends. China did not produce a fully formed "civil society," but individual grievances found new opportunities to coalesce into group dissent.[7]

Critical voices were more widely heard in the 1980s, and groups sharing common grievances began to emerge. Still, if the political elite had remained united and consistent in opposing any mass political action, the events of the Beijing Spring would not have escalated out of control. The previous rounds of student demonstrations were successfully contained, even though they showed an ominous tendency (from the standpoint of the leaders) to revive each time in enlarged form. What made the situation different in 1989 was the crumbling of unity within the elite and the implicit and explicit encouragement that the more ardent reformers within the leadership gave to students and others to raise critical voices. That encouragement seems to have been motivated by the increasing frustration that Zhao Ziyang and his followers felt over their difficulties in reviving reform momentum. Eventually many students and intellectuals came to feel that mass pressure was not only needed to promote the reform cause within a divided leadership, but that such pressure could also be effective in turning the tide against the conservatives within that leadership. The confidence (misguided, as it turned out) that bold public voicing of discontent not only would not be penalized but might actually produce desired results helped to energize active participation among the students and their allies. To be sure, there were some students who were very pessimistic about the prospects for change and who were willing to risk martyrdom nonetheless for their cause. However, if such pessimism had been generally shared, and if discontented students had faced a united and hostile elite, no escalating mass demonstrations would have occurred.

Even in the presence of widespread popular discontent, an opportunity to share that discontent with others, divisions within the elite, and some high-level encouragement of the demonstrators, the resulting demonstrations need not have gotten out of control. Indeed, given the sharp disagreements between the "not far enough" and "too far" groups, there were considerable opportunities for the leadership to foment con-

---

[7] Theorists of democratic transition argue that a civil society is a basic precondition for a democratic political system, and this view has been very influential among dissidents and reformers in Eastern Europe. Civil society involves the existence of a wide variety of organizations and associations that operate autonomously vis-à-vis the state. Such associations nourish a sense of citizenship that is protected from state infringement, and they provide vehicles through which group ideas and interests can be articulated and used to pressure the state. For an attempt to apply this concept to contemporary China, see Thomas Gold, "The Resurgence of Civil Society in China," *Journal of Democracy* (Winter 1990), pp. 18–31.

flict between groups as a way of keeping the situation from getting out of hand. In the previous major wave of student demonstrations, in 1986–87, this is precisely what happened. Leader statements and mass media accounts then portrayed the student demonstrators essentially as spoiled brats, concerned with improving their already privileged lives rather than with the problems of workers and peasants. The student demonstrations at that time attracted only minor public support from other groups in society and were relatively easily squelched.[8]

By 1989 the students had learned the lessons of earlier rounds of demonstrations, although some of this learning occurred only during the course of the Beijing Spring. Initially the students tried to exclude other groups from participating in their demonstrations, and in mourning former CCP general secretary Hu Yaobang, who died on April 15, they tended to focus upon issues (political reform and intellectual freedom) that were mainly of concern to other "not far enough" partisans. However, eventually this exclusionary policy was dropped and replaced by active encouragement of other groups to join them. In good Chinese fashion this participation usually took organized, corporate form, with individuals taking part as members of delegations from their schools or work units, complete with banners and signs, rather than as a heterogeneous mass. The appeals and demands raised by the students increasingly focused on issues that had broad popular appeal—to the "too far" groups as well as the "not far enough" ones. Increasingly the demonstrators' anger focused on inflation and corruption within the leadership, major problems that could unite the two disparate sides in hostility against the national elite.

Still, it took a further dramatic step to overcome the political and cultural gap between the students who initiated the demonstrations and the ordinary workers, cadres, and other urbanites who later joined them. That step was provided by the hunger strike launched in mid-May. The hunger strike testified in a vivid and relatively unconventional way to the students' position that they were not simply trying to benefit themselves but were laying claim to the moral legacy of righteous intellectuals in previous dynasties who were willing to risk their lives in their quest for justice. The dramatic act galvanized popular support for the students and led to a rapid escalation in both the size of the demonstrations in Tiananmen Square and in the number of

[8] It is important to keep in mind that minimal public support from other groups does not mean a total lack of sympathy in those groups. In a highly bureaucratized society such as China, with participation in any dissident activity easily detected and likely to have a dangerous impact on one's life and career, displaying public support for other groups is a brave act. Only when people feel a certain amount of assurance that they will not get into trouble are they likely to convert their sympathy into public acts.

supportive acts by other groups around the city. During this crucial period, splits within the leadership as well as problems in preparing for the Gorbachev visit prevented the elite from taking timely and forceful action to prevent the alliance between the "not far enoughs" and the "too fars" from being consolidated. Once that consolidation became apparent, a bandwagon effect set in, with more and more casual onlookers and thrill-seekers augmenting the ranks of committed protesters.

The unlikely alliance that had been forged to produce this popular uprising was visible in the symbols carried in Tiananmen Square and in countless smaller squares in provincial cities and towns. It is important to remember that demonstrations were not confined to Beijing. Not only provincial cities but many county seats and even small towns witnessed student demonstrations during the period of the Beijing Spring. Prominent in such demonstrations were Western symbols that conveyed themes favored by the "not far enoughs," such as slogans about freedom of the press and the Goddess of Democracy statue. However, also visible were competing non-Western symbols that reflected the views of the "too fars"—for example, the portraits of Mao Zedong that were borne aloft by many groups of demonstrators.

Consequences of the Beijing Spring

The mass demonstrations of the Beijing Spring were thus a product not merely of popular discontent but of a whole series of forces and contingencies. Furthermore, this chain of developments undermined the ability of the regime to unite the "too fars" and the "satisfieds" to fend off the challenge of the "not far enoughs." Instead, the "not far enoughs "were able to recruit support from the "too fars" in common opposition to the bureaucratic elite despite their many differences, while most of the "satisfieds" (China's peasants, in particular) remained on the sidelines. Under these circumstances, a disaffected and highly vocal minority almost succeeded in overturning the regime.

After the crackdown, the new conservative leadership coalition took a number of steps designed to stamp out organized opposition and prevent something similar from happening again. They ousted Zhao Ziyang and some of his key followers from the leadership and promoted into their ranks new leaders not closely associated in the public mind with the crackdown (notably Jiang Zemin, the new general secretary of the CCP) in an effort to forge an appearance of unity and stability. They increased political study and indoctrination activities, tightened the limits on cultural activities, and tried to stamp out harmful ideas and influences (for example, by jamming Voice of

America broadcasts). They reduced enrollments in key universities and initiated mandatory military training prior to enrollment in some institutions in an attempt to inoculate the young against "bourgeois liberal" ideas. They made it abundantly clear that voicing heterodox opinions could still get people into deep political trouble. They instituted measures designed to address the twin problems of inflation and bureaucratic corruption. And they attacked those who stimulated and participated in the demonstrations as unpatriotic, a theme designed to appeal to the nationalist sentiments of both the "too fars" and the "satisfieds."

Although such measures are designed to defuse both the sources of discontent and the precipitating conditions that led to the mass demonstrations, there are reasons to believe that the success of Deng Xiaoping's new conservative coalition in regaining control can be no more than partial and temporary. First, there are questions about how thorough and sustained these measures by the elite can be. Many provinces and localities are participating in the tightening of the political atmosphere only in a perfunctory manner, and even in Beijing many units are carrying out the new political study rituals and group criticism sessions in a formalistic and superficial way. Expressions of discontent are not being totally suppressed. Some individuals who have cooperated actively in the crackdown (for example, by turning in fugitives on the official arrest list) are now being subjected to public scorn. Furthermore, many of the familiar signs of elite disarray—conflicting messages in the mass media, unexplained disappearances and reappearances, rumors about schemes to gain more power—are apparent, making it difficult to persuade the public that the leadership will follow unified and consistent policies in the future. Even with the formal retirement of Deng Xiaoping from his last posts, it is obvious to everyone that the configuration of top leaders formed after the crackdown is of his making and is not likely to survive his death or incapacity. (The shift of mood in China is symbolized by the sad fact that many who in the early 1980s used to pray for Deng's longevity now hope for his early demise.)

All of these phenomena make it very unlikely that the genie of mass discontent can be put back in the bottle of quasi-Maoist controls. In addition to the grievances that existed prior to the Beijing Spring, there are new problems that will make the attempt by the conservatives to assert control highly problematic. There is now a powerful resentment unleashed by the crackdown itself, an outraged feeling that China's conservative leadership coalition has the blood of peaceful protesters on its hands. In addition, the economic situation has turned for the worse since the crackdown, producing new fears about stagnation and unemployment.[9] These new sources of anger are likely to make the reactions of the "too fars," who ordinarily might be expected to support the sort of curtailing of reform measures that has been launched since the crackdown, less than enthusiastic. In addition, the expressed commitment of the current leaders to continue the reforms and the "open" policy has prevented them thus far from formulating policies that would relieve the pre-1989 anxieties and hostility of the "too fars."

China's conservative leaders cannot simply turn back the clock and wipe out all consequences of the Beijing Spring, and the problems produced by the crackdown provide a strong basis for a continued union between "not far enough" and "too far" groups in the future. The Chinese political scene resembles a pressure cooker and is likely to do so for some time to come. Any crisis or rupturing of the enforced unity of the leaders is likely to unleash renewed popular anger, making the present "stability" a very precarious thing.

The paradox presented at the outset of this paper—of mounting discontent amid reform progress—is not so paradoxical after all. Dissatisfaction, pent-up consumer demands, and social tensions left over from the Mao era created extraordinary hopes and pressures that made the task of China's reformers very difficult. The initial progress of the reforms created public relief and gratitude but led to a thirst for more changes among some groups while fostering anxiety about future changes among others. Even in the wake of the June crackdown, the leadership has been unable to find a formula that will defuse popular hostilities and rebuild an effective alliance between those who think the reforms went too far and those who are relatively contented, in order to isolate the smaller but more articulate groups who do not think the reforms went far enough. Unless China's conservative leaders can find ways to defuse the situation, split the alliance of popular forces that oppose them, and rebuild popular support for their program of curtailed reforms, future explosions of mass discontent are quite likely.

---

[9] The picture on the economy is somewhat mixed. Inflation was reduced in the latter part of 1989 and a record grain harvest (in absolute, though not in relative, terms, given the continued growth in population) occurred in the same year. However, one of the causes of the decline in inflation is the retrenchment of the economy, and that has led to the closing of many enterprises, reductions in employment, and new efforts to force excess urban personnel to return to the countryside. These latter trends make popular perceptions of the economic situation considerably less than bullish.

4
China's Foreign Relations after 40 Years

Allen S. Whiting

As China's oligarchy of octogenarians reflected on the 40th anniversary of the People's Republic of China (PRC) on October 1, 1989, the few remaining revolutionary leaders could feel proud of their record in foreign relations. At the regime's founding Mao Zedong had declared that New China had "stood up" after the long-decried "century of shame and humiliation." His claim had indeed proved accurate. Beijing's place in the world was by now firmly established and duly acknowledged by Moscow, Washington, Tokyo, and others. In fact, the two superpower leaders both visited the Middle Kingdom capital in 1989 well before their Chinese counterpart met them on their home soils.

True, the course had been long and hard, in part complicated by the inevitable enmeshment of domestic politics with foreign relations. Thus in 1949 the revolutionary ethos of the newly ascendant Chinese Communist Party (CCP) prompted Beijing to ally with Moscow for economic development and national security. This in turn fueled Washington's anti-PRC fervor within the larger cold-war framework of Soviet-American confrontation. Again during the decade 1966–76 the revolutionary ethos became all-encompassing. Although the Cultural Revolution's origins and development derived wholly from domestic politics, its impact on foreign relations was dramatically demonstrated by Sino-Soviet border clashes in 1969 and the war alarms that followed.

But the domestic-foreign linkage had also had positive effects. In the decade after Mao's death in 1976, China's role in world affairs had won increasing respect as Beijing foreswore the revolutionary ethos in favor of joining the existing global political and economic system. Economic modernization became the primary domestic goal, requiring accommodation to international norms in foreign policy. This in turn brought China membership in major international economic organizations, expanded its diplomatic recognition, and reduced tension with all of its neighbors except Vietnam.

Moreover, China had never been more secure in this century. Persistent diplomatic efforts toward détente with the two superpowers permitted Beijing to relax its vigilance and reduce its military expenditures. The 1962 border war with India had established a line of control safeguarding Tibet against serious subversion and the critical Tibet-Xinjiang route from interdiction. Although the line remains unsanctioned by formal agreement, its stability is secure. In 1988 the People's Liberation Army (PLA) demonstrated its growing power in the South China Sea by smashing a small Vietnamese flotilla in the disputed Spratly Islands. Japan's increasing military strength warranted cautionary attention but provided no cause for immediate alarm.

Yet the spectacular fireworks over Tiananmen Square on October 1 could not blot out the dark spots in foreign relations that emerged in 1989 as a consequence of domestic politics. Not only was Beijing condemned by the advanced industrial world for the bloody suppression of unarmed student demonstrators and innocent bystanders on June 4, but the leadership also blamed the "counterrevolutionary rebellion" on a foreign plot to overthrow communist rule in China. Deng Xiaoping set the tone for his compatriots and the media in accusing "the international environment" in general and "U.S. influences" in particular of causing the domestic crisis. Beijing rejected foreign criticism as "interference in internal affairs" and charged Washington with having conspired against the regime from the 1950s to the present. In the last half of 1989 relations with the United States, Japan, and the European Community sank to their lowest level in the decade.

Ironically, events surrounding the long-awaited Sino-Soviet summit in May underscored the challenge that this domestic-foreign linkage posed for the Chinese leadership. Massive student demonstrations for political reforms prevented Soviet leader Mikhail Gorbachev, the premier political reformer, from visiting the Forbidden City and Tiananmen Square and forced him to enter the Great Hall of the People through a back door. His hosts were unwilling to risk hearing the humiliating attacks on themselves combined with praise for their guest.

The interplay of domestic politics and foreign relations in other socialist countries had serious implications for those countries' ties with China. The spillover effects of Gorbachev's reforms washed away communist leaders in East Germany, Poland, Hungary, Czechoslovakia, Bulgaria, and Romania, while Gorbachev struggled to salvage the party's power and multinational unity at home. By year's end, the cataclysmic East European developments had reawakened hope among the students and fear among the leaders that China would follow suit sooner or later, prompting a stormy exchange between a government official and a selected audience at Beijing University.[1]

The fall of Romania's Nicolae Ceausescu came only one month after his meeting with Qiao Shi, member of the Standing Committee of the Politburo and Secretariat of the CCP. Qiao had congratulated Ceausescu on "the successful convocation of the fourteenth [Romanian] party congress" and praised "the powerful leadership of the party."[2] The CCP marked the end of the congress with a call for "militant unity" between the two parties through "revolutionary friendship." The Romanian leader responded in the *People's Daily*, "Our two countries must take the initiative to resolve all kinds of difficulties."[3] Illegal wall posters at Beijing University later focused on his demise, with pointed implications for the future of Deng Xiaoping.[4] National security no longer depended on the PLA defending against an external military threat from foreign powers. Instead, 1989 found China's military called upon to suppress domestic dissidence through martial law in Lhasa (March) and Beijing (May), with foreign media reports and moral support for the dissidents playing a significant role. Tibetan lamas and Chinese university students alike attracted worldwide attention and strengthened their cause through the successful exploitation of foreign media. Paradoxically, while the threat of foreign attack was virtually eliminated by Beijing's improved relations with Moscow and Washington, the threat of foreign influence was greatly increased and proved far less amenable to counteraction. No matter how much Beijing jammed the airwaves, it could not wholly block BBC and Voice of America news bulletins. Local listeners transmitted the news through modern means of communication (such as fax) as well as traditional means, thereby thwarting the regime's efforts to control information about domestic as well as international events. Whether it came from emulation of American democracy or of Soviet *perestroika* and *glasnost*, the challenge to Deng's successors would be daunting.

As a further complication, Beijing's commitment to economic modernization and reform increased its dependence on foreign trade, loans, investment, and technology. This in turn increased the regime's vulnerability to economic sanctions such as those announced by Washington and Tokyo in mid-1989. It also lost credibility with for-

---

1 *New York Times*, December 29, 1989.

2 FBIS, *China Daily Report*, November 22, 1989, p. 17; *Xinhua*, November 22, 1989.

3 FBIS, *China Daily Report*, November 22, 1989, p.17; *South China Sunday Morning Post*, November 19, 1989, pp. 1–2.

4 *New York Times*, December 29, 1989.

eign banks and firms concerned about political instability and the fate of economic reforms, and thus the rate of foreign investment and technology transfer was slowed. Yet the greater the negative reaction abroad, the more the leadership reiterated its determination to reinstate Marxism-Leninism-Mao Zedong Thought as the guiding ideology and to resist the "bourgeois liberalization" transmitted by pernicious foreign influences.

Less immediately important but more perplexing over time was the problem of Taiwan. Four decades of threatening and cajoling had failed to persuade the Chinese Nationalist regime that its best interest lay in unification with the PRC. Although the United States could be blamed for encouraging Taiwanese separatism through arms sales, it was clearly Taipei and not Washington that held the key to the island's future. As with foreign relations in general, the record was mixed. On the positive side, trade and travel between the mainland and Taiwan surged as the late President Chiang Ching-kuo relaxed restrictions before his death in 1988. On the negative side, from Beijing's perspective, his Taiwanese successor, President Lee Teng-hui, represented the steady increase in political power by the island's native population as against its mainland component derived from the 1948 exodus. In December 1989 Taiwan's first genuine multiparty election not only resulted in 30 percent of the vote being awarded to non-Nationalist candidates but also saw independence for the island emerge as a campaign issue. Meanwhile, television coverage of the brutal killings in Beijing made mainland promises of "one country, two systems" less appealing than ever.

Concern over China's image abroad as well as over the reliability of PRC diplomats—50 reportedly defected after June 4—prompted the recall of all ambassadors for consultation in mid-summer. The concern proved justified by the absence of diplomatic representation from virtually all major powers at the 40th anniversary celebration in Tiananmen Square. Only in the Third World, China's self-proclaimed point of identity, did the PRC leadership enjoy continued acceptance, deliberately demonstrated by high-level visits and exchanges. At home Chinese media proclaimed defiant confidence in fighting off foreign influence and prevailing over economic sanctions. But the nationalistic rhetoric, typified by acerbic attacks on the granting of the Nobel Peace Prize to the Dalai Lama, betokened an outlook embittered by "interference in China's internal affairs" and embattled by the fall of communist rule abroad coinciding with continued opposition at home.

Throughout these developments, however, Beijing steadfastly insisted it would not change its foreign policy of "opening to the outside world" for economic and political interaction on the basis of the

Five Principles of Peaceful Coexistence. Specifically, it wooed foreign investment and trade, called on Japan to resume suspended aid and loans, and invited scientific cooperation through multinational conferences and bilateral exchange. Toward the world at large, nothing in China's posture had changed over the past ten years.

But for the Chinese population the open door required a fine mesh screen to keep out the "worms, flies, and mosquitoes" whose dangerous infections had poisoned the body politic, resulting in the "counterrevolutionary rebellion." Major newspaper and radio commentaries warned against the Western—read American—design to use trade, technology transfer, cultural exchange, and international conferences for the purpose of subverting communism in China. While conceding that much remained to be learned abroad and adopted at home, the Chinese media depicted the dangers of foreign influence in terms that at times approached xenophobia. This tone was particularly evident in the *Liberation Army Daily*, the journal of the PLA, but it permeated other newspapers as well.

Thus although foreign policy per se did not change in 1989, its interpretation underwent dramatic transformation for Chinese readers. Indeed, the rhetoric recalled that of the initial PRC founding in 1949–50 by differentiating between China's "true friends" and less trustworthy regimes with whom it was willing to do business at arm's length if they so desired. An assertive nationalism, recurringly manifest over the past four decades, threatened to cloud the atmosphere, if not the content, of foreign relations. Whether this atmosphere will improve when foreign sanctions are lifted and the present leaders, retired chairman Deng Xiaoping and President Yang Shangkun, die remains to be seen.

Sino-Soviet Relations

Gorbachev's May 15–18 visit to Beijing climaxed a decade of mutual probing for détente in Sino-Soviet relations wherein Moscow made significant concessions to Beijing on the latter's celebrated three demands: removal of Soviet troops from Mongolia and their reduction opposite China, withdrawal of Soviet forces from Afghanistan, and pressure on Vietnam to abandon its occupation of Cambodia. As the first top-level Soviet presence in China since Nikita Khrushchev's stormy arrival in 1959, the event had been anticipated by a steady improvement of relations, but in the end it was eclipsed by the Democracy Movement. Yet it remained important for its reestablishment of formal party relations as well as its benchmark role in state relations.

Political reforms in the Soviet Union and China, which had diverged sharply before the summit, moved even farther apart after the June 4 crackdown. This left party relations tacitly at odds, although a CCP delegation visited Moscow in September and a reciprocal delegation visited Beijing in late December. However, relations continued to improve with the piecemeal resolution of the border dispute, which settled most of the eastern frontier differences and made progress on the western front. While few details emerged, it was unlikely that agreement could be reached on Heixiazi (Bear Island) opposite Khabarovsk at the juncture of the Amur and Ussuri rivers, or on the high Pamir plateau at the trijuncture of the Soviet Union, Afghanistan, and China. This reduced the likelihood of a totally demilitarized border despite the two sides reportedly having discussed the possibility. Nevertheless, cross-border trade burgeoned, and the imminent completion of the Kazakhstan-Xinjiang railroad, which is largely financed by Moscow, augured well for further expansion in this area.

Nearly one-fourth of the joint communiqué that was issued after the May summit meeting addressed the Cambodian problem and reflected the separate positions of the two sides concerning its ultimate resolution. Differences remained over the role of the competing Cambodian factions following the Vietnamese withdrawal and the process toward general elections. These differences were shared by all the participants in the subsequent Paris conference and remained irreconcilable at year's end. The remainder of the communiqué held few surprises, for the most part expressing agreement on bilateral exchanges and principles of international relations.

However, in light of subsequent events, it seemed unlikely that Gorbachev's invitations to "Comrades Deng Xiaoping, Yang Shangkun, Zhao Ziyang, and Li Peng" for official visits to the Soviet Union would be taken up in the near future, if ever, by most of the list. Nonetheless, Moscow muted its comment and reported circumspectly on the Beijing massacre. In September Anatoly Lukyanov, first vice president of the Presidium of the Supreme Soviet, headed a delegation to Beijing, where he stated, "We cannot force the experience of one country onto another because the specific situations of the two countries are different. But, one point is common, that is, no reform is workable without the leadership of the party."[5]

Moscow's diplomatic discretion notwithstanding, Foreign Minister Qian Qichen minced no words concerning past Soviet perfidy in his 40-year review of foreign relations.[6] Omitting all reference to the mas-

[5] *Beijing Review* 32:39 (September 25–October 1, 1989), p. 11.

[6] Qian Qichen, "New China's Diplomacy: 40 Years On," *ibid.*, pp. 15–19.

sive and vital assistance in economic and military modernization rendered during the first decade of the Sino-Soviet alliance, Qian chose to recall "Soviet big-power chauvinist performances . . . breaching contracts, withdrawing experts, pressing for the repayment of debts, deploying heavy concentrations of troops along the border and provoking clashes. In the following two decades [1960–80], not once did the Soviet Union abandon its military threat against China." Then "after long confrontation, Sino-Soviet relations have finally been normalized." This did not betoken any mutual embrace, much less a return to strategic and tactical exchanges on military and political matters such as occurred in the 1950s.

In sum, Sino-Soviet relations fell far short of returning full circle to 1949 with the 1989 summit. Instead they struck a businesslike balance, eschewing both confrontation in bilateral relations and cooperation in world affairs. This served domestic economic needs in both countries by reducing pressure for military expenditure and increasing economic barter across the 4,650-mile border as well as at the state level. At the same time it preserved the independence of each to compete with the other in third areas, especially South and Southeast Asia, as well as to maintain a mutual distance with respect to domestic policy.

Insofar as this resembles the standard relationship of adjoining nations, it deserves the communiqué's term "normalization." Nevertheless, an ideological shadow remained at year's end to cloud this characterization of Sino-Soviet relations. Beijing did not inveigh publicly against Gorbachevian "revisionism" as it had against Khrushchev's earlier reforms in the 1950s. It could hardly do so with respect to economic reforms, for it had outpaced Moscow in this regard over the past decade, most notably with abandonment of communes for family farming. Yet despite the nominal agreement on domestic party roles during the May summit meeting, at no other point during the year did politics in the two countries approach convergence. On the contrary, virtually all of the political changes in Moscow over the past four years were without parallel in Beijing.

In November Li Peng contradicted the tenor of the joint communiqué as well as the assertions made during the summit by Deng and Zhao when he informed the German magazine *Die Welt:* "This normalization does not apply to the ties between the two communist parties; only the relations between the two sides have again returned to normal."[7] Then in late December informed sources re-

[7] FBIS, *China Daily Report*, November 24, 1989, p. 1; *Die Welt*, November 23, 1989, p. 6.

ported a secret directive expressing criticism of Soviet and East European reforms but warning recipients to keep this view private, except for minimal factual reporting.[8] The directive alleged that Gorbachev was responsible for the "subversion of socialism" in Eastern Europe and implicitly in the Soviet Union as well. Chinese press reports downplayed all related developments as instructed, but confidentially circulated translations of foreign media kept upper party and government levels fully informed. The successive collapse of one communist regime after another could not but undermine confidence in the Kremlin's course of action at home as well as abroad. The resulting impact on Sino-Soviet relations presumably prevents any agreement on domestic reforms. It also assures that Beijing will try to limit interaction between the two countries so long as it feels threatened by local political demands.

Sino-American Relations

The other leg of the once-vaunted strategic triangle deteriorated coincidentally with the strengthening of Sino-Soviet relations but, contrary to past conventional wisdom, there was no interrelated causality. The process began over a relatively minor matter with major symbolic significance during President Bush's "working visit" to Beijing following the funeral for the late Emperor Hirohito. Prior to Bush's arrival, the Chinese learned of a White House invitation planned for Fang Lizhi, noted astrophysicist and human rights advocate, and his wife, Li Shuxian, to attend the president's banquet. In diplomatic practice, this occasion would reciprocate the welcoming dinner and honor the local hosts, who would have some say in its handling. In political terms, the presence of some 500 guests would considerably dilute the visibility of the Fangs since they would not be at the head table or recognized in any remarks.

However, exchanges on the matter between the PRC Foreign Ministry and the American embassy apparently resulted in a deadlock. Both Li Peng and Zhao Ziyang sternly lectured Bush in separate conversations, warning that "a shadow" would fall over Sino-American relations if government officials were to "interfere in internal affairs" by raising the issue of human rights. Fang and his wife, together with the American couple escorting them, were prevented by a large police contingent from reaching the banquet and forced to walk some distance to the diplomatic quarter. Fang's press conference that night focused worldwide attention on the imbroglio. The Foreign Ministry

---

[8] *New York Times*, December 29, 1989.

spokesman declared that inviting persons unacceptable to the Chinese side could "only be interpreted as support to this kind of people and disrespect to the host country."[9] He also termed remarks by President Bush and Secretary of State Baker on their departure "irresponsible," occasioning "surprise" and "deep regret."

This minor incident foreshadowed what was to become a major impasse between Beijing and Washington when Fang and his wife won sanctuary in the American embassy following the Beijing massacre in June. The PRC thereupon declared them criminals to be arrested for having allegedly masterminded the "counterrevolutionary rebellion." Throughout the remainder of the year Chinese media excoriated the couple for having plotted the regime's overthrow together with "a small handful of people" and claimed that their refuge proved the nefarious role of "U.S. imperialism" in the Democracy Movement.

The Fangs symbolized the collision of values in Sino-American relations. More substantive damage to the relationship resulted from President Bush's announcement of sanctions that included the suspension of high-level contacts, Export-Import Bank loans and OPIC protection for American business in China, and all military-related sales. Bush further committed U.S. policy to persuading international organizations—mainly the World Bank—to suspend consideration of new loans to the PRC. He also granted waivers to an estimated 40,000 Chinese students in the United States when their visas expired, to save them from returning home and facing the consequences of their support of the Democracy Movement.

In the wake of a firestorm of American public reaction to the graphic television coverage of the Democracy Movement and its bloody demise, Congress responded more strongly than did the executive branch, with harsher language in speeches and far more severe sanctions in draft legislation. Although the final bill left discretion to the president for enacting the sanctions, he nonetheless vetoed it along with a separate bill extending special visa privileges to Chinese students in the United States. At the same time Bush announced administrative measures that would virtually duplicate the visa legislation.

Beijing reacted as might be expected, with fulsome outrage but limited measures. These included suspension of Fulbright lectureships and the Peace Corps program, along with cancellation of delegations to the United States and new restrictions on students planning to go abroad. The denunciations mounted through the summer as the Voice of America came under increased attack for "rumor-mongering" os-

---

[9] *Beijing Review* 32:11 (March 13–19, 1989), p. 12.

tensibly to stimulate "turmoil." A book was published that purported to document an American effort to destroy communism by promoting "peaceful evolution" through trade, aid, and cultural and scientific exchange. It accused successive officials from the Truman to the Bush administration of participating in this effort. Chinese media echoed and amplified this theme, going so far as to attack Richard Nixon, despite his repeated red-carpet treatment on visits to Beijing both when he was in and out of office. The recapitulation of American perfidy began with the U.S. role in the Korean War and intervention in the Taiwan Strait and continued to the present, with virtually no reference to positive developments after 1972, when President Nixon's trip to China began Sino-American détente.

In hope of repairing the situation, Nixon visited China in October, followed by former secretary of state Henry Kissinger in November. Deng Xiaoping bluntly told the ex-president, "Frankly speaking, the United States was too deeply involved in the turmoil and counterrevolutionary rebellion . . . . China was the real victim and it is unjust to reprove China for it."[10] Kissinger's visit proved no more successful.

The Bush administration had already moved to contain the damage to relations by secretly sending National Security Adviser Brent Scowcroft and Deputy Secretary Lawrence S. Eagleburger to Beijing in July, less than a month after the announcement of sanctions. A second Scowcroft-Eagleburger mission in December was announced simultaneously with its occurrence, after which news of the first one leaked out. Despite the exchanged formalities proclaiming friendship and the importance of Sino-American relations for "peace and stability," no resolution of the differences, including the impasse over the Fangs, had emerged by year's end. Neither had Beijing lifted martial law or relaxed its repression of those charged with directing the Democracy Movement. Nevertheless, Washington proceeded to approve the sale of three satellites to be used on Chinese launchers, ostensibly for civilian purposes, and lifted the Export-Import Bank and OPIC limitations. Work also continued on the US$500 million avionics package to upgrade Chinese fighter capability so that the equipment would be ready for delivery when the suspension on military-related sales was lifted.

In 1989 Sino-American relations manifested many of their attributes of the past 40 years. On the positive side both parties articulated the importance of strategic, political, cultural, and economic interests linking the two giant Pacific Ocean countries, much as they had since President Nixon's 1972 visit. On the negative side the two parties ar-

[10] *Beijing Review* 32:46 (November 13–19, 1989), p. 9.

ticulated contradictory ideological values, whose implementation in government actions evoked public anger that further exacerbated relations, much as had occurred from 1949 to 1972. Although the White House tried to turn the anger aside, Congressional moves thwarted it. In China official statements and the controlled media expressed anti-American sentiments, but it was impossible to assess their impact on the rural and urban populations.

As with Sino-Soviet relations, there was no full-scale return to the past, which in this case would have meant a total break. Both sides contained the substantive damage and maintained a semblance of dialogue in bilateral and multilateral forums. But this process depended on carefully calculated diplomacy and practical economics, there being no overriding strategic interest on either side in the wake of Sino-Soviet and Soviet-American détente. It also depended on no further developments occurring in Tibet or on the mainland that would trigger renewed accusations on both sides. Resolution of the Fang Lizhi problem could ameliorate but not remove the acrimony that followed the June 4 crackdown and the American reaction to it.

In both countries the impact of domestic politics inexorably poisoned the atmosphere within which Beijing and Washington conducted their business. This stood in sharp contrast to the relationship that both sides had toasted on the tenth anniversary of diplomatic recognition in December 1988. The previous ten years had seen isolated instances of value clash disturbing Sino-American ties, notably the issues of birth control and Tibetan dissidence. Nineteen eighty-nine, however, brought an increased intensity to divisive issues, as the American advocacy of human rights collided head-on with the Chinese leadership's insistence on control over its own people. The collision was exacerbated by a dynamic of action and reaction that neither capital was wholly able to stop.

Sino-Japanese and Sino-European Relations

In 1989 both Beijing and Tokyo managed to skate over the surface cracks that recurringly arise in their relationship and keep the more serious fissure of June 4 from creating a decline like that in Sino-American relations. Nevertheless, Japan's response to the events of June 4 halted the sense of improvement communicated by former prime minister Noboru Takeshita's visit in 1988 and the reduction that year in China's trade imbalance.

The most sensitive of the standard items in Sino-Japanese relations is the record of Tokyo's past aggression. In February the issue again flared briefly because of remarks in the Diet by Takeshita and a subordinate. The prime minister claimed that whether Japan's role in World War II was aggressive or nonaggressive was for future historians to decide, while the second official denied that the late emperor bore any responsibility for the war. China, along with other Asian countries, immediately protested, whereupon Takeshita and Foreign Minister Uno gave fulsome retractions. The incident closed quickly, in contrast with similar situations between 1985 and 1988, but betokened the continuing vulnerability of Sino-Japanese relations.

Premier Li Peng's visit to Japan in mid-April reciprocated Takeshita's but lacked the profuse and favorable publicity that had accompanied the latter's tour of Chinese cultural sites. Newly titled Emperor Akihito expressed his regret over past relations, and both governments agreed to establish a Sino-Japanese investment promotion organization. However, Li's effort to improve trade, increase technology transfer, and expand investment struck few sparks as Beijing's austerity program limited the prospects for profitable growth in joint ventures and special economic zones. The turmoil accompanying the June 4 events further darkened the business outlook as political instability coupled with economic retrenchment raised doubts in Japan about the regime's ability to manage either problem.

Tokyo's response to the brutal PLA crackdown fell far short of the condemnation voiced elsewhere, although as a member of the Group of Seven (which also includes the United States, Great Britain, France, West Germany, Italy, and Canada) Japan joined in criticizing the PLA actions in July. Restraint arose in part from Japanese sensitivity about reawakening Chinese resentment and in part from the lower level of public reaction in Japan to suppression of the Democracy Movement. Japan also lifted travel restrictions in time for participation in the October 1 national day celebration.

However, Japan announced it would delay implementation of the 810 billion yen aid program scheduled for 1990–94, linking implementation to the lifting of martial law in Beijing. This aroused belated but sharp Chinese criticism. At a November meeting with the Sino-Japanese Association on Economy and Trade, the minister of foreign economic relations and trade, Zheng Tuobin, charged that Tokyo had imposed the "strictest" sanctions in the Western bloc. In December after the second Scowcroft-Eagleburger mission, Japanese sources indicated the loan freeze would be partially lifted in early 1990, but no official announcement had occurred by the new year.

Japan also suspended high-level official contact. However, in mid-September Deng Xiaoping, Li Peng, and Jiang Zemin all separately received Masayoshi Ito, major Liberal Democratic Party figure and leader of the Parliamentarians for Japan-China Friendship. The reception reflected Beijing's effort to press Tokyo for better relations regardless of Washington's posture. Ito's past role in strengthening ties raised expectations for an immediate improvement. As expressed by Deng, "Sino-Japanese friendly ties must not change and will not change."[11] However, there were no new developments by year's end. In addition, Beijing failed to persuade Tokyo to deny Wuer Kaixi, the most prominent student leader of the May–June demonstrations, entry into Japan, and he held a series of highly publicized meetings there to attack suppression of the Democracy Movement.

Although the PRC could claim that out of 137 countries with whom it had relations, only "some 20" were critical of the June events, virtually all noncommunist Europe fell into that category together with Australia and New Zealand. In addition to the censure expressed collectively by the Group of Seven and the European Community, individual members expressed condemnation, the harshest being voiced by London and Bonn. France provoked sharp criticism from Beijing, initially in July when it gave refuge to Wuer Kaixi and Yan Jiaqi, both major figures in the Democracy Movement, after they had been rebuffed by Washington. A second wave of attacks followed in September when the First Congress of the Federation for a Democratic China met in Paris with headquarters provided in part by the French government. Norway also drew a strong PRC protest in December for awarding the Nobel Peace Prize to the Dalai Lama. In addition the World Bank deferred discussion of any further loans to Beijing, arousing the expected critical response.

The Third World: Better Prospects?

Ever since 1949 the PRC has managed to identify with Third World countries and advance its activities in them. Whether promoting the revolutionary ethos or supporting established regimes, Beijing's anti-hegemonical and anti-imperialist stance has found "friends" in Asia, the Middle East, Africa, and Latin America. Some friendships have proved more durable than others, depending on the basis of mutual interest and the ability to adapt to change in China's overall orientation. But as a rule, it has been the Third World that has provided continuity in China's foreign policy regardless of the shifts in relations with the superpowers and other major powers. Nineteen eighty-nine proved no exception in this regard.

In Asia, Zhao Ziyang visited Pyongyang, North Korea from April 24 to 29, just as the government-student confrontation was mounting

---

[11] *Beijing Review* 32:40 (October 2–8, 1989), p. 5.

in Beijing, which totally eclipsed his mission. However, no change occurred in the coolness of North Korean communications concerning China, reflecting continued displeasure in Pyongyang over Beijing's economic reforms as well as increasing interaction between Pyongyang and Seoul.[12] Following June 4 a greater Chinese desire for close relations was suggested by the reemergence in the Chinese media of the analogy of "lips and teeth" to describe the relationship, although the term was not reciprocated in the North Korean media. In September Beijing suddenly canceled a sizable South Korean business delegation that had anticipated an imminent exchange of trade offices between the two capitals. While this could have resulted from Beijing's rigorous retrenchment program, it had obvious appeal for Pyongyang. In November North Korean President Kim Il Sung suddenly visited Beijing "unofficially" and in complete secrecy, his red-carpet reception at the railroad station by Deng, Jiang, and Li only being revealed six days after his departure. Apparently the two regimes felt pressed by the rush of change in Eastern Europe and the Soviet Union, prompting high-level consultation on how to manage relations with these countries as well as their own bilateral affairs. According to the official announcement, "Their opinions on these issues were identical."

The situation in Cambodia required consultation between Bangkok and Beijing. Arming the Khmer Rouge guerrillas while negotiating with ASEAN, Phnom Penh, Hanoi, and Washington on how to handle the Vietnamese withdrawal and its aftermath provided a full agenda for the Thai foreign minister's visit to Beijing in mid-March and Prime Minister Chatichai Choonhavan's arrival in late October. Meanwhile Laos's leader, Kaysone Phomvihan, headed a government delegation to Beijing for his first visit in ten years, winning Chinese praise for the "normalization of relations." On Cambodia, however, China remained adamant, both continuing support for the Khmer Rouge and insisting that Hanoi had not really withdrawn all its forces.

Negotiations for the restoration of relations with Indonesia proceeded throughout the year, resulting in a PRC deputy foreign minister heading the first delegation to Jakarta since relations were broken in 1966. Sources in Indonesia indicated that agreement had been reached on all points for the two nations to resume formal diplomatic ties in 1990.

South Asia gained special prominence in the aftermath of Prime Minister Rajiv Gandhi's December 1988 visit, the first such Indian presence in the Chinese capital since that of his grandfather, Jawahar-

[12] For a summary analysis see FBIS, *Trends*, July 19, 1989, pp. 23–26.

lal Nehru, in 1954. In July 1989 the general secretary of the Congress Party of India came to continue negotiations on the disputed border, undeterred by the recent disturbances. In October Vice Premier Wu Xueqian arrived in New Delhi. The following month Premier Li Peng made his first trip abroad since June 4, touring Pakistan, Nepal, and Bangladesh. (President Benazir Bhutto had met with Li Peng in February to discuss Afghanistan, Cambodia, and other matters.) The *People's Daily* pointedly noted that it was "correct for China to regard the development of friendly relations with the Third World countries as the foundation of its foreign policy . . . . When certain Western powers are still exerting political and economic pressure on China, Premier Li Peng's successful visit to the three countries shows that the vast numbers of the Third World countries are our trusted, genuine friends."[13]

There was also activity in Chinese-African relations, with Beijing hosting the leaders of Mali, Burundi, Uganda, Togo, Burkina Faso, Ghana, and Sierra Leone. In addition the Ethiopian deputy prime minister visited the PRC, and Julius Nyerere, chairman of the Tanzanian Revolutionary Party, was Deng's first guest after he stepped down as chairman of the CCP Military Commission. In August Foreign Minister Qian made a whirlwind tour of Botswana, Lesotho, Zimbabwe, Angola, Zambia, and Mozambique, where he touted China's support for "serious North-South talks" on changing "the unreasonable international economic order and settlement of the African debt issue."[14] He also noted that "many African countries showed their understanding of the measures taken by the Chinese government to deal with the political disturbances that occurred in China."

However, minor reverses with possibly major implications occurred when one African and two Latin American countries—Liberia (October 9), Grenada (July 19), and Belize (October 11)—recognized the Republic of China (Taiwan), prompting the People's Republic to immediately break relations with them. All three cases reflected Taiwan's financial largesse in major aid projects, which prompted Beijing to lash out at "money diplomacy." This may have contributed to State Councillor Li Tieying's granting more than US$625,000 to the Congo and offering an interest-free loan of unspecified amount to the Central African Republic during his visit to those two countries in mid-November.

---

[13] FBIS, *China Daily Report*, November 22, 1989, pp. 14–15; *Renmin ribao*, November 22, 1989, p. 1.

[14] *Beijing Review* 32:49 (December 4–10, 1989), p. 15.

These developments had no precedent in the past decade but offered a suggestive parallel with the previous 20 years, when Taiwan and the mainland vied for diplomatic recognition in Africa and elsewhere by proffering competitive aid programs. With Taiwan's foreign exchange reserves in excess of US$70 billion, among the highest in the world, such competition would augur ill for Beijing were it to resume full force, given the desperate state of many Third World debtor nations.

Some compensation, however, came from the Middle East in April when Saudi Arabia, the only Arab nation without PRC diplomatic relations, opened a trade office in Beijing. Saudi ties to Taiwan remained firm for the time being, but in view of recent Chinese missile sales to Riyadh, such competition could redound in favor of the mainland. In May the new Iranian president, Hashemi Rafsanjani, was received by Deng, and in October, Yasser Arafat was welcomed as president of the State of Palestine. Li Peng offered a five-point Middle East peace proposal which called for an international conference to be presided over by the United Nations with attendance by the five permanent Security Council members "and other parties," direct dialogue between the Palestine Liberation Organization and Israel, an Israeli withdrawal from "the occupied territories," and mutual recognition between Palestine and Israel. Deng congratulated Arafat on his new presidential status and declared, "We have trusted and supported each other for several decades. Our relationship is not an ordinary one and friendship between us is eternal."[15]

Finally, in December President Yang made his first trip abroad since June 4, visiting Egypt, the United Arab Emirates, Kuwait, and Oman. As with Qian's August tour of Africa and Li Peng's November round in South Asia, Yang's Middle East visit brought no major announcements but served to strengthen China's image in the Third World so as to offset somewhat its lessened stature elsewhere.

Hong Kong and Taiwan

Last and perhaps of greatest long-run significance was Beijing's loss of credibility in Hong Kong and Taiwan after the June 4 massacre. Hong Kong virtually exploded, with an estimated one million persons demonstrating on behalf of the Democracy Movement. The long-time publisher of *Wen Wei Po* left his job with a bitter letter of denunciation. New China News Agency personnel joined in public protests, as did Bank of China employees. Prominent delegates to the Hong Kong

---

[15] *Beijing Review* 32:42 (October 16–22, 1989), p. 11.

Basic Law Drafting Committee resigned or spoke out critically against the PLA brutality. In London parliamentary and public opinion pressured the government to liberalize the restrictions on migration to the United Kingdom after the colony is taken over by the mainland in 1997, with some accommodation emerging at year's end.

Beijing reacted angrily to what it termed "subversive activity" in Hong Kong, while Governor David Wilson defended demonstrations as proper free speech. The issue sharpened as Hong Kong became an escape route for Democracy Movement dissidents and as one of China's noted Olympic swimmers who had fled to Hong Kong became a cause célèbre. When Guangdong authorities retaliated by refusing to accept captured illegal border crossers back into the PRC, the Hong Kong government retreated and promised it would not allow further anti-regime activity, whereupon the status quo ante was restored at the border. However, plummeting confidence in the colony's future was reflected in a sharp drop in the stock exchange in June and a continued flight of capital and managerial skill abroad. Beijing worsened the situation by unleashing a new campaign against "the internationalization of Hong Kong."

Taiwan reacted less vociferously than others to June 4, to avoid provoking Beijing, but it reaped political benefits by contrasting its relatively free and democratic election in December with mainland repression. Selected dissidents found refuge on the island, and Taipei gave support to Democracy Movement activities abroad. Travel to the mainland slumped after the massacre and was further deterred by the arrest of a Taiwanese journalist in the company of a dissident activist, but trade resumed its high rate of growth after a brief hiatus.

As already noted, Beijing's promise of "one country, two systems" lost much of its credibility in both Hong Kong and Taiwan after June 4. In addition, its increasingly aggressive propaganda campaign against "one China, one Taiwan" and Taiwanese independence reflected justified concern over the trend of island diplomacy and politics. The oblique threat of force reappeared after a long hiatus when President Yang remarked in Cairo: "A recent phenomenon is especially noteworthy. In recent elections in Taiwan, some people openly called for Taiwan's independence. There were foreign factors behind this, and some foreigners tried to use the incident to cause trouble. We think that it is very dangerous for Taiwan to seek independence . . . . We will never allow Taiwan to be independent. The Chinese Government will not sit idly by if Taiwan independence is becoming a reality."[16]

The phrase "will not stand idly by" recalled Beijing's warning in October 1950 that cautioned United Nations forces not to cross the 38th parallel into North Korea. When they did so, China intervened in the war, winning back the northern half of the peninsula. The congruence of Yang's words with the overall tone of assertive nationalism dominating the media in late 1989 provided a sharp contrast with 1988, previously characterized as "a red-letter year when reason and goodwill stepped out of the shadows into the limelight of world affairs generally and of China's foreign relations in particular."[17] A sense of siege mentality manifest in internal directives and public exhortations aimed at the PLA and the CCP revived xenophobic themes that had recurred up to 1977 but had since disappeared.

The constant caveats against foreign influence and plots of "peaceful evolution" allegedly promoted through foreign contact coexisted with assertions that the "open" policy must continue. The contradictory thrusts of this line suggested division within the leadership, although information thereon rests almost wholly on rumor. Should moderate reformers prevail in a succession struggle, the relaxed attitude toward foreign contact that prevailed prior to June 4, 1989, will return. Until that occurs, however, foreign relations will be seen by the Chinese ruling elite as posing an uneasy mixture of political threat and economic opportunity.

Ironically, this ambivalence characterized the original attitude of the new regime in 1949, succinctly stated by Mao in his celebrated essays at that time. Were it merely the view of the few remaining Long March survivors, the phenomenon might be attributed to the unreconstructed revolutionary ideology of one generation. But Li Peng and his cohorts have no such background. Their apparent acceptance of the "us" versus "them" world outlook does not augur well for China's accommodation to the present international system with its inevitable linkage of economic interdependence to media penetration and political interaction. Eventually such an accommodation will occur, but in the meantime Beijing is likely to stand fast in its resolve against "interference in internal affairs," regardless of the political or economic consequences abroad.

---

16 FBIS, *China Daily Report*, December 22, 1989, pp. 5–6; *Xinhua*, December 20, 1989.

17 Steven I. Levine, "Foreign Policy in 1988: Resolving Old Conflicts," in Anthony J. Kane, ed., *China Briefing, 1989* (Boulder, CO: Westview Press, 1989), p. 49.

5
The Crisis of Culture*

Leo Ou-fan Lee

The sudden outburst of youthful protest that erupted in Tiananmen Square in April 1989 thrilled people around the world. Thrill turned to shock on June 4 when the student demonstrations ended in a brutal, tragic crackdown. But the significance of these events went far beyond what was captured in the news media. Several years earlier a rising tide of cultural fermentation and agitation had already swept the major cities, paving the way for the student movement. These cultural activities were masterminded and launched by a large number of young and middle-aged intellectuals in various fields: creative writers, literary critics and theorists, and scholars in comparative culture and Chinese history and thought. They raised a series of intellectual concerns, all stemming initially from a profound disillusionment with the Cultural Revolution (1966–76), a decade of political terror and chaos that reduced Chinese life and culture to rubble.

Significantly, 1989 marked the 70th anniversary of the May Fourth Movement, itself a "cultural revolution" in which students took a prominent role. On that memorable Sunday, May 4, 1919, students from several universities in Beijing gathered to protest the humiliating decision of the warlord government to accept the terms of the Versailles Treaty, thereby relinquishing Chinese claims to the Shandong peninsula, birthplace of Confucius, when it passed from German to Japanese hands following World War I. This incident, however, was only the pivot of a large-scale movement ranging from a "literary revolution" in 1917, which ushered in a new vernacular mode of writing, to a vociferous series of iconoclastic assaults by intellectuals on all spheres of traditional Chinese culture. These intellectuals blamed tradition, and particularly Confucianism, for China's inability to adapt to

* Both the thesis and the material for this article are drawn from a collaborative research project now in progress, funded by the Luce Foundation, titled "China after the Cultural Revolution: Reassessments in Literature, Thought, and Politics." I am indebted to the Luce fellows from China as well as to the foundation for information and support.

the modern world. They argued that only a complete overhaul of culture, a revolutionary set of changes based on Western models, could save the Chinese nation from being "carved up like a melon" by the aggressive Western powers and their star pupil, Japan.

Since the beginning of 1989, the students in the universities in Beijing had been preparing for a large-scale demonstration to commemorate the 70th anniversary of the May Fourth Movement. The unexpected death of Hu Yaobang on April 15 served to advance it by half a month. As the university students marched to Tiananmen Square, they became aware of a double significance: they found themselves not only recalling the memory of May 4, 1919, but also reenacting the Tiananmen protest of April 5, 1976, when Zhou Enlai's death triggered a spontaneous demonstration in Beijing that eventually led to the downfall of the Gang of Four. If the commemoration of the May Fourth Movement was symbolic mainly in terms of cultural renovation, the reenactment of the April 5 demonstration clearly had more direct political connotations. Thus cultural and political memories were intermixed as the demonstrations gathered momentum and increased their scope. Like their predecessors on April 5, 1976, the students mourned a leader whom they considered to be upright and incorrupt, whose death followed a fall from political grace. Thus they were able to give voice to their discontent with official corruption and demand more radical reforms.

Large numbers of intellectuals were drawn into the student demonstrations. On May 16 they issued a six-point manifesto with more than 1,000 signatures supporting the students and advising the government to adopt democratic measures to cope with the political crisis. On the next day, May 17, a small group of intellectuals led by the political scientist Yan Jiaqi issued another more strongly worded manifesto that openly denounced Deng Xiaoping (without, however, mentioning his name) as a dictator and a *de facto* emperor.

The participation of intellectuals enlarged the ranks of the Democracy Movement and served as a catalyst that brought in people from different walks of life and from government units. A central coordinating council of student and intellectual leaders was established; daily meetings were held, with the student leaders sitting side by side with the intellectuals, discussing the daily agenda of activities. According to reliable reports, in late May intellectual members of this coordinating council persuaded student leaders to hold one last demonstration and then disband peacefully. But the orders were ignored by the demonstrators on the square, most of whom were new arrivals from the provinces. Had they gone along with the leaders' decision, the ensuing massacre in the long night of June 3–4 might have been avoided.

But it is not my intention to give a detailed narrative of the student movement itself, nor do I wish to analyze the complex relations between intellectual and student leaders during the period of the demonstrations. Rather, I am interested in exploring the broader background crisis of culture, for I believe that the relationship between culture and politics in contemporary China is as intricate as intraparty power struggles.

Amidst a general crisis of political faith in post-Cultural Revolution China, intellectuals found themselves confronting a cultural crisis as they began to address an overarching question: How does one account for a national catastrophe of such mammoth proportions that it adversely affected virtually all areas of Chinese life? Did the Cultural Revolution represent an abnormal development in the revolutionary process, or is it traceable to more deep-seated factors from the past?

By the mid-1980s, a kind of cultural soul-searching seemed to have enveloped large segments of the intelligentsia. A phrase coined by these intellectuals gained wide currency: *wenhua fansi*. Its literal meaning is reflection about culture, which implies active intellectual engagement with the cultural and historical ramifications of the Cultural Revolution rather than with its narrow political consequences.

As I shall demonstrate in the following pages, the assertiveness of culture as represented by the phenomenon of cultural self-reflection took on a decidedly political significance. It was, to borrow a phrase from the Czech playwright (and now president) Vaclav Havel, a form of "anti-political politics," which during the last three or four years had built a momentum of rising expectations from urban society vis-à-vis the party and the government. The Tiananmen demonstrations crystallized these expectations and turned them into a kind of "people power." Apparently, the movement became so threatening to Deng Xiaoping and other party leaders that they decided to put an end to the turmoil by resorting to a bloody crackdown. As a result, it is not impossible to imagine that the June 4 incident of 1989 will one day rival its May 4 predecessor in historical importance.

In some ways creative writers and literary critics have always been in the forefront of cultural movements in modern China. This was true of the May Fourth Movement itself, which was spearheaded by a literary revolution in 1917 that ushered in both the widespread use of the modern vernacular and a consciousness of new artistic forms. As Chinese intellectuals began to reflect on the meaning of the May Fourth Movement from a post-Cultural Revolution perspective, the historical ironies were clear. The May Fourth Movement is canonized in Chinese Communist Party (CCP) history because it marks the beginning of the communist movement. Marxism was introduced in

China by May Fourth intellectuals, leading directly to the founding of the CCP in 1921. Yet the subsequent history of the party is one of successive ideological campaigns against intellectuals, the very kinds of people who made the May Fourth Movement possible. The Cultural Revolution completed the process of the destruction of creative culture in the name of revolution.

The resurgence of the creative spirit and literary productivity in the post-Mao era was initially made possible when Deng Xiaoping revived the so-called Double Hundreds policy ("Let a Hundred Flowers Bloom, Let a Hundred Schools of Thought Contend") in late 1978. Mao Zedong had introduced this policy in 1956–57, but those who responded were immediately crushed in the Anti-Rightist campaign that followed. Despite similar campaigns against "bourgeois liberalization" and "spiritual pollution" in the early 1980s, most writers remained undaunted in the face of official pressures. They not only openly defied the attack from party conservatives but also began to evolve a series of artistic stances that in fact relegated to utter insignificance the party-sponsored tenets of socialist realism.

At first the challenge of culture to politics was indirect: the intellectuals and writers simply sought to remove cultural and literary activity from the party's immediate influence. But it was nevertheless a move contrary to the established guidelines, which left "politics in command" (a slogan from Maoist days) in the literary arena. It is clear that some of the CCP's dominant theories and models of cultural practice—for example, art and literature as instruments of policy, writers as "cultural workers" (not independent artists), and Marxism-Leninism-Mao Zedong Thought as the correct guide in all intellectual endeavors—have largely been replaced by the leaders in the cultural self-reflection movement with new theories and models, mostly derived from the modern West.

The process of culture challenging politics began in the late 1970s as a narrowly ideological discourse focused on the Cultural Revolution. But the official explanation, which attributed the catastrophe entirely to the wrongdoing of the Gang of Four, was found wanting. The "literature of the wounded," the first crop of literature echoing the new party line, presented a generally shallow picture. Some conscientious party intellectuals, particularly the journalist-writer Liu Binyan, were driven to uncover various facets of corrupt behavior among cadres at all levels. Liu's devastating reportage unveiled a society ridden with evil, which could not be explained solely by the Gang's erroneous policies. The roots lay deeper. For Liu and his followers, the entire body politic of the Chinese socialist system was rotten to the core and could be cured only by drastic reforms from within the party itself.

According to some Chinese scholars, the roots of this evil were embedded in Chinese culture itself—in the persistence of the so-called feudal remnants of cultural behavior, which needed to be excavated and analyzed. A number of young writers and artists, on the other hand, chose to propound a thesis of discontinuity: they argued that the political excesses during the "dark decade" of the Cultural Revolution had produced a cultural void or gap, something tantamount to a gigantic rupture in the cumulative layers of Chinese culture. More compelling than tracing the roots of political evil was transcending the problems created by the repressive ideology and bureaucratic apparatus of the CCP. According to this group, one had to go beyond politics in order to reappraise and reinvent Chinese culture from a fresh perspective.

This change in the cultural climate accelerated in 1985—so much so that the new cultural leaders took over most of the major cultural organs and arenas. Even the party's own *People's Daily* was subverted by conscientious reporters like Liu Binyan. What follows is a broad profile of the cultural self-reflection movement that unravels the various strands of literary and intellectual activity which converged in 1989 to provide the cultural background and climate for the student movement.

Chinese writers in their fifties or older, heavily steeped in Soviet-style socialist culture, continued to emphasize commitment to collective goals even as collective enterprises were being privatized. Their reigning artistic tenets were essentially those of socialist realism (exposing the ills of the old society and extolling the proletarian virtues of the new society under socialism). These writers were also inculcated with a spirit of revolutionary idealism in that they believed in personal sacrifice in order to realize the vision of a great future. It was this spirit that inspired an older writer like Liu Binyan to "intervene" in social life by exposing corruption no matter where he saw it.

Beginning in 1985, an emergent group of young fiction writers chose to place their art in the realm of culture, totally separated from party politics. This new turn away from politics and beyond old-fashioned realism not only made the young writers ready targets of the party's ideological criticism but also served to antagonize older writers like Liu Binyan who remain politically committed. The younger generation, all born "under the red flag," had become utterly disillusioned with all collective goals; they preferred to carve out a personal space removed from official ideology in their life and art.

With some exceptions (notably Wang Meng, former minister of culture, who introduced in his own fiction a stream-of-consciousness technique, and Wang Zengqi, a senior writer who started as a modernist in the late 1940s and is now regarded as something of a guru by the younger writers), the split of artistic stances clearly reflects a generational gap. This artistic "revenge" of the children against their parents is another strong echo of the May Fourth Movement. Still gathering momentum, it is a phenomenon fraught with political implications for those who came of age in the earlier movement and survive as party elders today. Ironically, literary avant-gardism and modernism in post-Mao China assume a larger political significance than did their counterparts in Europe half a century ago; Chinese writers and artists find themselves reacting against both the tyranny and (in their eyes) the philistine vulgarity of a corrupt official party culture that has lost its earlier revolutionary idealism.

This kind of iconoclasm was the ultimate hallmark of the May Fourth Movement. Contemporary Chinese intellectuals remain fervent anti-traditionalists because they see a continuing linkage between the current authoritarian state and society and the long-accumulated influence of China's feudal past. The peasant base of the communist revolution is seen as a contributing factor to authoritarianism: some even go so far as to assert that the CCP leadership contains a "gangster" (*banghui*) ethos stemming from peasant society. Another well-known example of anti-traditionalist scholarship is the thesis put forth by Jin Guantao, a young scholar, that China's dynastic legacy has given the political system a degree of ultrastability that ensures the continuation of essentially the same form of despotic government.

The celebrated television series "River Elegy" (*He shang*) provided the most articulate representation of this position. This six-part series was written and directed by three young intellectuals and was shown twice on government-controlled television in the summer of 1988, becoming an immediate *cause scandale* before it was banned. (After the June 4 massacre, the three authors of the series all became "criminals" hunted by the government; only one, Su Xiaokang, escaped abroad.) It has generated unprecedented controversy and passion, not only between the increasingly emboldened intelligentsia and the reactionary members of the party leadership, but also among intellectuals and other segments of the Chinese audience, which reportedly numbered more than 400 million.

The central metaphor of "River Elegy" is that Chinese civilization, symbolized by the Yellow River, has declined. The Yellow River was the cradle of ancient Chinese civilization, but heavy silting has now earned it the nickname China's Sorrow because of the destructive force of its periodic floods and changes in course. The creators of "River Elegy" argue that China's once-great civilization has accumulated a similar mass of "feudal" sediment that blocks progress toward modernization. While singing the dirge of its inevitable demise, the authors proclaim the arrival of a Western-oriented global civilization symbolized by the color of the ocean, azure. At the end of the last episode, as the camera slowly pans across a winding stretch of muddy yellow water flowing into the vast waves of the deep blue Pacific, the narrator comments in a tone of high seriousness:

> The characteristics of despotism are secrecy, autocracy, and arbitrariness.
> The characteristics of democracy should be transparency, popular will, and scientism.
> We are moving from turgidity to transparency.
> We have already moved from enclosure to openness.
> The Yellow River is fated to cross the loess plateau.
> The Yellow River will merge into the azure ocean.

This concluding metaphor proclaims a new historical inevitability: that China's destiny points toward the Pacific Ocean, in the opposite direction from the source of its ancient civilization.

What will this oceanic-oriented "new China" look like? It is not hard to find in the television series some glimpses of an initial vista: a shot of recently constructed skyscrapers in the new city of Shenzhen across the border from Hong Kong, scenes of brightly lit rooms full of computers, of American rockets launched into space, of the streets of Japan and Europe where fashionable women walk in high-heeled shoes. Are these shots meant to convey a sense of the new "azure" culture? Is China, now in the throes of the Four Modernizations (of agriculture, industry, national defense, and science and technology), destined by economic development to follow in the footsteps of its neighbors on the Pacific Rim?

Side by side with the effusive evocations of the "azure" West is a series of anguished meditations on China's ancient past and recent history. Interestingly, whereas the authors pay considerable attention to ancient taboos and myths, they gloss over the major part of 19th- and 20th-century history. The bulk of what can be called socialist culture has been neglected, perhaps for reasons of safety. What is left is a sharply drawn contrast between an archaic, muddled past and the Western-influenced present, from which the authors project a possibly brighter future for all of China.

As some critics have pointed out, the entire history of the CCP is passed over in "River Elegy" except for a few pointed reminders of some party leaders' sad fate during the Cultural Revolution. But one easily detects a pro-reformist stance. One episode argues unequivocally for the importance of intellectuals as the backbone of economic reform and modernization.

The often long-winded commentary (the series is like an academic treatise illustrated with visual material) written in a flowing literary style, while painfully ruminative about China, is glibly holistic about the West. The case for modernization and democracy is argued without any consideration of other alternatives. This dismissal of Chinese tradition and eulogy of the West's undifferentiated "azure" culture betrays, ironically, an undemocratic and authoritarian trait: the series is an intentional polemic built on a bifurcation between China and the West as simplistic as those of the conservatives. It revives old clichés about China and the West and about the need for total Westernization that recall the strident May Fourth stance against Chinese tradition. It seems that 70 years later this iconoclastic ethos is as compelling as before. In fact, the authors' next project, now aborted, was to have been a television series on the legacies of the May Fourth Movement.

This does not mean that tradition has no place in the current intellectual movement. One of the most noteworthy new scholarly institutions is the Academy of Chinese Culture established in 1985 by Tang Yijie, a Beijing University professor. Inspired by the Ming Neo-Confucian academies, it sponsored a series of lectures, seminars, and conferences on Confucian philosophy. Professor Tu Wei-ming from Harvard, an overseas Chinese intellectual who enjoys great renown in China due to his numerous and extensive visits, has taken a prominent role in arguing with his Chinese colleagues on the development of the third phase of Confucianism, following the first phase, early Confucianism, from the pre-Qin to the Later Han periods (5th century B.C.–2nd century A.D.), and the second phase, Neo-Confucianism, in Song-Ming times (10th–17th centuries). The debate is triggered partially by attempts to account for the economic miracles of the Four Tigers on the Pacific Rim (Taiwan, Hong Kong, South Korea, and Singapore), whose cultures all fall under the general influence of Confucianism.

Tu is not primarily interested in explaining economic success; rather he argues that these four modernizing societies should compel us to rethink the entire legacy of Confucianism—whether the long-evolving Confucian tradition has contained an inner dynamic that enables it to face the challenge of modernity and, more important, to respond to the spiritual crises resulting from a fragmented Western postmodern condition. Tu's position is generally affirmative: Confucianism is not dead, nor should it be relegated to the museum. It is actually going through a renewal and has reached a new phase in its development. Tu thus opposes his mainland colleagues' tendency to treat the rich legacy of Confucianism as a negative "feudal residue." He believes it constitutes the basis of the Chinese cultural identity, a powerful legacy despite its inner tensions. Another renowned overseas Chinese scholar, Lin Yü-sheng, has argued that a modern reexamination of this tradition should look into its potential for a kind of creative transformation, although he is, on balance, less sanguine about the possibility of realizing that potential.

Nevertheless, most young intellectuals inside China categorically reject any discourse on Confucianism out of emotional repulsion, because they equate it with "feudalism" as a source of traditional Chinese authoritarianism. "River Elegy" may be considered one extreme position resulting from the recent movement of cultural self-reflection. Because it was intended to be a polemic presented in a visual medium, its arguments had to be simplified. (The oversimplification may also be attributed in part to the fact that none of its authors had ever seen the "azure" West firsthand!) In contrast, the published writings of other intellectuals that examine the May Fourth legacy are much more subtle. I would like to introduce briefly a few influential samples of this more academic mode.

In a seminal article titled "Dual Variations on Enlightenment and National Salvation," the renowned scholar and aesthetician Li Zehou, who may be regarded as the liberal doyen of Chinese intellectuals, presents a dual thesis on the May Fourth Movement.[1] He distinguishes between the movement's two different, but mutually interactive, components: the political agenda of national salvation (*jiuwang*) and the cultural agenda of enlightenment (*qimeng*), that is, the opening up of the minds of the younger generation so as to assimilate new and foreign currents of thought. In Li's analysis, the anti-imperialist imperative of national salvation quickly eclipsed demands for enlightenment. The intellectuals, who first embodied the task of enlightenment, were themselves engulfed and "conquered" by the collective goal of national salvation and fervently embraced politics by adopting the revolutionary practice of Marxism-Leninism. Consequently, the May Fourth Movement was, in a sense, an abortive revolution, because its original goal of intellectual enlightenment remains unfulfilled. What makes this familiar argument distinctive is the underlying implication that this drift away from creative endeavors toward politics was not only a betrayal of the May Fourth spirit but also a disastrous course that landed Chinese intellectuals in trouble.

Liu Zaifu, a literary theorist influenced by Li, makes the case even more emphatically. The loss of the enlightenment spirit, in his view, was closely connected with the diminishing prestige of intellectuals in mod-

[1] Li Zehou, *Zhongguo xiandai sixiangshi lun* (Treatises on modern Chinese intellectual history). Beijing: Dongfang chubanshe, 1987, pp. 7–49.

ern China.[2] During the May Fourth period, the intellectuals still enjoyed an exalted position vis-à-vis the rest of the Chinese population. They were, in Liu's words, definitely the "subject," or those who did the enlightening, in relation to the "object," the people they wished to enlighten. Thus they positioned themselves in the vanguard of history. However, this self-assigned role was reversed by the communist revolution: the intellectuals became themselves the objects of the party's thought-reform campaigns, whereas the peasant masses had become the "subject" as the purported font of wisdom in Maoist ideology.

The reversal of roles again in the post-Mao era, when the leading position of intellectuals was reestablished, is not cause for joy. On the contrary, the lesson to be learned from this historical experience is that Chinese intellectuals should relinquish their self-appointed roles as prophets, saviors, or the vanguard and reconstitute themselves as a self-conscious group dedicated to the genuine intellectual enterprise of scholarship and reflection.

Liu emerged in the mid–1980s as the newly elected director of the Institute of Literature at the Chinese Academy of Social Sciences (CASS) and the reigning spokesman of literary theory. In his numerous works he propounds two literary theories: subjectivity (*zhuti xing*) and multiple composition of character (*xingge zuhe lun*).[3] What makes these abstruse formulations both provocative and daring is what is *not* said in them. In my view Liu is engaged in no less a task than the total dismantling of the Maoist canon on art and literature—not by frontally attacking it but by putting forward a theory of his own in its stead.

The goals of Liu's enterprise are clear: with the notion of subjectivity he wishes to reestablish the central position of the human subject—both authors and their fictional characters—in current Chinese literary discourse. The commanding position of the author with regard to the text is meant to restore writers of fiction to their May Fourth glory after half a century of being downgraded to mere propaganda agents for the party, while the emphasis on human characters is opposed to the socialist-realist view that fictional personae reflect types of social existence. Liu has gone into considerable depth in his analysis in order to "deconstruct" the extreme rigidities of the Maoist bipolarity, namely that char-

---

[2] Liu Zaifu, "Wusi wenxue qimeng jingshen de shiluo yu huigui" (The loss and recovery of the enlightenment spirit of May Fourth literature), in Lin Yü-sheng *et al.*, *Wusi: duoyuan de fansi* (May Fourth: pluralistic reflections) Hong Kong: Joint Publishing Co., 1989, pp. 92–122.

[3] See Liu Zaifu, *Wenxue de fansi* (Self-reflection on literature). Beijing: Renmin wenxue chubanshe, 1986. See also his *Xinge zuhe lun* (On the multiple composition of literary characters). Shanghai: Shanghai wenyi chubanshe, 1986. Liu's works have not received much attention in the West.

acters are designated in advance as either good or bad in accordance with their ideological function in the text.

Liu's daring challenge to the established principles of literature did not go unnoticed. He was attacked by two orthodox theoreticians, Chen Yong and Yao Xueying (the latter a famous novelist), who openly charged him with violating the sacred canons of Marxism-Leninism-Mao Zedong Thought. But Liu was undaunted and engaged them in heated exchanges in print. Yao once threatened to sue him, and several lawyers instantly offered their services to Liu. Thus, despite the renewed ideological campaign in early 1987 against bourgeois liberalization, including a major conference at Zhuozhou in February organized by the orthodox party theorists at which Liu was the central target of a planned attack, his reputation remained unscathed.

The extreme leftism exhibited by Liu's critics was a source of concern for the liberal-minded party leader Zhao Ziyang, who managed successfully to prevent these leftist backlashes from gaining strength.[4] But it was Liu's personal integrity and scholarly daring that made him enormously popular with liberal-minded writers and critics as well as the general reading public. Within the Institute of Literature, he also received enthusiastic support from his colleagues. That the director of the highest official literary research organ should have become an outspoken critic of the official line is indicative of the changed political climate since the mid-1980s as well as of the intellectual bankruptcy of the Maoist canon in literature.

As acknowledged leaders of the movement for cultural self-reflection, Li Zehou and Liu Zaifu have gained enormous popularity and received warm responses among young intellectuals, some of whom look up to the two men as their new "enlightened" mentors. For despite the scholarly verbosity of their arguments, they nevertheless represent a distinct position—a reversal of Mao's view, if you like—that places culture above politics. They would like to return to the true spirit of May Fourth—intellectual enlightenment—and continue with its unfinished task. However, for all their role reversals, they have not bridged the gap with the peasantry. The peasant masses remain largely silent and refuse to join in the intellectual discourse.

In a devastating article the young scholar Gan Yang has taken the entire Chinese intelligentsia to task. According to him, the problem with intellectuals lies precisely in their obsession "to speak for others

[4] The case of the Zhuozhou conference is being reopened by the current party leadership. An article in the *People's Daily* (Feb. 24, 1990) reaffirms the ideological correctness of the conference and denounces Zhao Ziyang for his alleged collusion with some Hong Kong journals in leaking the conference materials to Hong Kong for "besmearing." See the Hong Kong journal *Jiushi niandai* (The nineties, March 1990), p. 36.

and to speak the truth to others who have not seen the truth."[5] But this self-professed monopoly on truth was long ago destroyed by the CCP, and the "masses," whether enlightened or not, no longer need the intellectuals to speak for them. On the contrary, Gan Yang charges that this May Fourth discourse has been appropriated by the party and reshaped into its own ideology of "serving the people." Gan urged that the intellectuals of the post-Mao era reflect critically on an ironic legacy of history: namely that their "knowledge" has become a constituent element of the party's "power." (The wording and theory come from the French philosopher Michel Foucault, whose works have been translated into Chinese.)

It is not hard to see that behind Gan Yang's critique is a profound discontent with the lack of a genuine spirit of self-reflection among Chinese intellectuals. The relevance of this critique to the situation of intellectuals during the past four decades is obvious. In the name of nationalism, they seem so singularly dedicated to a dominant political belief that they have not pondered the implications of a number of related issues. Why is it that in the midst of prolonged calamities, from the Anti-Rightist campaign to the Cultural Revolution, Chinese intellectuals have not demonstrated a genuine individual conscience? With a few exceptions (notably the personal essays by the veteran writer Ba Jin in the late 1970s) there has been no significant introspective writing about the Cultural Revolution that departs from the typical public confessions or accusations.

Instead, as the "River Elegy" has shown, post-Mao political discourse remains essentially in the Maoist mode even as most of the intellectuals are becoming vehement anti-Maoists. In other words, their rhetoric is "monologic": it pronounces its own truth as self-evident without giving any room for alternative views or solutions. According to Liu and other critics, Chinese intellectuals must liberate themselves not only from Maoism as an all-embracing ideology but also from the prison house of Maoist language. The persistence of the Maoist mode has so governed their own thinking that it is difficult for them to have a genuine and in-depth understanding of other cultures and other traditions. Thus a true "opening up" (*kaifang*) in thought means the introduction, or even invention, of new terms and phrases that do not belong in the Maoist rhetoric. In an interesting parallel to the May Fourth language revolution (in which the modern vernacular, *baihua*, became the new language for literature and other forms of public discourse), the young literary intellectuals since 1985 have become in-

[5] Gan Yang, "Ziyou de linian: Wusi chuantong zhi queshi mian" (The idea of freedom: the deficiency of the May Fourth tradition), in Lin Yü-sheng *et al.*, *op.cit.*

creasingly committed to a consciousness of style and language: they want to go beyond the standard ideological tropes used in official works of socialist realism in order to create new artistic worlds through their inventive language.

It was generally agreed that 1985 marked the beginning of a new movement in literary theory, when a few daring critics based in Amoy and supported by Liu Zaifu tried (and failed) to apply to literature major theories from the social sciences, such as cybernetics, systems analysis, and information theory. A few younger writers and critics, despite their admiration for his personal integrity, considered Liu's theory old-fashioned. Although most of them do not know foreign languages, they eagerly grabbed all the Chinese translations they could find from contemporary Western sources—from Russian formalism and French structuralism to German phenomenology and Derridian deconstructionism. Western literary theory has attained a fairly solid footing among young academicians, whether or not they are able fully to grasp its complex language through translation.

This craze for all things Western reminds us once again of the May Fourth period, when the quest for modernity became a reigning ethos. But the current search for novelty conceals a negative passion. Liu Zaifu observes that "Chinese writers use Western literature to negate themselves—or rather to negate those concepts and models of recent tradition that bind the writer's soul. It is precisely this desire to negate themselves that inspires such unusually ardent admiration of Western literature among Chinese writers."[6] In other words, "Western learning" was being used not only to fill an intellectual vacuum but also to cleanse the writer's soul and hence liberate it from the grip of recent ideology.

It is not surprising, therefore, that many writers openly embrace Western modernism in order to liberate themselves from the burden of all the persistent "feudal" influences from Chinese culture. For instance, Liu Xiaobo, a young radical critic who denigrated Li Zehou and Liu Zaifu and belittled the entire literary harvest of the last decade, rated as worthy only the works of James Joyce and T. S. Eliot. (For all his reckless radicalism in literary matters, Liu Xiaobo took a prominent role during the last phase of the Tiananmen demonstrations as a moderate force in persuading the student hunger strikers to stop and other students to make an orderly retreat from the square. He was arrested after the June 4 massacre.) Other writers ranked

[6] Liu Zaifu, "Chinese Literature in the Past Ten Years: Spirit and Direction," *Chinese Literature* (Autumn 1989), p. 155.

Franz Kafka, Nathaniel Hawthorne, and Gabriel García Márquez as their "only" models.

The felt need for new methods of intellectual inquiry and reflection also prompted translations of Western philosophy and social science. Understandably, these translations largely eschewed the Marxist canons. By concentrating on Western theories other than Soviet Marxism, the translators attempted to orient themselves away from the closed world of Marxist-Leninist-Maoist orthodoxy. Gan Yang, himself a young researcher in the Institute of Philosophy of the Chinese Academy of Social Sciences with no official connections, was the editor-in-chief of a dozen series of translations of modern Western masters of social thought—from Max Weber to Isaiah Berlin—totaling more than 100 titles. Another series called Marching toward the Future was edited by a young scholar, Jin Guantao (whose theory of ultrastability was mentioned earlier). In addition to promoting new translations, both men also published their own journals geared to the young readership in the urban areas.

The most prestigious and influential journal in China and abroad was *Dushu* (Reading), published by the Joint Publishing Company, a government publishing house with a semi-independent branch office in Hong Kong that not only distributes the journal overseas but also independently publishes its own editions of the major thinkers and writers in the cultural self-reflection movement. With its small format and unassuming cover, this monthly intellectual journal consistently featured highbrow but readable articles on the state of contemporary Chinese culture as well as reviews of important books, both Chinese and Western.

The immense popularity of these journals and translations in China's intellectual circles bespeaks a cultural climate that is increasingly open and international. As the movement spread, new and less academically inclined journals mushroomed that were even bolder and took greater risks. I would like to mention two unusual cases of enterprising journalism that occurred in late 1988 and early 1989.[7] The *Eastern Record* (*Dongfang jishi*), which was supported financially by the Jiangsu Literature and Arts Press, a state-owned provincial publishing house, was edited by a dozen Beijing-based writers and intellectuals who were all friends and shared a common avant-gardist stance. Without official interference, the group, with each member taking

---

[7] My account of the two journals as well as of the Dule Bookshop is drawn entirely from Zha Jianying, "Notes on the Emergence of a Counter-Public in China," unpublished paper prepared for the Center for Psychosocial Studies, Chicago (January 1990), and used with the author's permission.

charge of a specific column, embarked upon a daring intellectual enterprise of reinvestigating political scandals and reexamining the Cultural Revolution, the role of intellectuals, the condition of women, the cultural influence from the West, and many other issues—all from a critical perspective.

Perhaps the most provocative reportage was that by Dai Qing, a woman writer connected with the higher echelons of the CCP, who chose to reexamine the party documents concerning a notorious case during the Anti-Rightist campaign. Dai had also published a devastating piece about the party's execution in 1947 of Wang Shiwei, a writer who had figured prominently in the Yan'an literary scene. Such daring investigative journalism of the party's past history was unheard of, and it landed Dai Qing in jail after the June 4 massacre.

The other enterprising journal was published in the far south, in the Special Economic Zone of Hainan island, where a group of writers from Hunan province had flocked to seek their fortunes. Nicknamed the Hunan Brigade, they planned to publish a popular magazine in order to make enough money to establish a publishing house for serious books. This purposeful commercial venture became a great success: the first issue of the *Hainan Reportage* contained, among other things, a sensational exposé of Chairman Mao's private life. It sold 500,000 copies instantly. Unfortunately, the journal was suspended after the massacre and is currently under government investigation.

Yet another case of intellectual/business venture was the Dule (Capital Joy) Bookshop, opened by a young woman with private funds in 1988 and reputed to be the first private bookstore in Beijing. The basement café, later added to this otherwise mediocre bookshop, soon became the meeting place of reformist intellectuals. In late January of last year, a group of leading intellectuals including astrophysicist Fang Lizhi gathered to promote their privately funded, independent new journal, the *New Enlightenment* (*Xin qimeng*). After much animated speech-giving to an audience of both locals and foreign reporters, the first two issues were given out and drinks were served. But a couple of months later the bookshop was forced to close down, and the meetings of the journal editors were harassed by the police and eventually forced to stop.

What amazes outside observers and insiders alike is that the young advocates of avant-garde art seemed to gain enormous popularity, their works appearing in prestigious journals such as *Shanghai Literature* (*Shanghai wenxue*), *Beijing Literature* (*Beijing wenxue*), *October* (*Shiyue*), and *Harvest* (*Shouhuo*)—so much so that senior and more established writers were pushed aside, some unable to have their works published or reviewed.

The initiators of this avant-garde trend were the young practitioners of "obscure poetry" (*menglong shi*) associated with the unofficial journal *Today* (*Jintian*) in Beijing. The trend soon spread to poets in Shanghai, Sichuan, and other regions, then to literary critics and theorists who wished to construct new systems of analysis. The literary trends of the past few years merit attention because their responses to the current state of cultural crisis have taken a more radical and imaginative form than those found in scholarly or journalistic writings.

According to some of the participants, the crucial event that served to consolidate the group identity of the young avant-gardists was a conference in the city of Hangzhou in November 1984, sponsored by the journal *Shanghai Literature*. About 20 young writers and critics, mainly from Beijing and Shanghai, attended. It was the first "pure" literary conference in that neither the attendees nor the program had any hidden political agenda. In the shadow of the official Anti-Spiritual Pollution campaign that was being launched in nearby Shanghai, they discussed the current state of creative literature and Chinese culture. What emerged from eight days of intense discussions was a renewed interest in regional culture as a way to "decenter" the party-dominated official culture.

Whatever their faults of immaturity or impetuosity, these younger-generation writers and critics have, since 1985, managed to bring theory and creativity to bear on each other and produced a harvest of notable works, especially in fiction, whose artistic quality is in my opinion superior to most, if not all, revolutionary works produced in the past four decades. Their leading champion, Li Tuo, characterized the current scene in creative writing (that is, since 1985) as containing two interrelated tendencies: a search for the roots of Chinese culture in distant or marginal regions by the "roots" (*xungen*) school, and a zestful exploration of the new possibilities of form and language by the "experimental" school.

As I have written elsewhere to introduce an English collection of their works, the roots for which writers from the first school were searching were not so much familial or genealogical as they were cultural and historical; these writers believed that they had been cut off from their cultural roots by the ideological campaigns of recent decades, which had also deprived them of a true sense of self.[8] They stood, as it were, on shallow ground underneath which the deeper layers of Chinese culture had been destroyed. In view of this double deprivation, each of the writers identified with this school was in

[8] See my introduction to Jeanne Tai, tr. and ed., *Spring Bamboo: A Collection of Contemporary Chinese Short Stories* (New York: Random House, 1989), pp. xi–xvii.

search of a unique and authentic world that presumably lay beneath the surface of social life or beyond the pale of socialist ideology.

In constructing their "other" fictional worlds these writers wished not only to debunk the dominant Han culture, now atrophied by the burden of politics, but also to probe the depths of what could be called the collective unconscious of the Chinese people. By emphasizing regional culture they demonstrated their interest in the minority cultures of the border areas (for example, Tibet) as well as in the more "exotic" or ancient regions and cultures of China, rich with myth and folklore. Among the most prominent practitioners of this mode of writing are Han Shaogong from southern Hunan province, Jia Pingwa and Shi Tiesheng from Shanxi province in the northwest, Zheng Wanlong from the Xing'an mountains in Heilongjiang province, Zhaxi Dawa from Tibet, and perhaps the most famous of them all, Mo Yan from Shandong province (whose novel *Red Sorghum* was later made into a successful film). Their promoter and guiding spirit was Li Tuo, who hailed originally from the Dawuer tribe in Manchuria.

The second mode of writing, emerging after that of the roots school but sharing certain technical traits with it, was the so-called experimental fiction that first attracted critical attention in about 1986. The characteristics that distinguish these new writers from those of the roots school are a greater concern with fictional language and, by experimentation with language, the construction of a personal and subjective vision. If the "roots" writers are still interested in the deeper structures of Chinese culture and the nation, the "experimentalists" tend to be more abstract and existential, probing the psychic contours of isolated and abnormal individuals who lead solitary existences fraught with premonitions of madness, mysticism, and death. For instance, the stories of Can Xue are constructed in a series of dark and chilling images expressed in a disconnected syntax that makes their content distinctively opaque and hard to absorb, thereby posing a welcome challenge to the avant-garde theorists and critics. The newly discovered writer Yu Hua, now only 27 years old, seems obsessed with various forms of death in his flamboyant and lyrical depictions of violence. On the other hand, some writers (Ma Yuan, for instance), under the influence of Jorge Luis Borges, are more interested in exploring the mystical possibilities of time and space and the capacity of fictional language to comment on its own narrative process.

Whether engaged in experimenting with new techniques derived from the West or exploring artistically their own regional roots, this young generation of avant-garde writers has definitely abandoned the long-established tradition of literature as a vehicle for social conscience and political action (or legitimation). That these writers have chosen to shock the party establishment with their radical experimentalism in art reminds us, in fact, of the artistic stance of European modernists. But it is a modernism that speaks to a cultural crisis of unprecedented proportions. Around the same time that the roots movement captured the literary scene, a large-scale "cultural craze" was raging in intellectual circles. Some insiders argue that in fact the literary movement had a direct impact on the intellectual movement in that it led to similar interests in cultural theory and comparative culture. As Gan Yang has convincingly argued, this form of cultural consciousness itself represented a continuation of the intellectual revolt against the Cultural Revolution.[9] Like its literary counterpart, it was at once political and apolitical in the sense that it both frontally attacked the "pan-politicization" of Chinese life (as summed up by the Maoist slogan "politics in command") and attempted to break away from the trammels of politics so as to give the cultural realm a true measure of autonomy.

By early 1989 this crescendo of cultural activity had reached a peak. The young writers and artists were openly defiant. In January an exhibition of avant-garde art attracted large crowds: among its many unconventional artistic displays was a live performance of a shoot-out in a telephone booth. As police eventually surrounded the exhibition building, local passersby shouted their support for the artists.

On another front, an open letter drafted by Fang Lizhi asking for the release of the dissident Wei Jingsheng on the tenth anniversary of his imprisonment soon turned into a signature campaign: 33 names, including those of some of the intellectuals mentioned in this chapter, were collected in the first group of signatures. The initiative came from Bei Dao, an otherwise apolitical poet and former editor of the unofficial journal *Today*. Two successive groups of signatures followed, one from scientists and the other consisting mostly of names of journalists and scholars from the Institute of Literature. These acts of courage were unprecedented in the party's 40-year history. That these intellectuals became so emboldened as to infringe upon the party's exclusive domain of policymaking was further evidence of the radically changed relationship between culture and politics in early 1989: instead of controlling culture by means of political campaigns, the party for the first time found itself politically on the defensive against the onslaught of culture.

It is against this background that we must view the student demonstrations in April, May, and June of 1989, for in my view the germina-

[9] Gan Yang, ed., *Zhongguo dangdai wenhua yishi* (Contemporary Chinese cultural consciousness). Hong Kong: Joint Publishing Co., 1989, p. ii.

tion and development of the student movement can be linked to this large-scale sociocultural crisis. A long process of cultural reflection and activity had paved the way for the emergence of a new mentality, which the students also embodied—a new view of life centered on the provenance of the self, a new view of society as a sphere of public life separated from and even opposed to the party-state, and a new view of the Chinese nation as no longer identifiable with the party-state but defined instead as a larger entity trying to transform itself into a state of modernity. The student demonstrators themselves did not invent any of these concepts, but they were influenced by the intellectuals in the literary and cultural arenas.

To give some concrete examples, the students in a dozen universities I visited in a lecture tour in 1986 were all familiar with the theories and controversies described in this chapter. Interestingly, most of the writers and critics discussed here, especially those who claimed a clear avant-gardist artistic stance, participated actively in the Tiananmen Square demonstrations as supporters of the students (whereas the social realists of the older generation did not). One of the reasons may have been that they shared the outlook of the students and spoke the same language—a language of cultural iconoclasm and defiance.

But these writers and critics also sought further constitutional guarantees of a larger sphere of freedom—of speech, the press, and congregation, and the right of demonstration itself. These demands for freedom and democracy articulated the voice of the "new people" (that is, no longer the ideological collective as defined by the party but rather its transfiguration in urban society)—the newly awakened popular power of a gathering of forces (students, intellectuals, local residents, and, to some extent, workers) in an emergent public sphere that dared publicly to pose challenges to the party-state.

The mushrooming of literary and intellectual journals, each clamoring for an independent voice, was a significant phenomenon reminiscent of the May Fourth intellectual scene 70 years earlier. But it was all the more remarkable because these recent endeavors were launched against a much more mammoth state, a monolithic political structure within which the latter-day intellectuals attempted to open up new spaces and avenues of expression. These spaces in turn constituted a sphere of public opinion that betokened the emergent power of a societal culture that could hardly be contained by official orthodoxy.

What the ruling gerontocracy has failed to realize is that the past decade of "opening" and reform also effected major changes in Chinese society—to such an extent that an infrastructure of new institutions has developed with exchanges of people and ideas both within China and abroad. Chinese graduate students studying in the United

States sent articles back to journals like *Dushu* on topics ranging from democracy to feminism and postmodernism. Chinese universities and other research institutions invited guests as various as Milton Friedman and Fredric Jameson in an almost frenzied competition for new ideas from abroad. (Jacques Derrida was scheduled to go in September; he would have arrived with a distinguished delegation of French and German scholars had the June 4 massacre not occurred.)

New semi-independent research institutes and think tanks also sprouted, ranging from the privately supported Academy of Chinese Culture to the Social Science Research Institute of the Central Iron and Steel Company. Informal *shalong* (salons) became an urban fad: held mostly at private homes or on university campuses, these intellectual gatherings provided forums for focused discussions on what their members considered to be pressing issues in the fields of art, literature, and even politics. (The student leader Wang Dan had been a member of a salon on democracy.) In sum, the government policy of encouraging individual entrepreneurs (*getihu*) in the economy also spawned a new species of entrepreneurs in cultural production, and the groups and institutions with which they were associated linked together to form within the existing political structure a kind of burgeoning public sphere in which the party's hegemony in Chinese life was challenged.

In some ways Tiananmen Square can be seen as a material representation of the emergent public sphere: it is both a concrete public space, the largest public square in the world, and a symbolic space, which during the brief period of the Beijing Spring crystallized the aspirations of all these new societal forces. While the students certainly spearheaded the demands, they no longer spoke as one abstract body but purposely flaunted a polyphony of voices. From mid-April to mid-May, the party leadership, torn by its internal power struggle, seemed unable to adopt a consistent policy toward the students.

In the midst of the power vacuum, a carnivalesque atmosphere gradually set in: amidst much singing, talking, and meeting, various groups presented different platforms addressed not only to the government but to each other. Their rhetoric and slogans contained appeals to the general good and an incredible density of verbal puns and cultural cross-references. The Western media captured visually the vividness of the imagery on the square, but not the intellectual content of the students' discourse. Nor did it pay much attention to the role of intellectuals in the movement.

The celebratory atmosphere was punctured, of course, by the hunger strikers, who used this effective but essentially masochistic ritual to force the government to come to terms with the student demands.

When Zhao Ziyang lost and martial law was declared by Premier Li Peng on May 20, the carnivalesque mood gave way to more desperate diatribes against government leaders. The various groups were forced into one strident opposition, its demands and tactics becoming increasingly radical. Polarization led to eventual bloody suppression. The erection of the Goddess of Democracy was a last rallying ritual—a bold gesture intended not only to link the movement with Western ideals of democracy and freedom but also, perhaps more important, to disrupt that old symbolic axis formed by Mao's portrait on the wall of the Forbidden City and his mausoleum on the square.

The June 4 massacre has put an end (at least temporarily) to the organized form of the movement itself, but certainly not to the flow of its ideas. Now that some of its leaders no longer occupy center stage politically, their forced silence or exile provides them with more time and mental space for reflection. The ranks of Chinese intellectuals in exile are divided into two general positions. One position, represented by the Paris-based Democratic Front, is concerned with the political agenda of overthrowing the CCP's monopoly of power and establishing a multiparty system and a Chinese federation of states (including Taiwan and Hong Kong) in the future. Some of the people holding this position formerly belonged to Zhao Ziyang's think tanks or were associated with the commercial enterprise of the Stone Company, China's most successful computer company, founded by Wan Runnan, now a leading exiled dissident. The other position, represented by intellectuals who are disillusioned with both intraparty reform and political activity, argues that not only must the task of cultural self-reflection be continued but new categories and perspectives of analysis must also be sought. The failure of the student movement has revealed, among other things, the poverty of its underlying theory, particularly with regard to the meaning of democracy.

The traditions and paradigms of Western science and democracy, which had been transfigured by the May Fourth leaders into two popular personifications (Mr. Science and Mr. Democracy, in Chen Duxiu's famous appellation), are now receiving renewed interest from most Chinese intellectuals in exile, especially as a result of the failure of the student Democracy Movement and the obstacles facing the Four Modernizations. Other issues being explored include the notions of individualism and selfhood, the problems of totalitarianism and the power of the "public sphere" (lessons from Eastern Europe), and the complexities of modernity and post-modernity in Western societies and in Taiwan and Hong Kong, as well as the new theories of cultural comparison and the new contexts of literary and artistic expression. None of these is likely to yield concrete solutions to China's immediate problems of political oppression and economic instability. But advocates of this intellectual position are convinced that without a qualitative change in thinking, China's political course is doomed to repeat itself no matter who seizes power.

As of the time of writing (March 1990), the forces of official reaction are crashing down on the entire cultural movement. Old campaigns are being renewed (for example, the campaign against "bourgeois liberalization") and old dissidents (such as Liu Binyan) attacked. New campaigns are being planned or launched by the leadership. One such campaign, still in the planning stage, reportedly sets as its principal targets three leading figures in the cultural field: Wang Meng, Li Zehou, and Liu Zaifu. The other intellectual leaders described in this chapter have either been arrested or forced into exile, or have disappeared. Their jobs at their own work units have been taken over by their enemies, who suffered intellectual defeat and now seek vengeance, or by otherwise obscure figures of the orthodox ilk. For instance, Wang Meng, the minister of culture, was ousted and replaced by a Maoist conservative, He Jingzhi.

The Writers' Association, a relatively liberal organ, is now under the control of party conservatives of little or no literary renown. The entire Chinese Academy of Social Sciences has been occupied by party-delegated "work teams," and a few upstarts are now seizing the opportunity to advance their own career ambitions. A prime example is the case of He Xin, a researcher at the Institute of Literature at CASS, who had written to Deng Xiaoping as early as late April with suggestions on how to punish dissident intellectuals and who also appeared on nationwide television after June 4 attacking the leaders of the cultural self-reflection movement.[10] However, for all his self-promotion, He Xin has not gained much political ground among his colleagues, who retaliated with charges (written on wall posters) that his former associations were infected with elements of "bourgeois liberalization."

As the case of He Xin indicates, despite various measures of oppression, the majority of Chinese intellectuals have neither joined the ranks of new power nor betrayed the movement. This is in sharp contrast to their abject behavior of confession and mutual accusation during the Anti-Rightist campaign in 1957 and during the early phase of the Cultural Revolution. From all possible sources it would seem that this time they are putting up a silent front of passive resistance by

---

[10] I am indebted to Geremie Barmé of Australian National University and to Chinese friends for the information on He Xin. Barmé has also translated He's letter to Deng Xiaoping into English.

merely going through the empty rituals of thought reform and covering up their own or their friends' activities in Tiananmen Square. In view of this passive resistance, whether or not the official campaigns will achieve their intended results remains to be seen. With increased pressures from above, students and intellectuals seem not to have "reformed" their views but rather to have grown even more cynical in their attitudes toward party and state.

The situation in early 1990 looks, at least temporarily, gloomy indeed. However, as the Chinese word for "crisis" (*weiji*) implies, it is precisely at the critical juncture of danger that a new opportunity for change presents itself. And despite the bleakness of the current political situation in China, there is still ground for hope that the vital pulse of the cultural "lifeblood" (*mingmai*) has not been stopped and that the task of reflection and creativity goes on.

6
One Country, Two Systems: The Future of Hong Kong

Frank Ching

By far the most important developments affecting Hong Kong during 1989 were the dramatic events of May and June in Beijing. One million people took to the streets of Hong Kong to show their support for the student-led pro-democracy demonstrations. The bloody crushing of those demonstrations, the fall of Zhao Ziyang and his supporters, the rise of a hard-line faction within the Chinese leadership, and the ensuing crackdown in China all had a major impact on the territory. In Hong Kong too the Chinese leadership cracked down, charging that the British colony had become a base of subversion against the mainland. These developments determined the final form of the Basic Law, Hong Kong's post-1997 constitution, which was adopted by the Basic Law Drafting Committee (BLDC) on February 16, 1990, and by the National People's Congress (NPC) in Beijing on April 4, 1990.

Even before the events of late May and early June, however, there was a sense of growing unease in Hong Kong about the direction in which events had moved since 1984, when the Sino-British Joint Declaration on the Question of Hong Kong was signed. The Joint Declaration provided for the return of all of Hong Kong to China on July 1, 1997. In it China outlined its basic policies toward Hong Kong and promised to constitute the territory as a Special Administrative Region (SAR) that would enjoy "a high degree of autonomy" for 50 years under the concept of "one country, two systems." The socialist system would not be imposed on Hong Kong, the territory's legal system would stay the same, and Hong Kong's life-style would remain unchanged. The territory would govern itself, and its legislature would be constituted by elections.

The near euphoria that had greeted the Joint Declaration in 1984 had gradually been replaced by the cynical view that China would not allow Hong Kong true autonomy and that Britain was merely looking for a graceful exit. The deep-seated distrust of the Chinese communists on the part of many people in Hong Kong had by no means dissipated, and increasing numbers were leaving the colony each year, creating a substantial drain of skilled workers and professionals as well as of capital.

Pressure groups emerged, most of which sought dialogue with Beijing while occasionally also lobbying the British government. By early 1989 it was clear that Britain's policy toward Hong Kong was undergoing a reexamination amid mounting international concern. By the end of that year it was equally evident that China had decided not to underestimate the threat that the tiny territory might pose to its socialist system.

Within Hong Kong, 1989 opened much as 1988 had closed, with political debate focused largely on the drafting of the Basic Law, in particular on the degree to which the legislature would be popularly elected. Other issues that engendered much heat were whether Britain had an obligation to allow Hong Kong British subjects the right to live in the United Kingdom, especially since it was turning the territory over to a communist dictatorship, and how to cope with the growing numbers of Vietnamese boat people streaming into the colony.

The Joint Declaration

In the 1950s and 1960s the British attitude had been that 1997, the year in which the United Kingdom's lease on the greater part of Hong Kong was due to expire, was too far away to be much cause for concern. The British believed that China recognized the value of Hong Kong's retaining its political and economic system. They pointed out that in 1949 the communist troops had stopped at the border instead of swooping down to "liberate" the British colony. Even during the xenophobic Cultural Revolution, they pointed out, Chinese leaders were able to limit the impact of events on Hong Kong and made no attempt to take over.

During the Cultural Revolution the British did not think it possible to negotiate a reasonable agreement with the radical leadership in Beijing. That assessment changed with the rise of Deng Xiaoping after the death of Mao Zedong. In 1979 the governor of Hong Kong, Sir Murray MacLehose, paid an official visit to China and met with Deng to sound him out on the future of the British colony. On that occasion, the Chinese leader made his famous remark, "Investors in Hong Kong should set their hearts at ease."

By 1982, however, with the lease on the New Territories, which account for 92 percent of the land area of the colony, due to expire in 15 years' time, it was no longer possible for the business community in Hong Kong to be content with that simple reassurance. For one thing, banks had to decide whether they could offer mortgages that extended beyond 1997. There was a feeling, particularly on the part of the business community, that the Deng administration offered the best chance of negotiating a continuation of British administration in Hong Kong, if not a renewal of the lease itself.

It was to initiate a resolution of the Hong Kong problem that Prime Minister Margaret Thatcher visited Beijing in September 1982. The atmosphere was frosty as Mrs. Thatcher insisted that the 19th-century treaties under which Britain had obtained control of Hong Kong were valid, while the Chinese repeated their characterization of them as "unequal treaties" that were null and void. The two sides did agree, however, to begin to negotiate. Two years later, in September 1984, the draft of the Sino-British Joint Declaration was initialed.

The Democracy Issue

Before the signing of the Joint Declaration, the Hong Kong legislature had been wholly appointed. The Joint Declaration implied that a post-1997 Hong Kong would be governed democratically, although the scope of the legislature's authority and the manner of elections (direct or indirect) were not specified. Indeed, British officials made a point of linking democratic development to Britain's withdrawal from Hong Kong. In April 1984, after Britain had agreed in principle to return the colony to China in 1997, the British foreign secretary, Sir Geoffrey Howe, flew to Hong Kong and announced at a press conference that "it would not be realistic to think of an agreement that provides for continued British administration in Hong Kong after 1997." At the same time, he declared, "During the years immediately ahead, the government of Hong Kong will be developed on increasingly representative lines."

In July the Hong Kong government issued a Green Paper outlining its plans for democratic development. (Green Papers offer the public a chance to comment on policies before they are officially announced in White Papers.) The goal, it said, was "to develop progressively a system of government the authority for which is firmly rooted in Hong Kong, which is able to represent authoritatively the views of the people of Hong Kong, and which is more directly accountable to the people of Hong Kong."

On September 24, the day the draft of the Joint Declaration was initialed, a special session of the Legislative Council was held during which the governor, Sir Edward Youde, unveiled the accord and said it would "allow scope for the development of Hong Kong's governmental system as the years progress. As you know, our objective in the years immediately ahead is to use that process to root political power in the community where it belongs."

This series of actions, so much at variance with Britain's previous reluctance to grant any degree of democracy, indicated that London was paving the way for its exit from its last major colony. The British government early on had said that any agreement reached with China had to be acceptable both to the people of Hong Kong and to the British Parliament. It knew that, for the agreement to be acceptable to Parliament, Britain could not be seen as handing over 5.5 million people to a communist government but had instead to leave behind an autonomous Hong Kong that enjoyed a system of representative government.

The Chinese did nothing to discourage the growing notion that a post-1997 Hong Kong would be truly democratic. In fact, by promoting the slogan "Hong Kong people ruling Hong Kong" as their motto, Chinese leaders encouraged the belief that they would have no objection to the development of representative government. Zhao Ziyang, then premier, responded to a letter from university students in Hong Kong by pledging that the territory would be governed democratically after 1997.

If there was one warning signal, it was a declaration by the Chinese Foreign Ministry, issued at the time of the July 1984 Green Paper, that China would not be bound by anything done by the British in Hong Kong.

Throughout late 1984 and early 1985, when the British government was working to get the Joint Declaration ratified by Parliament, promises of democratization were made in Hong Kong and London. To determine whether the agreement was acceptable to the people of Hong Kong, an Assessment Office was set up to receive opinions from the public. Its report in November said:

> The provision for the legislature of the Hong Kong SAR to be constituted by elections was hailed by many . . . as "far-sighted and progressive." There should be (as the Hong Kong government plans) a progressive development or a more representative system with seats filled by direct election . . . . The new political structure should be established by the late 80s or early 90s so as to enable Hong Kong people to practice self-administration before 1997. . . . After the most careful analysis

> and consideration of all the information received, the Office has concluded that most of the people of Hong Kong find the draft agreement acceptable.

While all this was going on, the Chinese kept silent. It was not until November 1985, six months after the Sino-British accord had gone into effect, that China's representative in Hong Kong, Xu Jiatun, head of the local New China News Agency (NCNA), held an unprecedented news conference at which he accused Britain of violating the Joint Declaration with its planned political reforms.

Chinese officials advanced the concept of convergence, which meant that whatever Britain did before 1997 had to be consistent with China's plans for post-1997 Hong Kong. By January 1986 Britain had accepted the Chinese position.

In November 1984, as a result of popular reaction to the July Green Paper, the Hong Kong government had promised a review of political reforms in 1987 to determine whether direct election to the legislature should be introduced in 1988. It issued another consultative Green Paper in May 1987 and set up a Survey Office to receive public views on it.

Although direct elections in 1988 were the focus of public discussion and a bone of contention between the Chinese and British governments, the May Green Paper did not limit itself to this issue. Instead, it covered a wide range of issues, many of a technical nature. These included the role and composition of district boards, the size of the Urban Council and its relationship to the district boards and the Regional Council, the composition of the Legislative Council, the possibility of setting up an electoral college, the sequence and timing of elections, and the age of entitlement to vote.

The findings of the Survey Office, which indicated that direct election in 1988 had the support of a very small minority of the population, took most people by surprise. All earlier surveys not conducted by the government had indicated that those favoring direct elections in 1988 overwhelmingly outnumbered those who were opposed. The finding of the Survey Office on direct elections was challenged by professional pollsters, newspaper editors, political activists, and other groups. Nevertheless, the government announced in February 1988 that direct elections would not be held until 1991, at which time ten seats would be so elected.

With Britain having decided on a pause in Hong Kong's political reforms, China began the process of devising a mini-constitution for the territory. The 59 members of the Basic Law Drafting Committee were appointed by China's National People's Congress in 1985; of those, 36 were from the mainland and 23 from Hong Kong. Chinese officials declared that the Hong Kong public would be fully consulted during the drafting process, and much time was spent soliciting public views. A first draft of the Basic Law was published in April 1988, and the public was consulted in the ensuing months on five topics: the relationship between the People's Republic of China (PRC) and the Hong Kong Special Administrative Region (HKSAR); the fundamental rights and duties of residents; the political structure; the economy; and education, science, culture, sports, religion, labor, and social services.

The draft came in for widespread criticism. As was to be expected, the relationship between Hong Kong and the central government as well as the future political structure of the territory received the most attention, since they concerned the extent to which Hong Kong would be autonomous. The draft provided for an executive-led government and presented several options for the makeup of the future legislature. Debate, therefore, focused on the means of elections, or rather the number of legislators to be directly elected by the public, since there was strong resistance on the part of the conservative business community, and from China, to direct election of all seats.

In 1985, when the British allowed a minority of the seats in the Legislative Council to be filled through elections, no legislators were directly elected by the public. Some were chosen by electoral colleges, a substantial number of whose members were appointed by the government, while others were elected by functional constituencies, such as doctors, lawyers, and teachers. The functional constituencies gave disproportionate weight to the financial sector and professional groupings, whereas other bodies, such as labor unions, had much smaller voices than their numbers would suggest.

At this time, a dichotomy emerged between liberals, who wished to move relatively quickly toward full direct election, and conservatives, who sought to proceed more slowly. This division was carried into the process of drafting the Basic Law. The first Basic Law draft offered four alternatives, two of which provided for 25 percent of the legislators to be chosen through direct elections, one for 30 percent, and the most liberal for "no less than 50 percent."

After the five-month consultation period, the BLDC and its various subgroups produced a second draft, which contained major revisions. As far as political structure was concerned, it did away with the four options and adopted what it called a mainstream political model, which provided for a 55-seat legislature in 1997 with 15 seats filled through direct elections. "Representatives from the industrial, commercial, and financial sectors" were allocated 16 seats, "representatives from the professions," 12 seats, and "representatives from labor, social services, religious communities, and other sectors," 12 seats. This was dubbed the "Cha-Cha" model within Hong Kong, since it had been proposed by two drafters both surnamed Cha.

The "Cha-Cha" model provided for a gradual increase in the number of directly elected members so that, by the beginning of the legislature's third term in 2003, half the members would be directly elected. The draft allowed for the possibility of a legislature whose seats were all directly elected. It provided for a possible referendum to be held during the legislature's fourth term, that is, after 2007, to decide whether the entire legislature should be selected through direct elections. The referendum would be held with the endorsement of a majority of the legislature, the consent of the territory's chief executive, and the approval of the Standing Committee of the NPC. The result would only be valid if more than 30 percent of eligible voters voted for it.

The "Cha-Cha" proposal aroused a storm of protest in Hong Kong, chiefly on the part of liberal groups. Even many conservative and moderate groups felt that too many restraints had been placed on the development of representative government.

The beginning of 1989 saw the convening of a plenary session of the BLDC in Guangzhou. From January 9 to 15, the drafters discussed the new draft. The following month, after approval by the Standing Committee of the NPC, the second draft was released for another five-month consultation exercise in Hong Kong.

There was general agreement that, aside from the limitations on the number of directly elected seats, there were major improvements in the second draft. The section on human rights, for example, included a provision that restrictions on rights and freedoms must not contravene the two United Nations covenants on human rights—the International Covenant on Civil and Political Rights and the International Covenant on Economic, Social, and Cultural Rights as applied to Hong Kong. The phrase "as applied to Hong Kong" reflected the fact that Britain had entered into the covenants certain reservations when extending them to Hong Kong. For example, it reserved the right not to establish an elected Executive Council in Hong Kong. That reservation will continue after 1997.

In addition, Chinese laws that would apply to Hong Kong after 1997 were limited to six, listed in an annex. This removed ambiguity as to just which mainland laws would apply. These six laws were largely noncontroversial, dealing with such things as the national anthem, the national emblem, National Day, the territorial sea, diplomatic privileges, and nationality.

Another major step forward was the agreement between British and Chinese diplomats to adopt the "through train" formula, so that the last legislators of the British colony could also serve as the first legislators of the HKSAR, with their four-year term straddling 1997 so as to minimize disruption and provide continuity.

The Basic Law was thus being shaped in a two-pronged process, with China sounding out Hong Kong opinion on the one hand and negotiating with Britain on the other. The former process was open, since meetings of the BLDC were covered by the Hong Kong press. The latter process was secret.

The Nationality Issue

Despite progress on the Basic Law, pervasive distrust of the Chinese communists continued in Hong Kong, with skeptics pointing to what they saw as Chinese unwillingness to grant true autonomy to Hong Kong in the crucial areas of political structure and the independence of the judiciary. The draft Basic Law not only provided for less than half of the legislature to be directly elected but also concentrated power in the hands of a chief executive, who would be appointed by Beijing after "consultation" or "elections" in Hong Kong. In addition, even though the Joint Declaration provided for a final court of appeals in Hong Kong, the Chinese insisted that the right to interpret Hong Kong's constitutional instrument, the Basic Law, lay with the Standing Committee of the NPC rather than with the Hong Kong courts.

Fear that China would not allow Hong Kong true autonomy led to a growing exodus. In the mid-1980s about 20,000 people a year left the colony. This number rose to 30,000 in 1987, 45,000 in 1988, and 42,800 in 1989. A disproportionate number of those leaving were well-educated people who were working as professionals or in middle management. At the same time, people who had left earlier returned armed with foreign passports, which would enable them to leave Hong Kong should things go badly after 1997.

The desire of many people for such an "insurance policy" led to widespread agitation for British subjects in Hong Kong to be given the right to live in the United Kingdom. This right was lost through a series of acts of Parliament from the 1960s to the 1980s, when British immigration and nationality laws were changed. By late 1988 and early 1989 the correspondence columns of Hong Kong's newspapers were filled with letters accusing Britain of having abandoned its 3.25 million British subjects in Hong Kong. The campaign to restore the right of abode in Britain to British subjects in Hong Kong was strongly opposed by the British government, and by the Home Office in particular, although many private citizens came out in support of it.

It was probably this clamor for the restoration of full British citizenship rights that gradually caused some members of Parliament to conclude that not all was well with Britain's policy toward Hong Kong and that a reassessment was called for. In addition, the sensitive issue of nationality caused a split to appear between the British administration in Hong Kong and the parent government in London. In February 1989 the Foreign Affairs Select Committee of the House of Commons announced that it would hold an inquiry into British policy toward Hong Kong. This was an acknowledgment by the committee that problems existed in the implementation of the Joint Declaration.

In his appearance before the committee in London, the British foreign secretary, Sir Geoffrey Howe, argued against restoring the right of abode, pointing to the large numbers of Hong Kong British subjects—3.25 million eligible for the British dependent territory passport. The foreign secretary was followed by Sir David Wilson, the governor of Hong Kong, who took a different line. "[The nationality issue] is a matter of intense feeling in Hong Kong," he said. "There is a great deal of bitterness on this subject, a great deal of bitterness about the fact that progressively from 1962, the Commonwealth Immigrants Act, onward, the right to come and settle in the United Kingdom, which some people in Hong Kong formerly had, has been taken away from them." Governor Wilson told the committee that many people were leaving Hong Kong to get a foreign passport, then returning to the territory. If Britain gave them the rights of full British citizenship, they would have "an insurance policy without having to leave."

This was very much the argument being voiced in Hong Kong. Restoration of the right of abode in Britain, it was argued, would stop the brain drain. The outflow of skilled workers not only exacerbated a tight labor market but also caused salaries to spiral upward, fueling inflation, and threatened to slow the colony's economic expansion.

In April, when the Foreign Affairs Select Committee held hearings in Hong Kong, many private groups appeared before it. All those who gave evidence, liberals and conservatives alike, urged Britain to restore the right of abode to Hong Kong British subjects, most of whom had gained that status by virtue of birth in British territory. Government officials appeared before the committee on April 21, led by Sir David Ford, chief secretary of Hong Kong, who called on Britain for "action as well as words."

The Democracy Movement

While the committee was taking evidence in Hong Kong, dramatic events were taking place in Beijing. Only hours after Chief Secretary Ford called on Britain for action, tens of thousands of students in the Chinese capital began pouring out of campuses across the city and marching toward Tiananmen Square in the country's biggest spontaneous demonstration since the Cultural Revolution. In this volatile atmosphere, the Foreign Affairs Select Committee flew into Beijing. The highest official with whom the group met was Vice Foreign Minister Zhou Nan. The committee asked Zhou for China's position on the right-of-abode issue. Zhou replied that this was an internal British matter and did not concern China.

Events in Beijing were shown on television around the world, but no one watched as avidly as the 5.6 million people in Hong Kong. Groups of students rallied in support of their Beijing counterparts, but the numbers were small at first. That changed radically on May 20, when Beijing proclaimed martial law. On the same day, Hong Kong was struck by a typhoon. As a result, schools and offices were shut. Tens of thousands took to the streets to demonstrate solidarity with the people of Beijing. It was by far the biggest turnout Hong Kong had seen in decades. But that figure was dwarfed in the following days and weeks when more than a million people—one-fifth of the population—took part in marches and rallies.

The strong reaction to events in China reflected deep-seated emotions in Hong Kong. Ever since the signing of the Joint Declaration, discontent had been simmering. Many felt betrayed by the British. Frustration turned into resentment of both Britain and China. The majority of the people of Hong Kong were legally British but ethnically Chinese. Few, if any, thought of themselves as British, but neither did they identify with China.

Until 1949 the population of Hong Kong, both Western and Chinese, was largely transient. The Chinese for the most part came from neighboring Guangdong province, hoping to make some money before returning to their native villages. If they died in Hong Kong, their bodies were shipped home for burial. The communist victory in China changed the situation. Over a million people poured into Hong Kong, planning to wait for things to settle down on the mainland so they could return home. They thought of themselves as sojourners, not settlers, but they were cut off from China in the ensuing decades.

Their children changed the demographics of Hong Kong. By the 1970s, for the first time, more than half the Hong Kong population had been born there. Unlike their parents, the members of the new generation did not think of themselves as being from any particular village in China. Hong Kong was the only home they knew, although their cultural identification with China remained strong.

If the Chinese in Hong Kong did not identify with the British, neither did they identify with the communist dictatorship in China. After all, most of them were either refugees from China or the children of such refugees. Many felt pride at China's achievements, including its status as a nuclear power. But on the whole, they were afraid of the communists.

Then came the Tiananmen protests. Now, it seemed, there were people and forces within China who stood for values with which many people in Hong Kong could identify, values such as democracy and human rights, free speech and a free press. Doubts about Hong Kong's future melded with hopes for China itself turning into a free society. Many thought they were witnessing the beginning of a process of peaceful transformation in China that would eventually lead to a democratic system.

A new organization, the Hong Kong Alliance in Support of the Patriotic Democratic Movement in China, was formed. Its leaders were the same people who had spearheaded the democratic movement within Hong Kong. The Hong Kong Alliance, which instantly enjoyed mass support, declared that until China became democratic there was no hope for Hong Kong to be democratic.

The alliance raised millions of dollars to support the Beijing students, largely through a huge pop-music concert. Tents, blankets, and other supplies were sent to Tiananmen Square. Hundreds of thousands of dollars in cash were taken to Beijing.

Virtually overnight, a consensus emerged that the colony needed to hasten the development of democracy. On May 25 the *Hong Kong Standard* said in an editorial:

> A week ago it could not have happened. Businessmen and trade unionists, left and right, conservatives and liberals, all agreeing on a political issue. A week ago even the liberals could not agree among themselves. Today, all are united behind Beijing's students, speaking with one voice to condemn the imposition of martial law and, more importantly, to call for the speedier introduction of political reforms in Hong Kong.

A survey published that same day showed that 92 percent of the population wanted better safeguards for democracy after 1997 built into the Basic Law. The day before, the members of Omelco (Office of Members of the Executive and Legislative Councils, the two top bodies) decided unanimously that the pace of democratization should be speeded up, with 50 percent of the legislature directly elected by 1995, and 100 percent by 2003.

Omelco's stance reflected a certain defiance of China, since the draft Basic Law provided for only 27 percent of the legislature to be directly elected in 1997. The Omelco decision reflected a shift in Hong Kong society. Events in Beijing caused a closing of ranks in Hong Kong and a feeling that the development of democracy had to be stepped up, although there were still differences over speed.

Martial law united Hong Kong; the massacre created horror and anger. As China moved to impose a news blackout, many in Hong Kong acted to counter it. The local radio station began Mandarin-dialect broadcasts beamed at the mainland. People poured news into China, in newspaper articles sent by mail and fax and in videotapes showing the brutality of the massacre. When the Beijing authorities announced lists of wanted student leaders and set up a hot line for the use of informers, people in Hong Kong tried to jam the line by repeatedly calling that number. Some helped create an underground railroad for those on Beijing's wanted list. They managed to spirit out dozens of political dissidents, including the student leader Wuer Kaixi and political scientist Yan Jiaqi.

The massacre also put new urgency into demands for the right of abode in Britain. A new group, Hong Kong People Saving Hong Kong, was formed to fight for this right. It collected 600,000 signatures almost overnight. Other groups sprang up, including ROAD, or the Right of Abode Delegation, consisting of local businesspeople. Another group, Honour Hong Kong Campaign, was set up by leading British businesspeople with the same goal.

For a few weeks in the summer of 1989, fear verging on panic caused many people to grab at straws. Ideas seriously advanced ranged from getting China to lease Hong Kong to the United Nations for 100 years to recreating Hong Kong in northern Australia. The day after Singapore announced it would accept 25,000 Hong Kong families in the next five to eight years, the Singapore Commission was mobbed by more than 10,000 people seeking application forms.

Then China extended its crackdown to Hong Kong. Pressure was brought to bear on the Hong Kong government to ban the Hong Kong Alliance and to prevent the use of the territory as a base for subverting the Chinese government. Some community leaders called on the alliance to disband on the ground that it was fueling Chinese anger. The government refused to ban the alliance but agreed that Hong Kong would not be a base for subversion.

Chen Xitong, the mayor of Beijing, stressed Hong Kong's role in the pro-democracy uprising in a report to the NPC. Chen pointed out that supporters in Hong Kong had supplied tents, enabling the students to "set up 'villages of freedom' and launch a 'democracy university' on the square." A few days earlier, on July 11, Jiang Zemin, the new party chief, had declared to three Hong Kong visitors, "We practice our socialism and you may practice your capitalism. 'The well water does not interfere with the river water.' We will not practice socialism in Hong Kong, Macao, and Taiwan, but you should not transplant capitalism onto the country's mainland."

The well water and river water metaphor was used by Jiang to explain Beijing's "one country, two systems" policy. The price to pay for China's not interfering in Hong Kong affairs, Jiang warned, was for Hong Kong not to try to meddle in mainland politics. While this sounded reasonable enough, some critics in Hong Kong felt that China's policy was not applied in an even-handed manner: while Beijing warned Hong Kong not to support democracy on the mainland, it felt no compunction about opposing democracy in Hong Kong. Some in Hong Kong also asserted that Chinese nationals in Hong Kong had a right to participate in national affairs.

In July the official Chinese Communist Party newspaper in Beijing, the *People's Daily*, published an article condemning "a small handful of people in Hong Kong." It criticized the chairman and vice chairman of the Hong Kong Alliance, Szeto Wah and Martin Lee—without mentioning their names—and accused them, and others, of "undertaking all sorts of activities to subvert the Chinese government." "According to recent press reports," the article continued, "this handful of people is preparing to set up a so-called political party. The 'one country, two systems' principle will certainly be sabotaged and Hong Kong will be in deep trouble once these people gain power."

Repercussions of Tiananmen

Beijing's attitude toward Hong Kong changed after June 4. Previously, China may have viewed the colony's population as largely nonpolitical, concerned primarily with making money. After the massive display in support of pro-democracy students, however, China had to reassess Hong Kong's impact on the rest of the country, and its potential impact after 1997. That is undoubtedly why, when the NPC met in March 1990, Premier Li Peng again issued a call for vigilance against "a small number of people" who used the territory as a base for subversion against China. China had always had to pay a political price for the economic benefits it derived from Hong Kong; in the wake of the events of May and June 1989, however, it evidently decided that the survival of the Communist Party, not Hong Kong, was paramount.

Among those engaged in the spontaneous outpouring of emotions during May and June were employees of official Chinese organizations in Hong Kong, including the New China News Agency and the Bank of China. Even Xu Jiatun, China's *de facto* ambassador, met and spoke solicitously with Hong Kong hunger strikers.

Two communist newspapers—*Ta Kung Pao* and *Wen Wei Po*—joined the other Hong Kong papers in castigating the Chinese government. Li Tse-chung, the director of *Wen Wei Po,* who had been a supporter of the communist cause for four decades, denounced the party. Eventually, NCNA sent a vice director to *Wen Wei Po* and announced that Li's resignation—submitted many years ago but never acted upon—had been accepted. This was the first official admission that these papers were under China's control. Previously, a polite fiction had been maintained that they were run by local "patriots." The actions of employees of state organs in Hong Kong also caused Beijing to tighten control over these bodies. By late 1989 it was known that Xu Jiatun would be replaced by hard-liner Zhou Nan.

The massacre disrupted relations between China and Britain as it did those between China and other Western countries. Britain called off a session scheduled for June of the Sino-British Joint Liaison Group (JLG), which had been set up to resolve issues in the implementation of the Joint Declaration. Britain also began to change its position on two key issues: nationality and democracy. The very limited room that Britain had for maneuver became apparent in July, however, when the Foreign Affairs Select Committee issued its report on Hong Kong. The report stated that Britain had no choice but to hand Hong Kong back to China in 1997. Its options lay in what it could do in the remaining years of British rule to help increase Hong Kong's chances for survival as an autonomous region of China, and what it could do for the people in Hong Kong who do not want to live under the sovereignty of a communist government.

Concerning the right of abode, the Foreign Affairs Select Committee ruled out any proposal to allow all British subjects in Hong Kong the right to live in Britain. It did suggest that certain people who were especially vulnerable, such as Crown servants in sensitive positions, be accorded that right. It recommended that full democracy be introduced to Hong Kong before 1997. However, it was clear that Britain was not in a position to force China to leave intact whatever Britain might put into place in Hong Kong before 1997.

In July, after the publication of the committee's report, Foreign Secretary Howe told the House of Commons that Britain would try to convince China to take steps to boost confidence in Hong Kong, such as refraining from stationing the People's Liberation Army in the territory, delaying promulgation of the Basic Law, and improving its provisions. More important, he promised to step up the development of representative government and devise a nationality package to give key people in Hong Kong the confidence to remain up to and, it was hoped, beyond 1997.

At the same time, Britain sought to bolster international support for its position on Hong Kong. Prime Minister Thatcher brought up the Hong Kong issue in major international forums, including the European Summit in Madrid, the Group of Seven economic summit in Paris, and the Commonwealth head-of-government meeting in Kuala Lumpur. This incurred the wrath of China, which accused the British of "internationalization" of the Hong Kong issue. On September 1 the *People's Daily* published an article that warned against pinning Hong Kong's future on foreign powers. Two months later the theme was taken up again, with the *People's Daily* claiming that such attempts to garner international support were a violation of international law and a breach of the Joint Declaration. It said that Britain's motive was to use international pressure to thwart China's effort to resume sovereignty over Hong Kong.

In December 1989 Britain unveiled its nationality package. This offered full British nationality to 50,000 key people and their families, a maximum of 225,000 people, in the hope that such an "insurance policy" would, in the words of the new foreign secretary, Douglas Hurd, "anchor them in Hong Kong." About one-third of the passports would go to the civil service and two-thirds to the private sector.

China denounced the move, claiming that it violated the Joint Declaration. In retaliation, China introduced a provision in the draft Basic Law limiting legislators who held foreign passports or who had the right to live in foreign countries to no more than 15 percent. Chinese officials said they would not recognize such passport holders as foreign nationals and would deny them British consular protection after 1997.

The tumultuous events of May and June disrupted the Basic Law drafting process. Two members of the BLDC, publisher Louis Cha, an author of the "mainstream" model, and Anglican bishop Peter Kwong, resigned. Two other members, lawyer Martin Lee and teacher Szeto Wah, both members of the Legislative Council as well as leaders of the Hong Kong Alliance, declared that they would not serve as long as the "Deng-Li-Yang clique" remained in power, referring to senior leader Deng Xiaoping, Premier Li Peng, and head of state Yang Shangkun. Later, the NPC declared that the two had engaged in activities inconsistent with the status of BLDC members and suspended them.

China rejected calls for new concessions and instead stiffened its provisions, adding a clause against subversion. But the most sensitive issue was still that of political structure and democratization. In September the conservative New Hong Kong Alliance (not to be confused with the Hong Kong Alliance led by Lee and Szeto) proposed a bicameral legislature after 1997. The idea found favor in Beijing but was widely denounced in Hong Kong. When the BLDC resumed work in December 1989, it adopted a new "mainstream" model that allowed 18 of the 60 seats of the 1997 legislature to be directly elected, 12 to be returned by an electoral committee, and 30 to be chosen by functional constituencies. (The "Cha-Cha" model had provided for a 55-seat legislature with 15 seats filled through direct election and 40 through functional constituencies.) In 1999 the directly elected seats would rise to 24, offset by a drop in the electoral committee seats, with the number of functional constituency seats unchanged. Then, in 2003, the electoral committee would disappear altogether, and half the seats would be returned through direct elections and half through functional constituencies. In addition, this model devised a voting plan that resembled the bicameral proposal: those elected by functional constituencies would vote separately from the other legislators. Only one Hong Kong drafter supported this proposal, but it was easily carried because of the large mainlander majority on the BLDC.

In January 1990, after the BLDC adopted its new "mainstream" model, Hurd visited Hong Kong for the first time as foreign secretary. He promised that Britain would soon unveil its plans for representative government but did not promise to adopt the Omelco consensus, which called for 30 seats to be directly elected by 1997 as opposed to the BLDC proposal of 18. Hurd made clear that Britain's objective was still to reach agreement with China but, failing that, Britain would make its own decisions. Time was running out, as the Chinese timetable called for the Basic Law to be completed in February and promulgated by the NPC when it convened in March.

While the BLDC was meeting, secret discussions were taking place between British and Chinese diplomats. This latest round had begun in November 1989, when Sir Percy Cradock, the prime minister's foreign policy adviser, made a secret trip to Beijing. The talks were continued into the new year by the British ambassador, Sir Alan Donald.

In late February 1990 the four-and-a-half-year-long process of drafting a Basic Law for Hong Kong came to an end. On February 16 the BLDC adopted the final draft. The day before, the news was leaked that Britain and China had reached agreement. This was confirmed when the BLDC, meeting on its last day, adopted an amendment to provide for 20 seats to be directly elected in 1997. Minutes after the package was approved by the drafters, the Hong Kong government announced that 18 seats would be open for direct elections in 1991 and "not less than 20" in 1995.

In London, Foreign Secretary Hurd told the House of Commons that although the rate of progress "would not be as rapid as many people in Hong Kong, or we ourselves, would have liked to see . . . it would be a considerable improvement on the position reached in December."

The Repatriation Issue

In the fall another crisis erupted when the Hong Kong government refused to send back a Chinese champion swimmer, Yang Yang. The young man, who said he was a member of a pro-democracy organization, claimed he faced persecution in China. NCNA said that, under a series of agreements regarding immigration matters (none of which has ever been published), the Hong Kong government was obliged to send all overstayers back to China. After the Hong Kong government allowed Yang to leave for the United States, China retaliated by refusing to take back from Hong Kong its illegal immigrants.

The repatriation to China of illegal immigrants had been agreed upon almost a decade ago, and this was the first time China had refused to cooperate. The deadlock created serious pressures on both sides. In Hong Kong there were fears of a flood of illegals crossing the border when word spread that they would no longer be repatriated. Within China there was also fear of a wave of unemployed people from different provinces swarming into Guangdong province on their way to Hong Kong.

With such pressure on both sides, an agreement to resume repatriation was reached after several weeks of secret talks. But the agreement itself precipitated a new dispute. The Hong Kong government said that no concessions had been made to arrive at the agreement. The claim provoked a stinging response from NCNA. At an unusual press conference, Chinese officials accused the British of lying and threatened to disclose the contents of a written agreement that allegedly contained undertakings made by the Hong Kong government. The following day, the text of a letter written to NCNA by Hong Kong's political adviser, William Ehrman, was published on the front page of the *South China Morning Post*. The letter, dated October 23 and addressed to Ji Shaoxiang, head of NCNA's foreign affairs department, reiterated that "the Hong Kong government has no intention of allowing Hong Kong to be used as a base for subversive activities against the People's Republic of China." After the publication of the letter, both sides declined to make any further comment, and the issue was allowed to fade.

The Boat People

Another issue that beset Hong Kong throughout 1989 was the perennial problem of Vietnamese refugees. The year saw the greatest influx of boat people in a decade; about 34,000 arrived, stretching the colony's capacity to house and feed the arrivals to the breaking point.

The international community had decided in 1979, at a conference in Geneva, that the countries of Southeast Asia would offer initial asylum to Vietnamese refugees, who would eventually be resettled in the West. However, over the years, the resettlement countries had become more restrictive. In 1988 Hong Kong introduced a policy under which all arrivals from Vietnam would be made subject to a screening procedure to determine whether they were genuine refugees with a well-founded fear of persecution. Those screened out would be treated as illegal immigrants, subject to repatriation to Vietnam.

In June 1989 another conference was held at Geneva, at which the international community endorsed the screening policy and agreed in principle to the repatriation of nonrefugees. But it did not endorse mandatory repatriation. In effect, it asked Hong Kong to persuade Vietnamese screened out to go home voluntarily. However, few volunteered. Between November 1988 and October 1989, only 264 Vietnamese went home voluntarily.

Pressure grew in Hong Kong for mandatory repatriation. Britain agreed. Despite strong American opposition, Britain reached agreement with Vietnam on forcible repatriation.

On December 12, 1989, Hong Kong security officials, in riot gear, made a predawn sweep and rounded up 51 Vietnamese boat people, mostly women and children, escorted them to the airport, and put them on a plane for Hanoi. This triggered a wave of condemnation, particularly by the United States.

Another Geneva meeting was convened and Hong Kong was able to win the support of most participants for a six-month moratorium during which nonrefugees would be persuaded to go home voluntarily before mandatory repatriation was resumed. The United States insisted on a one-year moratorium. Vietnam, appalled by the publicity, refused to continue mandatory repatriation. In mid-February 1990 a British official, Francis Maude, held talks in Vietnam but made no visible progress.

With few signs of an early solution to the problem, pressures rose inside the Vietnamese camps. There was a rash of suicide attempts and, on February 18, 1990, the first fatality occurred when a Vietnamese man who had been screened out hanged himself. Clashes broke out between rival groups of Vietnamese as well as between Vietnamese and security forces. The Vietnamese refugee issue has given Hong Kong bad press internationally, even though technically Britain is responsible for decisions that have foreign policy implications.

The greatest, and perhaps the only, opponent of mandatory repatriation of Vietnamese is the United States, which is increasingly being depicted within Hong Kong as upholding a double standard, since the United States itself repatriates illegal immigrants. The United States is seen as unreasonable for not accepting these people itself, yet blocking their return to Vietnam. Furthermore, Hong Kong is saddled with the costs of maintaining the Vietnamese camps, for neither the United States nor the United Nations High Commissioner for Refugees will pay to house people whom they do not define as political refugees.

The Future of Hong Kong

In an attempt to project an image of a government in charge and with a vision for the future, Governor Wilson, in his annual address to the legislature on October 11, 1989, unveiled a plan for enhancing Hong Kong's prosperity. The plan includes the construction of a new airport on the island of Lantau capable of handling 80 million passengers a year, or more than three times the current capacity of Kai Tak, with the first of two runways to open by early 1997. This would entail building a high-speed rail system, a six-lane highway, and a new town for at least 150,000 people. At the same time, the governor outlined plans for a new port that would increase container throughput fivefold. With 80 million tons of cargo a year, Hong Kong is already the world's busiest container port. The cost of these projects is estimated at HK$127 billion. The government hopes that the private sector can account for 40 to 60 percent of the financing.

The governor also announced ambitious plans in other areas. On education, he set a target of providing first-year university places for over 18 percent of the relevant age group by 1995, compared with 7 percent in 1989. On housing, he said the Housing Authority aimed to produce 527,000 public housing units for rental and sale by the year 2001. On the environment, he said that the government proposed to spend at least HK$20 billion in the next decade to bring pollution under control. These government goals were, on the whole, welcomed.

China, however, warned Hong Kong to cut its cloak according to its cloth and indicated that the colony must not count on Chinese financial support. Locally, educators wondered out loud where teachers could be found, even if school buildings could be erected, since large numbers of teachers were emigrating.

By spring 1990 the airport development plans were turning into another bone of contention between Hong Kong and China. Banks were reluctant to help finance the project without clear Chinese endorsement, and China made plain its reluctance to endorse the project without first being fully informed about it. NCNA suggested that the Hong Kong government provide it with studies done by consultants on the airport project. This seemingly reasonable request could be the thin end of the wedge by which China gradually insinuates itself into Hong Kong's decision-making process well before 1997. China's desire to be fully involved in the administration of Hong Kong was made explicit on April 27, 1990, when Guo Fengmin, the new Chinese head of the JLG, told a press conference that China expected to be consulted on all major decisions involving Hong Kong before 1997.

The events of June 3 and 4 had an impact on the Hong Kong economy. The travel industry was badly hit, largely because tourists avoided China. Property prices were also affected. A choice site in the central financial district, originally expected to fetch US$500–640 million, was sold for US$346 million. Despite the sharp drop, however, the fact that there were bidders was in itself seen as a sign of a return of confidence. A group led by Wharf (Holdings) Ltd. won the license to develop the territory's first cable television network. The joint-venture company said it would invest between HK$4 billion (US$512 million) and HK$5.5 billion (US$705 million) in the project. This was interpreted as another sign of confidence, since the venture is not expected to turn a profit until after 1997.

In recent years Hong Kong companies have set up factories in southern China, taking advantage of the low cost of land and labor, and today they employ about 2 million workers in the Pearl River Delta, more than the number of workers in Hong Kong itself. However, in the aftermath of Tiananmen, businesspeople held off on new investments in China and many sought ways of diversifying. Many companies have followed the lead set by Jardine Matheson in 1984 by establishing corporate domiciles outside Hong Kong.

Major foreign institutions are reassessing their positions. The exposure of American banks to Hong Kong is estimated at US$20 billion, ten times their exposure to China. One U.S. corporation, Citibank, pledged its commitment to Hong Kong and announced plans to acquire more office space. Others are likely to be more circumspect and adopt a wait-and-see attitude.

Beijing's promise to allow Hong Kong "a high degree of autonomy" is based on self-interest, since the colony accounts for between one-third and 40 percent of China's foreign exchange earnings and two-thirds of its foreign investment. For this reason alone, China is unlikely to want to do anything that will damage Hong Kong's business climate. The problem is that, where Beijing is concerned, economics takes a back seat to politics.

The return of China to a degree of normalcy gave Hong Kong a chance to reassess its situation. It is one that has been permanently changed by the events of June 3–4 and their aftermath. Within the colony, there has been a politicization—almost a radicalization—of large segments of the population that had previously been described as politically apathetic.

The reassessment, and China's new bellicose attitude toward Hong Kong, caused many groups and individuals formerly considered pro-Beijing to distance themselves from the Chinese government. Identification with China, developed to its highest point during the demonstrations of May and June, has fallen to a new low. A new political party, the United Democrats of Hong Kong, led by Martin Lee and Szeto Wah, declared at its founding in April 1990 that it would not involve itself in Chinese politics but would focus on Hong Kong affairs.

The cataclysmic events of 1989 showed that cleavages within Hong Kong could be quickly narrowed. Millions of people reacted in almost exactly the same way to the crisis in Beijing. There was also a shift in the spectrum of opinions within Hong Kong. Those previously suspicious of China had their fears strongly confirmed, while others who had been cautiously optimistic about the relationship became aware of the enormous difficulty of making China's formula of "one country, two systems" work after 1997.

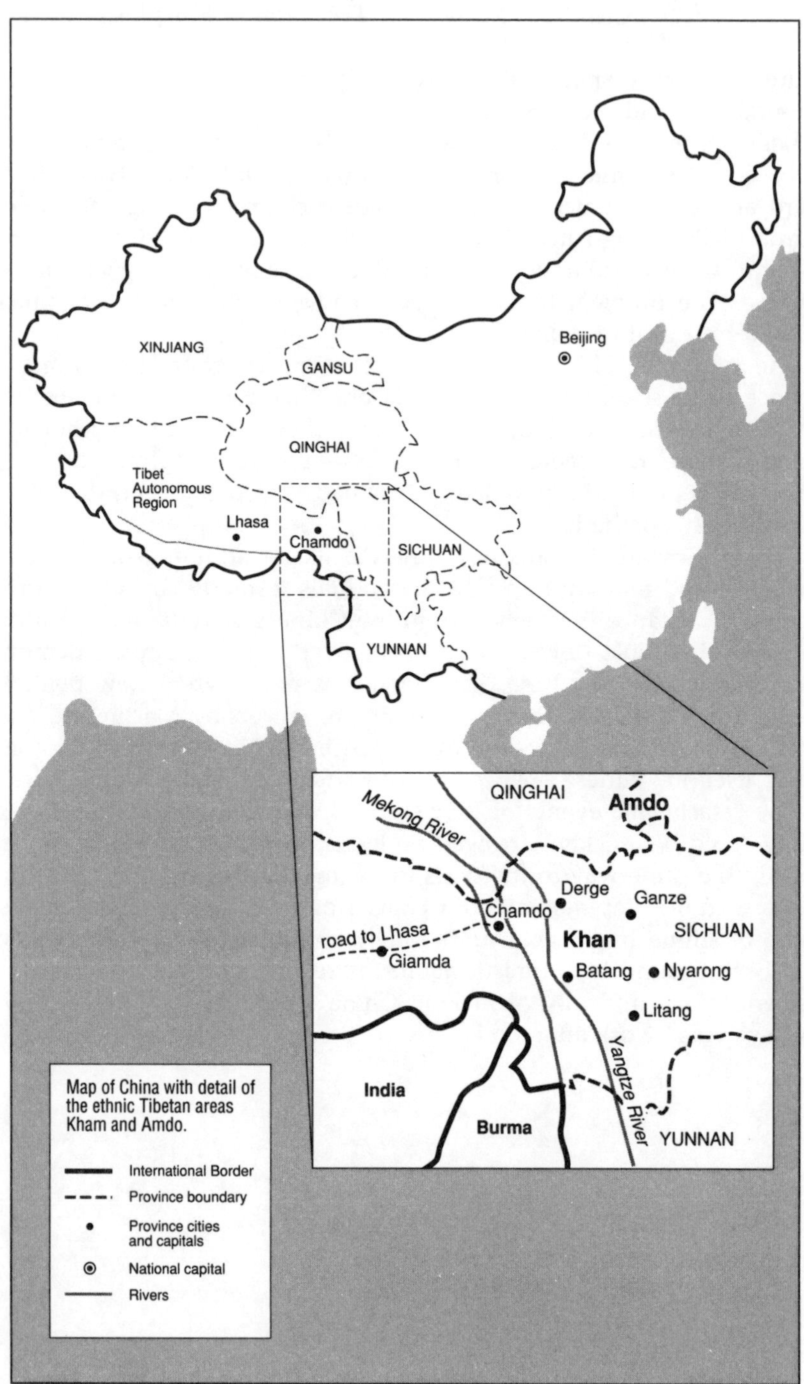

Map of China with detail of the ethnic Tibetan areas Kham and Amdo.

7
The Dragon and the Snow Lion: The Tibet Question in the 20th Century

Melvyn C. Goldstein

On March 5, 1989, Tibetan monks and nuns demonstrated in Lhasa in support of Tibetan independence, precipitating the fourth and worst riot in a series that began on October 1, 1987. The extent of the anger and violence exhibited by Tibetans in these riots took the Chinese government by surprise, simultaneously embarrassing, infuriating, and frustrating it. Beijing believed that its post-Mao Tibet policy broke with past excesses and was conciliatory and sympathetic to the economic and cultural aspirations of the Tibetan people. But now, despite this reform, the government was faced with repeated demonstrations and violent riots. As a result of the unrest, China imposed martial law in Lhasa on March 7, 1989.

Nineteen eighty-nine was also the year that His Holiness the Dalai Lama, the former ruler of Tibet who now resides in Dharamsala, India, received the Nobel Peace Prize. His acceptance speech did not describe a Chinese reform policy in Tibet but rather presented a grim picture of events there, claiming terrible systematic violations of fundamental human rights.

The pervasive tendency of both the Tibetan exiles and the Chinese leadership to describe events in Tibet in either black or white—horrendous oppression or magnificent reform and development—pressures the nonspecialist to choose one side and accept its version in entirety. This chapter attempts to provide an alternative; an interpretation in which shades of gray are explored and the complex historical antecedents of today's situation are presented. While it is possible that this approach may irritate some in both Dharamsala and Beijing, I hope they will take it as it is intended—as an attempt to set out for Americans a balanced account of a volatile and complex issue.

The recent disturbances in Tibet are the current manifestation of the longstanding conflict over what the political status of Tibet vis-à-vis China should be: the "Tibet question." Throughout the 20th century China and Tibet have sparred over this issue, each shifting positions and strategies, gaining temporary advantages but unable to achieve the elusive goal both seek—a permanent, mutually agreeable solution. The individual players who began the competition have long since died, but the game continues, with today's players launching new strategies to compel the antagonist to accept their conditions as the appropriate conclusion.

The complexity of the issue is such that one cannot even begin to examine the contrasting perceptions of conditions in Tibet without precisely defining what is meant by "Tibet," since the referent of this term has become badly confused. The Dalai Lama and the Tibetan exile community generally subsume under "Tibet" not only the actual political entity (state) that was ruled by the Dalai Lamas until 1959 but also all the ethnic Tibetan areas in the adjacent Chinese provinces of Qinghai, Sichuan, Gansu, and Yunnan. Many Westerners, knowingly or unwittingly, have followed suit.

These areas, however, have been under Chinese control for centuries, as noted by Tibetologist Hugh Richardson in distinguishing between "ethnographic" and "political" Tibet.[1] The current Tibet Autonomous Region (TAR) is virtually identical to the political entity the Dalai Lamas ruled. In this chapter, therefore, I use "Tibet" to mean the political entity that was equivalent to Tibet in the 1930s and 1940s, that is, to today's TAR, and not the artificially conceptualized "greater Tibet" that Tibetans in exile would like to see created.

The Historical Context: Tibet under the Qing

The political entity we know as Tibet became subordinate to China in the early 18th century during the height of the Qing (Manchu) dynasty. China's overlordship, however, was never formalized—the mutual rights and obligations of the two sides were not delimited in treaties or other written agreements. Tibet became a loosely linked protectorate of China, but Tibetan officials governed their country with their own officials and laws. Manchu influence and authority were implemented at the top through imperial commissioners (called

---

[1] Hugh Richardson, *Tibet and Its History* (Boston: Shambhala Press, 1984), pp. 1–2. See also Josef Kolmas, *Tibet and Imperial China* (Canberra: The Australian National University, 1967), pp. 41–42, and Eric Teichman, *Travels of a Consular Officer in Eastern Tibet* (Cambridge, England: Cambridge University Press, 1922), pp. 1–8.

amban) who were stationed in Lhasa together with a small bodyguard force. The Qing emperors of China were not interested in incorporating Tibet and administering it as a province. They were content to ensure that Tibet's activities and policies did not conflict with their interests. As Manchu power eroded during the 19th century and China became preoccupied with the onslaught of Western imperialism, its hegemony over Tibet became increasingly symbolic.

British initiatives at the turn of the 19th century changed this, setting in motion a series of events that altered the status quo dramatically. Tibet suddenly assumed center stage in an international drama that continues to this day.

The British Thrust

British influence on the Indian subcontinent was extended to the border of Tibet when it subordinated the string of Himalayan states and principalities, particularly when Sikkim, an ethnic Tibetan principality lying along the main trade route from Tibet to India, was converted into a protectorate in 1861. The British then tried to establish cordial relations with Tibet, but failed because the Tibetan government was disinclined even to hold discussions let alone to permit travel and trade. Britain turned to China, the *de jure* overlord of Tibet, to gain access. The Anglo-Chinese Tibetan Trade Regulations of 1893 gave British merchants the right to travel to the Yatung trade mart in Tibet and permitted British government officials to reside there to oversee British trade. Tibet, however, was not a party to this agreement and refused to accept its terms.

In 1899 Lord Curzon appeared on the scene as the new viceroy of India. Curzon escalated the importance of British contact with Tibet by linking the political situation in Tibet to the security of India. In particular, he raised the possibility that Tibet might fall under Russian domination.

Curzon quickly decided that China's inability to exert control over Tibet rendered working through Beijing an exercise in futility. He pressured Beijing to arrange for a meeting with Tibetan officials and in late 1903 sent an expedition across the border to a Tibetan administrative headquarters about 15 miles north of Sikkim. Lhasa, however, was unwilling to discuss matters and insisted that the British leave Tibetan territory at once. Faced with the embarrassing specter of another British failure to open Tibet, London agreed to permit the mission to proceed farther north. Although the objective was to open negotiations rather than to invade per se, the British officers and officials ultimately led their Indian troops deeper and deeper into Tibet.

They easily defeated the ragtag Tibetan forces they encountered along the way and in 1904 became the first Western troops to conquer Lhasa.

Throughout this period the Chinese imperial commissioners in Lhasa urged the 13th Dalai Lama to negotiate with the British expeditionary force, but the Dalai Lama ignored this counsel and fled to Mongolia, presumably to seek Russian support against Britain. The regent he left in his place was forced to accept British terms (in the Lhasa Convention of 1904) to ensure the withdrawal of British/Indian troops. Signed only by Tibet and the British head of the expeditionary force, it excluded any other foreign power from exercising political influence in Tibet, a clause that was vague enough to exclude China as well as Russia.

With British India now poised to subordinate Tibet under its ever-expanding political and commercial umbrella, London responded negatively to the conquest of Tibet, virtually repudiating the expedition's occupation of Lhasa. Even more important, London promptly entered into negotiations with China to obtain the latter's acceptance of the Lhasa Convention, thereby reaffirming China's *de jure* control over Tibet. The resultant 1906 Anglo-Chinese Convention restated the Chinese overlord position in Tibet and restricted the British role primarily to commercial affairs.

China's Response

The invasion of Tibet and the Lhasa Convention of 1904 dramatically altered Chinese policy toward Tibet. Until then, the Qing dynasty had evinced no interest in directly administering or Sinicizing Tibet. The British thrust, however, now suggested to Beijing that unless it took prompt action its position as nominal overlord in Tibet might be lost. China, although enfeebled and on the brink of collapse, responded with surprising vigor. It launched a two-pronged policy aimed at administratively incorporating the ethnic Tibetan territories in Sichuan province and taking a more active role in day-to-day affairs in Tibet proper. The 13th Dalai Lama's overture to the Russian czar proved futile, and his position in exile became precarious. He had been "deposed" by the Chinese government in 1904 because of his flight. Although Tibetans never questioned his legitimacy as their ruler, the increased domination of affairs in Lhasa by the imperial commissioners made him unwilling to return to Lhasa without first achieving some accommodation with the Chinese.

In 1908 the Dalai Lama went to Beijing, which ultimately agreed that he could return to Tibet to rule, but when he arrived in Lhasa in late December 1909, he learned that a Chinese army of several thousand troops from Sichuan was on its way to ensure that he toed the line. For a month he vacillated as to how to respond and then, as this army entered Lhasa in February 1910, he again decided to flee into exile, this time south to his former enemies in India. China again deposed the Dalai Lama and redoubled its efforts to expand its control over Tibet.

The Tibet Question: 1913–51

Tibet seemed set on a trajectory that would have ended in its incorporation into China proper when the Qing dynasty was suddenly overthrown in 1911. The 13th Dalai Lama (still in exile in India) organized a military force that quickly expelled all Chinese officials and troops from Tibet. He triumphantly returned to Lhasa in 1913 and unequivocally declared himself the ruler of Tibet, no longer acknowledging even symbolic subordination to China.

The Simla Compromise

The new Chinese republican government, however, continued to claim Tibet as a part of China. In fact, because one of the fundamental goals of the Chinese nationalists was the reunification of all parts of what had been the Chinese empire, control of Tibet took on great symbolic significance. It was, therefore, obvious to the Dalai Lama (and the British) that unless some agreement could be reached regarding Tibet's status, Tibet would have to militarily defend the *de facto* independent position it had established in 1913. A tripartite conference was convened by Britain in Simla, India, in 1913 to settle this issue. Attended by Chinese, Tibetan, and British plenipotentiaries, it produced a draft convention in 1914 that set the background for the next three and a half decades.

Tibet wanted the conference to declare it independent. The only way to achieve this aim would have been for Great Britain to strongly champion the Tibetan cause, but British strategic aims were not congruent with those of Lhasa. His Majesty's government decided not to support an independent Tibet or even to threaten to do so if China proved recalcitrant at the conference. Great Britain was unwilling to face the international criticism from Russia and China that support for Tibetan independence would have engendered. The British were fearful of harming their trade interests in China and Hong Kong, and, to a degree, were also fearful that an independent Tibet might soon become "independent" of British influence.

Britain proposed that Tibet be accepted as a self-governing dominion nominally under China but with Chinese influence and power severely limited. The reduction of Chinese influence and power in Tibet would create a buffer zone along India's northern border where British commercial interests could thrive. Tibet ultimately agreed to the Simla compromise because it guaranteed Lhasa complete control over its affairs, including its own army, money, and so forth. The price it paid was that it had to accept China as its suzerain.

The political dimension of the Tibet question, however, turned out to be easier to accommodate than the territorial one. Tibet and China found it impossible to agree on where to draw the boundary between Tibet and China. The 13th Dalai Lama's government demanded (as the Dalai Lama does today) that ethnic Tibetan areas east of the Mekong-Yangtze divide (in Qinghai, Gansu, Yunnan, and Sichuan provinces) be ceded to Tibet, while China demanded that the boundary be established only 125 miles east of Lhasa at Giamda (see map), an area well west of the Mekong River. The British tried to broker a compromise, but the new Chinese government found the territorial compromise unacceptable and immediately repudiated the Simla Convention. Britain and Tibet then signed an agreement binding each to the terms of the unsigned Simla Convention, including a statement that so long as China refused to sign the agreement it could not enjoy any of the privileges included in it. However, since China did not agree to the convention, the Tibet question really remained unresolved. Great Britain had achieved its goals, but Tibet obtained no *de jure* status accepted by China.

These events precipitated a major confrontation between two factions within Tibet. On the one hand, a group of pro-British, aristocratic officials argued for modernization including the development of a strong, modern military. This faction had the ear of the Dalai Lama until the early 1920s, when a conservative, religious-led faction convinced him that this policy was a mistake. These conservatives believed that alien Western values were a greater threat to Tibet's theocratic state than was China, since in the long term, the diffusion of atheistic Western ideas would weaken the dominance of Buddhism in Tibet. The Dalai Lama's decision to scale down dramatically the plans for modernization led to new overtures from China for bilateral talks without British involvement. Initiatives continued but little was accomplished, and no Chinese officials were permitted to reside in Tibet throughout the period 1913–33.

Chinese fortunes in Tibet improved somewhat after the death of the 13th Dalai Lama in 1933; nevertheless, when the Kuomintang government of Chiang Kai-shek fell to the communists in 1949, the Tibetan question was still no closer to settlement than it had been at the time of the fall of the Qing dynasty in 1911. The relevant Western countries were content to adhere to the convenient Simla conditions, acknowledging *de jure* Chinese suzerainty over Tibet while dealing directly with Tibet as if it were a *de facto* independent state. Much of the current confusion over Tibet's political status derives from this double standard on the part of the Western nations concerned.

For example, in 1948 when the Tibetan government sent a trade mission to the West, British officials in Hong Kong stamped the Tibetan passports with entry visas valid for three months. The Chinese government (of Chiang Kai-shek) discovered this and asked London how it could take Tibetan passports when it did not accept Tibet as an independent state. The British Foreign Office assured the Chinese that a mistake had been made, promising that in the future no more visas would be issued on Tibetan passports. Consequently, when the Tibetan mission requested renewals, it was advised that these visas would be issued on separate pieces of paper called "affidavits of identity." The Tibetans, surprised and indignant, refused to accept these. The British Foreign Office solved the problem by crossing out the words "three months" on the expired visa stamps and substituting "nine months." Thus, Great Britain kept its promise to the Chinese government, since these were not new visas, and at the same time mollified the Tibetans by admitting them on passports issued by the Tibetan government.[2]

The 17-Point Agreement

The establishment of the People's Republic of China (PRC) in 1949 set in motion events that two years later broke the post-1911 deadlock. The new Chinese government insisted, as had Chiang Kai-shek, that Tibet was an integral part of China, and it achieved in two years what its predecessors had not accomplished in three decades of diplomacy, intimidation, and outright force: it propelled Tibet to the negotiating table by invading across the Yangtze River in October 1950 and quickly capturing the bulk of the Tibetan army stationed there. The road to Lhasa was now virtually open. China, however, clearly wanted to "liberate" Tibet peacefully, not conquer it militarily, so the People's Liberation Army (PLA) halted its advance while Beijing demanded that Lhasa open negotiations to settle the Tibet question. The Tibetan government sought help from the United Nations, the United

---

[2] Melvyn C. Goldstein, *A History of Modern Tibet, 1913–1951:The Demise of the Lamaist State* (Berkeley: University of California Press, 1989), pp. 598–601.

States, India, and Britain, but none was forthcoming so it sent a negotiating delegation to Beijing in 1951. Once again, as they had been forced to do in 1904, Tibetan delegates reluctantly signed an agreement—the "17-Point Agreement for the Peaceful Liberation of Tibet." In it, Tibet formally acknowledged Chinese sovereignty over Tibet in exchange for Chinese agreement to maintain the Dalai Lama and the traditional politico-economic system intact.

The 17-Point Agreement established a set of mutually agreed-upon ground rules for Tibetan-Chinese relations for the first time since the fall of the Manchu dynasty in 1911. But both sides soon found that putting it into practice would be neither straightforward nor easy.

Tibet and the PRC

Coexistence: 1951–59

The years between 1951 and 1959 were marked by increasingly serious levels of conflict and discontent, particularly after 1955 when the situation deteriorated, ending in the abortive Tibetan uprising of March 1959 and the flight of the 14th Dalai Lama into exile in India.

Many conservative monk and lay officials were from the start openly opposed to a sizable Chinese presence in Tibet. Their expectation (or perhaps empty hope) was that accepting Chinese sovereignty over Tibet and letting China conduct Tibet's international relations and defense would sufficiently mollify Beijing that it would allow Tibet to continue governing itself internally without political, economic, or social change. They were, therefore, offended and responded with overt hostility when the first groups of Chinese officials and troops entered Tibet with their red flags and irritating propaganda about Tibet being liberated from imperialism and being once again part of the great "motherland."

On the other hand, the Dalai Lama and the majority of the leading government officials felt that they must try in good faith to develop cooperative relations with the Chinese in order to make the agreement work and preserve the integrity of Tibet's religious polity. Although they did not like the active Chinese role in Tibet, they were still in charge of its administration, for the Chinese were being careful to ask the traditional government to issue any orders they wanted promulgated. The Tibetan government's strategy appeared to be to yield on peripheral issues so as to protect the essential one—continuity of the Dalai Lama's rule and religion.

Beijing's view of the agreement bore little resemblance to the conservative Tibetans' view. The Chinese believed that the issue of whether Tibet was an integral part of China had been decided and that eventually, when Tibetans were more receptive, socialist reforms would be implemented as was currently being done among the Chinese peasants. But since Tibetans were clearly not then receptive, the Chinese adhered to the terms of the 17-Point Agreement, refraining from instituting any reforms regarding land, economy, or class structure among the mass of Tibetan peasants and nomads. Most villagers, therefore, never laid eyes on a Chinese person between 1951 and 1959.

Instead the Chinese tried to win popularity among Tibetans by showing that they respected Tibet's religious institutions. Every year the Chinese gave money alms (*gye*) to the 20,000 monks of Lhasa's great monasteries, and they also refrained from verbal attacks on the traditional socio-economic system. Chinese propaganda in Lhasa in 1951 focused on eliminating so-called imperialist influences and on helping Tibet to modernize rather than on communizing it. Many Tibetans were given trips to China to see what modern Chinese cities looked like, and schools and clinics were established with the approval of the Tibetan government. Women's and youth groups were started and were well received by many members of the aristocracy and trading community who had been thwarted in their attempts to modernize Tibet before 1950.

But there were problems, the most obvious of which was a consequence of the arrival in Lhasa of large numbers of Chinese troops and officials. The sudden need to feed thousands of Chinese, together with the Chinese policy of paying with silver dollars, created an instant shortage of grains and substantial inflation as early as 1952. This gave impetus to strong anti-Chinese feelings among many Lhasans and to the formation of a secret association (the People's Assembly) which demanded that the Chinese repatriate most of their personnel.

Moreover, many of the Tibetan officials who were trying to make things work distrusted Chinese long-term plans for Tibet. But despite such problems and doubts, the years 1951–55 passed with the Tibetan government still in control, and the traditional system continuing to function as it had before 1951. At this juncture, events outside Tibet proper changed the situation within Tibet for the worse.

The liberal terms laid down in the 17-Point Agreement were valid for the Tibetan state ruled by the Dalai Lama but did not cover the adjacent ethnic Tibetan areas east of the Yangtze River that had been under Chinese administration. The Chinese government, therefore, had no qualms about beginning socialist reforms there. These moves initially provoked a few small outbreaks of violence, but the reforms continued, and in 1955–56 major revolts occurred in which a large number of Chinese soldiers, officials, and citizens were killed. The PLA harshly quelled these revolts by late 1957, but they resulted in a sizable immigration of armed and bitter Eastern Tibetans into Tibet proper.

The Dalai Lama and the Tibetan government now feared that the Chinese would begin to implement socialist reforms in Tibet, and the Dalai Lama began seriously to consider fleeing into exile. In late 1956, when he was visiting India with his entourage, he precipitated a crisis by deciding not to return. In early 1957 Mao Zedong publicly announced that reforms in Tibet would be postponed for six years, and if Tibetans were still not willing to accept reforms after that time, they would be postponed again, for decades if necessary. With this commitment, the Dalai Lama returned to Lhasa.

But Chinese distrust of the leading officials in Lhasa and intrusiveness in government continued to increase. By March 1959 events deteriorated to the point where the Dalai Lama's key officials prevailed upon him to flee again. He did so, and in his wake about 100,000 Tibetans sought refuge in India, Nepal, Sikkim, and Bhutan. Simultaneously, a Tibetan uprising took place and was quickly quelled by the PLA. From that point on, the traditional society ended and Tibet came under the direct administration of China. In 1965 Tibet was formally restructured as the Tibet Autonomous Region.

Nineteen fifty-nine, therefore, marked the reemergence of the Tibet question as an international issue, with the Dalai Lama and his government-in-exile denouncing the 17-Point Agreement as invalid. The exiles began to accuse the Chinese of human rights violations and to seek international support for Tibet's self-determination and independence. These activities continue to the present.

Direct Chinese Rule

China employed harsh measures to suppress the 1959 uprising in Lhasa: many Tibetans were killed in the fighting around the Dalai Lama's palace, and others were arrested or sent to labor camps. Beijing soon decided, however, that the Tibetan peasantry was not ready for a major transformation of its economy into communes, so it adopted a policy of bringing Tibet to socialism gradually, implementing some changes but not others. For example, although the mass of monks were sent home from their monasteries, individual Tibetans were still permitted to practice their Buddhism. The overwhelming majority of peasant households kept the fields and animals they held in 1959, and economic decisions, as well as all income, remained under the control of individual households.

The emergence of the "Great Proletarian Cultural Revolution" in 1966 eventually changed that. Over the next four years farming and pastoral nomadic areas were restructured into communes. Farmers and nomads became "owners" of shares of the commune, but in reality they were simply laborers who worked in accordance with the commune leaders' orders. As in the rest of China, individuals earned food, goods, and cash by their labor, accumulating work points throughout the year. Although no attempt was made to resettle Chinese (Han) farmers in rural farming or nomad areas during this period, Tibetan traditional culture came under severe attack.

The policy known as "destroying the four olds" (old ideas, old culture, old customs, and old habits) was energetically implemented with the aim of creating a new homogeneous and atheistic communist culture in place of the traditional one. Private religious activities were forbidden, religious buildings (including monasteries, temples, and even prayer walls) were torn down, and Tibetans were forced to abandon deeply held values and customs that went to the core of their cultural identity. The class struggle sessions conducted by Tibetan cadres and the constant barrage of propaganda contradicting and ridiculing everything Tibetans understood and felt created severe psychological dissonance. In short, Chinese policy during this period sought to destroy the social and cultural fabric of Tibet's traditional way of life.

Chinese Policy in Tibet in the Post-Mao Era

The death of Mao Zedong in 1976, the fall of the Gang of Four, and the rise to power of Deng Xiaoping created a new cultural and economic ideology in China. The full impact of these changes reached Tibet only in 1980 when the highest echelons of the Chinese Communist Party (CCP) stepped in to investigate a controversy over conditions in the TAR, in effect to examine the consequences of China's 20 years (1959–79) of direct rule in Tibet.

Assessing Conditions in Tibet

While China was discarding Maoist ideology and policies in China proper and assessing how to rectify the damage done there, Ren Rong, the Han first secretary of the CCP in Tibet, was reporting that political conditions in Tibet were excellent and that Tibetans were solidly behind the party and the motherland. At about the same time, the Dalai Lama's brother Gyalo Thundrup and representatives of the Chinese government held preliminary talks in Hong Kong at which both sides expressed an interest in settling the Tibetan question. This led to Beijing's inviting the Dalai Lama to send a delegation in 1979 to travel and observe conditions in Tibet. Beijing obviously believed that the delegation would be impressed by the progress that had been made in Tibet since 1959 and the solidarity of the Tibetan people with the nation.

This first delegation included another brother of the Dalai Lama and several officials from Dharamsala, the headquarters of the Dalai Lama's government-in-exile. The Tibetan delegation first visited part of Amdo (in Qinghai province), where it received a tumultuous welcome. Beijing, embarrassed by this expression of support for the Dalai Lama, contacted Ren in Lhasa asking him what would happen if the delegation were to continue to Lhasa according to plan. Ren is said to have replied that the people of Lhasa were more ideologically developed than the simple farmers and herders of Amdo and strongly supported the ideals of the Communist Party; there would be no such problems in Lhasa. So strongly did the local administration in Tibet believe this that it organized neighborhood meetings in Lhasa just before the arrival of the delegation to exhort the local Tibetan "masses" not to let their hatred of the "old society" provoke them to throw stones or spit at the Dalai Lama's delegates, who were coming as guests of the Chinese government.

The Tibetans agreed politely and then gave the delegation a welcome surpassing anything it had received in Qinghai. Thousands upon thousands of Lhasans mobbed the delegation. Many cried and prostrated themselves, others offered ceremonial scarves, fighting to touch the Dalai Lama's brother, and a few shouted Tibetan nationalistic slogans such as "Tibet is independent" and "Han go home." Since Beijing officials were accompanying the Tibetan refugee delegation, there was no way for Ren, who was known to be unsympathetic to Tibetan cultural, religious, and language reforms, to cover up this fiasco and his utter misreading of the sentiment of the Tibetan masses.

This incident revealed to Beijing the extent to which Tibetan nationalism and identification with the Dalai Lama still existed among the Tibetan masses, who presumably were at the bottom of the "old society" and should have been grateful to China for "liberating" them from "feudalism." Twenty years under China apparently had not extinguished Tibetans' belief in the sanctity of the Dalai Lama and his position as leader of the Tibetan people. It also apparently had not extinguished their feeling that Tibet should be ruled by Tibetans in accordance with Tibetan values.

When the Tibetan refugee delegation returned to Beijing it informed the Chinese leadership that it was appalled by the massive religious and cultural destruction and the overall poverty, backwardness, and lack of material progress it had witnessed in Tibet. This shocked the highest reaches of the CCP and forced Beijing to reassess the situation in Tibet and begin a process of readjustment that continues to the present.

After considerable preliminary investigation, Hu Yaobang and Vice Premier Wan Li made an unprecedented fact-finding visit to Tibet in May of 1980 to see conditions for themselves. They apparently were not pleased by what they saw and heard, and acted immediately, taking Ren back to Beijing with them, presumably so that he could not thwart their reform plans. Hu publicly announced a sweeping six-point report on Tibet that addressed political, economic, cultural, and educational issues.

This public statement was apparently mild compared with the secret report and speeches Hu made to the party cadres, in which he is said to have equated the previous 20 years of Chinese rule in Tibet with Western colonial occupation. This decision of Hu Yaobang and the Central Committee of the CCP to support those inside and outside China who criticized conditions in Tibet formed the basis on which a series of reform measures was implemented in Tibet in the following years.

China's New Reform Policy

The reform policy represented Beijing's attempt to redress the wrongs that had been done to Tibetans, albeit within the framework that Tibet was an inalienable part of China. It had four salient dimensions: quickly improving the standard of living of individual Tibetans; developing the infrastructure and economic potential of Tibet to launch sustained growth in the years ahead; alleviating charges of cultural deprivation by allowing more real autonomy for Tibet, particularly with respect to cultural and religious practices; and decreasing Han-Tibetan friction by reducing the Han presence in Tibet through the return of large numbers of Han cadres (and their families) to China proper.

This policy was also aimed at the Tibetan exile community headed by the Dalai Lama. First, it would blunt the negative criticism about Chinese oppression and poverty in Tibet, enabling Beijing's new leadership to portray itself in the Western media as moderate and forward-thinking with regard to Tibet. It would also make Tibetans in the TAR less susceptible to the propaganda of the exiles and possibly even persuade the exiles and the Dalai Lama that they could realize their economic and cultural-nationalistic aspirations with Tibet as part of the PRC.

Improving the standard of living of Tibetans, particularly the rural farmers and herders who constitute 80 to 90 percent of the population, was immediately addressed through the dissolution of communes and the introduction of the responsibility system. As in China proper, farmland and animals were divided up among commune members, and households were permitted to produce and sell in accordance with market forces. Beijing, however, went much farther in the TAR than in the rest of China, exempting farmers and nomads in Tibet until 1990 both from taxes and from the contract system, that is, from having to sell a quota to the government at below-market prices, as Han farmers must. This exemption has been very effective, allowing Tibetan families to generate surpluses in a traditional system of production. Although there are still pockets of rural poverty in Tibet due to poor soil quality and climatic factors, by 1987 the majority of Tibetan farmers and nomads were using surpluses to purchase new commodities and start renovating old houses or building new ones.

Tibetans in urban areas such as Lhasa have also fared well. Tibet is classified as a hardship area because of the high cost of living, so salaries for cadres are very high. A new Tibetan cadre/researcher just out of college, for example, received a starting salary of about 200 yuan a month from the Tibet Academy of Social Sciences in 1987, roughly double what he or she would have received in Beijing. Private individuals and small co-ops opened restaurants, "sweet tea" shops, bars, grocery shops, and the like, many of which did very well. In fact, by 1985 Lhasa was engaged in a frenzy of consumption and consumerism. The markets were filled with Japanese televisions, cassette recorders, radios, and other imported luxury items (the TAR government having convinced Beijing that the harsh Tibetan environment required imports rather than Chinese-made products). It was not unusual to see Tibetan traders wearing swords and traditional native dress riding big new Honda motorcycles. There was also a thriving business within the Tibetan community for traditional Tibetan luxury items such as icons, silver bowls, and the like. Economically, therefore, the quality of life for Lhasans and rural folk improved markedly during the 1980s, particularly after 1984.

The government also launched a major program to develop the economic and administrative infrastructure of the TAR. A series of 43 major projects costing about 300 million yuan was begun in 1983, including a 1,200-room luxury hotel in Lhasa, a new gymnasium, improved geothermal electric facilities, and so forth. The target date for completion of these was August 1985, the 20th anniversary of the establishment of the TAR.

In 1983 the "open" policy was expanded to Tibet. Tourism, which had begun as early as 1980, was greatly expanded, and by 1986 there were between 30,000 and 40,000 tourists visiting Lhasa per year (whereas before 1985 there were only about 1,500). Similarly, foreign businesses as well as other provinces in China were invited to help develop Tibet, and beginning in 1985, Tibet opened somewhat to Western and Japanese academics. China obviously felt it had nothing to hide in Tibet.

On the level of Tibetan culture, a major series of reforms occurred, not all at once to be sure, but incrementally. Traditional secular and religious books were published in Tibetan, and an effort was made to foster modern Tibetan literature through the development of several literary magazines and the publication of poems and short stories in newspapers. Lhasa Television began broadcasting programs on a second channel in Tibetan, with foreign and Chinese shows often dubbed. The Department of Tibetan Language and Literature at Tibet University was expanded.

Individuals were allowed to practice traditional Tibetan Buddhism. They could worship openly by circumambulating holy sites, turning prayer wheels, erecting prayer flags on their houses, going on visits to monasteries and temples, and making monetary and other offerings (such as butter lamps) to deities, monks, or monasteries. Altars could be maintained in houses, new statues could be built and consecrated for such altars, and by 1985–86, monks could be invited to perform prayers in people's houses. Pictures of the Dalai Lama were openly for sale in the Lhasa marketplace, and local Tibetans wore Dalai Lama buttons.

Institutional religion—monasteries and nunneries—also saw a renaissance, although here the government retained considerable control. Beginning in the early 1980s, money was allocated to rebuild and renovate several hundred of the more important monasteries and temples that had been destroyed during the Cultural Revolution. Other monasteries were permitted to be rebuilt with funds donated by private citizens. By 1987 Lhasa's three great monasteries (Ganden, Sera, and Drepung) contained about 1,000 monks, far fewer than the 20,000 they had contained in 1959, but still impressive considering that there were none when the new reforms began.

For Tibetans in Tibet, this was a heady time. Their devotion to Buddhism could be expressed by prayers and deeds, and their perception of the worth of their traditional culture had been vindicated. The old customs and values that had been so severely denigrated during the "destroy the four olds" campaign reappeared, and people were thrilled at the changes that had occurred. Parents took their small children on religious visits to monasteries so that they would learn their culture, and pilgrims from all over Tibet and the ethnic Tibetan areas of Qinghai, Sichuan, and Gansu flocked to Lhasa to visit the Jokhang temple and other holy sites.

Other policies were aimed at transforming the TAR politically into a more truly "Tibetan" autonomous region. First, a program was started with much fanfare wherein many Han cadres were withdrawn and the number and proportion of Tibetan cadres were increased. Although this did not proceed as well as planned, by 1986 about 60 percent of all TAR officials were ethnic Tibetans. In 1987 a blue-ribbon committee was formed to develop a plan to make the Tibetan language (written and spoken) the official working language throughout the TAR by the year 2000. There was also public recognition in Beijing that Tibet was different from the other autonomous regions in China because of its unique history. Many Tibetan cadres believed that Beijing would soon initiate a second wave of reforms that would establish a special autonomous status for Tibet in which all officials would be ethnic Tibetans and the language of government would be Tibetan.

Simultaneously, a set of policies aimed at developing new linkages with the Tibetans in exile began very successfully. From 1979, Tibetans in exile could visit Tibet to see relatives and Tibetans could leave for visits (with some constraints). Between 1986 and 1988, many Tibetans in exile did in fact visit Tibet, even though they had to accept Chinese visas as "overseas Chinese" to do so. A number of Tibetans abroad expressed interest in doing business in Tibet. There was a feeling of possibility in the air. For the first time some Tibetans in exile began to wonder whether the new Chinese policies might not make it possible for Tibet to be a part of China yet retain the essential elements of Tibetan culture and values. Such Tibetans themselves generally had no thought of resettling, but they were beginning to like the idea of being able to travel back and forth, so long, of course, as Tibet continued along the path to more complete cultural autonomy. This was still China to be sure, and political freedom of expression and assembly as we know them in the West were not permitted, but great strides had been made in permitting Tibetan culture to flourish.

The Beijing–Dalai Lama Discourse

Beijing's leaders in 1979 appear to have been eager to put the Tibet question behind them. They saw themselves as reformers committed to a policy of improving conditions in Tibet and rightly considered normalization of relations with the Dalai Lama to be in their long-term interest. Not only would it silence one of China's most vocal critics abroad, but it would also send a positive signal to Hong Kong and Taiwan. It would undermine the small nationalist underground that existed in Lhasa, help to satisfy the Tibetan people as a whole, and allow Beijing to concentrate its attention on its real problem—revitalizing China's decrepit economy.

Nevertheless, Beijing set clear parameters regarding the political status of Tibet. Tibet was an inseparable part of China, and self-determination was not an acceptable issue for discussion. The only issue on the table (as it had been in 1914 at Simla and 1951 in Beijing) would be the terms of Tibet's autonomy. The Chinese goal apparently was a "cultural" solution—allowing the TAR to satisfy the religious and cultural aspirations of Tibetans but leaving the current political structure intact. However, Beijing indicated to Dharamsala that it would discuss anything short of independence.

From the Dalai Lama's vantage point, this was also a propitious time. The Maoists were discredited and out of power, and the reformers were turning China upside down as they worked to open China to the West. Vocal though the Tibetan exile community had been about independence, it consisted of only 100,000 members, a minuscule number in comparison with the roughly 2 million Tibetans in the TAR (and roughly 3 million in the bordering Chinese provinces). It was obvious that the long-term future of Tibetans and Tibetan culture lay with the Tibetans in China, and the Dalai Lama apparently felt a responsibility to try to intervene on their behalf. It now seemed possible that an acceptable compromise might be worked out. The question for the Dalai Lama was how much autonomy short of independence was sufficient to permit reconciliation.

By 1982 relations had warmed sufficiently for the Dalai Lama to send a high-level delegation to hold talks in Beijing. The substance of these discussions is not completely known, but it appears that the Tibetans saw the meeting as primarily functioning to educate and "feel out" the Chinese rather than to fix the exact terms of Tibetan autonomy within the PRC. In addition to presenting their interpretation of the history of Sino-Tibetan relations, they discussed the substantial differences between Tibetans and Chinese in culture, race, and religion and the problematic conditions in Tibet and the adjacent ethnic enclaves. It also appears that the Tibetan side insisted that any settlement must include reuniting the ethnic Tibetan areas of Qinghai, Sichuan, Gansu, and Yunnan provinces with Tibet proper. The exiles also presented their views that Tibet should become a demilitarized zone, meaning that all Han troops should be withdrawn. Discussions also took place about the possibility of the Dalai Lama making a visit to Tibet within the next year or two. No serious progress was made on the terms of autonomy, apparently because Dharamsala was unwilling to discuss a compromise that would address the cultural issues but leave the political structure—continued rule by the Communist Party—intact.

While these discussions were in progress, the exile government and its friends continued to accuse the Chinese of heinous and systematic human rights violations and to lobby worldwide for independence. Highly inflammatory rhetoric was widely used, including the repeated accusation that the Chinese were committing genocide in Tibet.[3] And although the Dalai Lama on occasion indicated that things had improved somewhat in Tibet, this assessment was overshadowed by the torrent of emotional anti-Chinese rhetoric.

In 1984 a second face-to-face meeting between negotiators from Dharamsala and China took place in Beijing. No statements have been made about the content of these talks, but it appears that China was not pleased by the way the discussions were stalemated or by the refusal of the Dalai Lama to ease up on anti-Chinese propaganda, despite the major reforms it was instituting. It decided to fire a shell across the Dalai Lama's bow by making public a five-point proposal that the Tibetan delegation had just rejected. These points included the suggestion that if the Dalai Lama returned to China to live, he should live not in Tibet but in Beijing. This position represented a substantial hardening of the Chinese attitude and shocked the exile community. It is not clear what the Beijing leadership hoped to accomplish by making the proposal public.

Constraints on the Dalai Lama

Beijing's criticism that Dharamsala was unwilling to negotiate for a realistic settlement—that is, one that focused on greater autonomy within the communist state system rather than on a separate government—is probably accurate. On the other hand, this was no easy matter for the Dalai Lama since despite his obvious desire to reach some

[3] It is clear that there was never any Chinese policy aimed at eradicating Tibetans by singling them out and murdering them as was the case in Nazi Germany with Jews. Those Tibetans who died unnaturally in Tibet during this period did so through revolts and famines, not through a deliberate policy of genocide. There was also no policy of eliminating Tibetans by forcing them to utilize birth control. For a discussion of the population dimension of this issue, see Melvyn C. Goldstein and Cynthia M. Beall, "China's Birth Control Policy in the Tibet Autonomous Region: Myths and Realities," *Asian Survey*, forthcoming, 1990.

sort of rapprochement with Beijing over the status of Tibet, there was no consensus among the exiles as to what terms short of independence would be acceptable. Within the exile community many factions were already unhappy that secret negotiations were going on and were vehemently opposed to the renouncing of the cherished dream of independence, let alone to a Tibet with the Dalai Lama in Beijing rather than Lhasa.

The Tibetan exiles are divided into regional, religious, and, to a lesser extent, political factions. Regionally, the cleavage is between three groups: the Tibetans from Central and Western Tibet (i.e., those from political Tibet), and the two ethnic Tibetan subgroups from the Chinese border provinces, the Eastern and the Northeastern Tibetans (Khampas and Amdowas). Traditionally there was considerable interregional hostility, particularly between Central and Eastern Tibetans, who spoke different and sometimes mutually unintelligible dialects. In exile, some Eastern Tibetans set up refugee operations completely independent of the Dalai Lama's government-in-exile, and others nominally accepted affiliation with Dharamsala but continued to argue about rights and prerogatives. In the area of religion, some Tibetan Buddhist sects also kept their distance from Dharamsala or operated separately. And politically, the Tibetan Youth Association generally took a much more militant stance than Dharamsala, at varying times advocating violence and terrorism to achieve independence.

Since the government-in-exile had no coercive sanctions at its disposal, the Dalai Lama saw his main role as keeping the various factions in the exile community together. Consequently, he has assiduously avoided taking extreme positions that would generate conflict and flame the preexisting regional and religious animosities. The strategy of his leadership has been to unite the exiles by focusing attention on goals that all share: the preservation of religion, language, and culture and the fight for independence.

All of this constrained the Dalai Lama's options in the 1980s. First, the regional differences made it virtually impossible for him to negotiate with the Chinese over the TAR alone, even if he had wanted to, for this would be impossible to justify to the Eastern and Northeastern Tibetans in exile. Consequently, he has demanded that all ethnic Tibetans must be united in a new Tibet, just as the traditional Tibetan government demanded at Simla in 1914, and he now talks about Tibet as if it had really included these ethnic areas in the 1930s and 1940s. In fact, he now talks of China invading Tibet in 1949 (rather than in 1950, as was the case for political Tibet), since that is when the PLA took control of the provinces adjacent to political Tibet that contained ethnic Tibetans.

Politically, Dharamsala has insisted for more than two decades that the refugees are only temporarily in exile. It has actively urged Tibetans not to accept Indian, Nepalese, or Bhutanese citizenship—that is, to remain stateless—since it feels that becoming citizens of another country would diminish their moral claim to Tibet and perhaps foster their assimilation into the host country. This focus on waiting for Tibet to regain its independence, however, has made it difficult for the Dalai Lama to suddenly inform his refugee followers that something less than independence is now acceptable.

Dharamsala's longstanding accusations about Chinese abuses created a similar constraint because it portrayed Chinese communists one-dimensionally, as monsters. While this may have been true during the Cultural Revolution, it clearly was not in the 1980s. Internally, this approach was highly effective in keeping nationalistic sentiment alive, but it also made talking positively of Beijing's post-1980 efforts in Tibet very difficult within the exile community, if, in fact, Dharamsala ever had any interest in doing so.

There was a similar problem externally. Moderating the virulent anti-Chinese propaganda was also rendered difficult because Dharamsala's most effective weapon against Beijing had been its ability to utilize the very strong human rights and anti-communist interest that flourished in Washington during the Reagan administration to secure new support from influential groups, in particular, members of the U.S. Congress. Dharamsala had attacked China on human rights grounds since 1959 with considerable justification, but now, despite the changing situation in Tibet and China, it was unwilling to relinquish its newfound audience. While the Dalai Lama certainly understood the dimensions of the reforms going on in Tibet (presumably that is why he felt negotiations might be fruitful), he opted to allow a barrage of misleading and dissembling charges, apparently believing such rhetorical confrontation would compel Beijing to agree to better terms for Tibet. Thus, while Beijing continued to improve conditions in Tibet, it received no credit in the West due to the very effective propaganda effort of Dharamsala.

All of this created a vituperative atmosphere not conducive to constructive negotiations. Not surprisingly, as 1985 came to a close the Dalai Lama had still not visited Tibet. The faint hope of 1979 was fading fast. Not only was Beijing angry at Dharamsala's virulent attacks, but events in Tibet seemed to be moving on a course that favored the Chinese and made Dharamsala and the exiles less important to Beijing.

Beijing's Gains

By 1985–86, there was optimism in Tibet that the TAR would be able to develop and implement new language and cultural policies that would make it again a distinctly Tibetan autonomous region. And in addition to the gains discussed earlier, China scored several international successes—with the British, it completed the plan for Hong Kong's return, the United Nations organized development projects in Tibet (as did the Swiss Red Cross), and major leaders such as Helmut Kohl and Jimmy Carter planned to visit Tibet in 1987.

Beijing also appeared to be making headway in wooing the Lhasan masses. Although this is a simplification, Tibetans in Lhasa in 1985–86 can be divided into three subgroups. There was a small group (about 10 percent), mainly high officials, who were strongly pro-Chinese. Another small group (also about 10 percent) of Lhasa's Tibetans consisted of die-hard Tibetan nationalists who believed that no matter how long it took, Tibetans should resist, or even fight, the Chinese to reestablish an independent Tibet. In between were the mass of workers, cadres, and businesspeople. Their feelings and loyalties were mixed. Although they were bitter at how Tibet had been treated by China and probably shared the aspirations of the activist nationalists, they did not consider independence a realistic goal. Thus, they were unwilling to support the nationalists' position with action. For Beijing, this meant that if it could convince this majority of Tibetans that conditions in Tibet were improving culturally and economically, they were likely to accept Tibet as part of China. On the other hand, if things became worse, they could easily be pushed to support the die-hard nationalist faction actively, compelling China to resort to the use of sheer force to hold Tibet. In essence, therefore, influencing the attitudes of this cohort was a key element in the struggle between Dharamsala and Beijing in the 1980s.

As the new reforms took hold in Lhasa, it began to seem that Beijing's new policy would continue to develop and meet the needs of these Tibetans. One sign of this was the absence of a mass flight of Tibetans to India or Nepal during the 1980s comparable to the recent migration from East to West Germany. Since the importance of a settlement with the Dalai Lama decreased in proportion to the increase in satisfaction on the part of the masses in Tibet, Beijing appeared in 1985–86 to be holding the winning cards. An indication that Beijing believed this to be the case was its insistence that an official Dharamsala fact-finding delegation scheduled for 1986 had to accept visas as "overseas Chinese." When it refused, the trip was canceled.

For the exiles, the possibility that Beijing's reform policy was winning the struggle for the mass of Tibetans and gaining international respectability represented the worst-case scenario. Suddenly Dharamsala found itself in danger of becoming irrelevant to the political process in Tibet. Dharamsala responded by launching a major counterattack whose aim was to attract international attention and support for the Tibetan cause, thereby showing China that it must come to terms with the Dalai Lama and Dharamsala.

Dharamsala's Offensive

The Dalai Lama's greatest problem was that although there was sympathy for Tibet's cause in the West, no major government anywhere had ever backed its quest for independence. The U.S. government does not support this goal, nor do the governments of Great Britain or India. Thus the exiles' propaganda, though effective in garnering sympathy and embarrassing Beijing, did not represent a direct threat to China's *de jure* claim to Tibet. However, the exiles' increasing contact with and support among the human rights and anti-China factions in the U.S. Congress offered a new, and potentially powerful, tactic for increasing the costs to Beijing of not coming to terms. The strategy was simple. Because China's economic development needed support from the United States and other Western nations, any influence the exiles could exert on U.S. congresspeople (and others) to place stumbling blocks in the way of U.S.–China relations because of China's treatment of Tibet could dramatically increase Dharamsala's leverage in Beijing, even without a change in official U.S. policy with regard to independence. Dharamsala apparently believed that this added leverage would ultimately compel Beijing to accept a different political structure for Tibet as the solution to the Tibet question.

The new Dharamsala offensive had four main components: the Dalai Lama for the first time would himself carry the exiles' political message to the West, where he would make overtly political speeches to government forums; large-scale letter-writing campaigns to Congress would be coordinated by members of Buddhist and other pro-Tibetan organizations in the United States; civil disobedience would be encouraged in Tibet so as to support the exiles' accusations in the West and refocus the attention of the Tibetan people; and the Dalai Lama would demonstrate his reasonableness and flexibility by proposing terms to solve the Tibet question that did not demand full independence.

In late 1986 and early 1987 several high-level meetings of senior Tibetan exile leaders and other "friends" were held in London, New

York, and Washington, D.C., to plan this strategy—in particular the political aspects of the Dalai Lama's visit to the United States in late 1987. The Dalai Lama arrived in the United States on September 19, 1987, and addressed the Congressional Human Rights Caucus two days later, making a proposal that called for the withdrawal of Chinese troops and military installations from Tibet (including ethnic Kham and Amdo) and the resumption of negotiations between Dharamsala and Beijing.

Laced with emotion-laden statements and assertions of human rights abuses and environmental degradation certain to gall Beijing, this proposal was geared to the Western, not the Chinese, audience. Nevertheless, it did not talk of independence, and it openly asserted that the Dalai Lama wanted to hold talks on Tibet's future. Though vague, the proposal played well with Congress and the press in the West.

The First Riot—October 1, 1987

All of this was eagerly followed in Lhasa, as many Tibetans knew Chinese and regularly listened to the Voice of America radio broadcasts and the Dalai Lama's visit to the United States had been shown on Lhasa television. Less than a week after the Dalai Lama's speech and while he was ending his visit to the United States, nationalistic monks in Lhasa demonstrated in support of his initiative.

On September 27, about 27 monks from Drepung Monastery (located just west of Lhasa) walked around the circular path in the main market area of Lhasa, the heart of the traditional city. Holding a handmade Tibetan flag, they shouted slogans like "May the Dalai Lama live 10,000 years" and "Chinese should leave Tibet." The monks went around the always-crowded path five times. No one interfered with them, since the police had not expected such a demonstration and were not around. After their fifth turn, the monks walked down the main thoroughfare to the TAR government's headquarters and protested there. At that point the police appeared, and the monks were arrested and taken away.

Four days later, on the morning of October 1, 1987, Chinese National Day, another group of between 20 and 30 monks came to the Lhasa market area to show support for the earlier group and demand their release from jail. Police took them into custody and started beating them inside the police station. Some Tibetans on the upper floor of an adjacent building saw this and began to shout from the windows, "Stop beating the monks." A crowd of Tibetans had already gathered outside the police headquarters demanding the release of the monks, and before long this escalated into a full-scale riot. In the end, the police station and some vehicles were burnt, a number of Chinese stores were destroyed, and anywhere from 6 to 20 Tibetans were killed when police (including ethnic Tibetans) fired at the crowds.

Beijing was stunned by the riots and the anti-Chinese anger they expressed. There had been clandestine nationalistic incidents for years in Lhasa, but these were small, isolated activities that were easy to deal with. Now Beijing had to contend with thousands of average Tibetans who were angry enough to face death and prison by participating in a massive riot against Chinese rule in Tibet. This riot was particularly humiliating to Beijing because it coincided with the attacks of the Dalai Lama and U.S. congresspeople and seemed to prove to the world that they were true.

The Chinese initially claimed that the demonstration was inspired by Dharamsala, and in a sense they were correct. Many Tibetan monks had traveled to Dharamsala and Nepal over the previous three years, and Tibetan refugees from India and Nepal were allowed to visit and live in Lhasa for months on end. Thus the mechanism for such instigation was readily available. And, while it is not clear whether Dharamsala (or other exile elements) actually asked one or more of the Drepung monks to organize a demonstration, it *is* clear that the demonstration was meant to support the Dalai Lama's new initiative in the United States while he was there.

The Tibetans in Lhasa interpreted the events in the United States in the context of their own system of government and therefore saw the Dalai Lama's speech to Congress as a potential turning point in Tibetan history. With no knowledge of concepts like checks and balances, it was natural for Tibetans in Lhasa to believe that the support shown by members of the U.S. Congress reflected general U.S. government support for the Dalai Lama and Tibetan independence. Many people believed that this meant the United States would soon force China to "free" Tibet. Beijing inadvertently reinforced this belief by launching a string of vitriolic attacks in the Beijing and Lhasa media about the U.S. Congress's interference in Chinese affairs, which seemed to confirm that the events in the United States were indeed extremely important. Thus, while there is reason to believe that Tibetans in exile actually encouraged the monks to stage a demonstration, it is equally plausible that the monks' belief that this was a turning point in Tibetan history produced the demonstration without any direct request from abroad. Whatever the truth of this matter, certainly no one dreamed of provoking a bloody riot.

The real cause of the riot—as distinct from the earlier small demonstration—is complex. Despite the reforms, a residue of bitterness and resentment against the government (which in Tibetans' minds was synonymous with the Han Chinese) remained. And like unseen flammable fumes, this anger and frustration needed only to be ignited. The sight of police beating monks set it ablaze.

The reasons for this residual anger are several. Tibetans were still bitter about the personal and collective (ethnic) suffering they had experienced since 1959 under direct Chinese rule. They saw themselves as engaged in a struggle to keep their culture and national identity afloat in a world of 1 billion Han. In addition, Tibetans resented the condescending attitudes of many Han in Tibet, who appeared to consider them uncouth barbarians and view their culture as inferior. The presence of large numbers of poorly educated Han in Lhasa fueled the problem, creating a myriad of face-to-face encounters that opened past wounds. Not surprisingly, Tibetans invariably interpreted events in Tibet ethnically—Han versus Tibetan. For example, although both Han and Tibetans complained about the Cultural Revolution and about corruption, the Han blamed the Gang of Four (a political faction) while Tibetans invariably blamed the Han and were reluctant to believe that the transition from Mao to Deng Xiaoping signaled a major qualitative change, since Han still dictated the Tibetans' fate.

Moreover, the Chinese insistence on a crash program of economic development in Tibet inadvertently created new problems. One such problem was the large influx of Han Chinese into Tibet after 1983. Ironically, this does not appear to have started as a deliberate Chinese scheme to swamp Tibet with Han "colonists," as is often charged, but rather was an outgrowth of the government's wish to develop Tibet quickly, particularly with respect to large construction projects, and its decision to import thousands of Han workers to achieve this goal. This created a demand for scores of new Han restaurants, shops, and services, and thousands of petty capitalist Han followed to fill these needs. These tradespeople expanded their scope to sell Tibetans all sorts of products imported from eastern China and abroad, as well as traditional items such as incense and prayer scarves for religious offerings at temples. They also came to dominate the industries that repair bicycles, watches, radios, and televisions in Lhasa, and at higher levels, have co-opted much of the private trade in wool, skins, and cashmere between Tibet and the rest of China. Their success sent a message to the surrounding provinces that there was profit to be made in Tibet, and this drew large numbers of new Han annually. Even Han beggars got the message, and by 1988 there were teams of Han with monkeys begging throughout Lhasa.

The explosion of tourism beginning in 1985 added to the influx of Han, who came to dominate the tourist trade as drivers and guides. The general economic prosperity among Tibetans in Lhasa also gave the Han tradespeople plenty of customers in the local service sector. The Han in Tibet are extremely industrious and hard working, and even very nationalistic Tibetans often hired Han rather than Tibetan carpenters because they were cheaper and less trouble (for example, they accepted poorer-quality food while they worked and did not demand the traditional gifts of home-brewed Tibetan beer).

These Han are not colonists in the normal sense of the word. They do not see themselves as permanent immigrants but are, by and large, petty entrepreneurs who have come to Tibet to make money and then return to Sichuan or Qinghai. Moreover, no Han have come to Tibet to move into villages and farms or to compete with the nomads as ranchers. Nevertheless, although this is understood by Lhasans, it does not mitigate their anger and resentment toward the Chinese influx that has made them a minority in their own city. There are obvious economic reasons for this resentment, since Han control increasingly large segments of the local economy. However, while the influx is a frequent topic of conversation and complaint, in reality there is still enough work to go around. Again, the anger is largely ethnic in character, with Tibetans feeling that Lhasa is being transformed into a Han city.

The program of development in Tibet highlighted a related point—the Tibetans' feeling of discrimination vis-à-vis the Han. There is no official program of favoritism to Han in the TAR; to the contrary, many Han themselves complain of discrimination, since entitlement programs often give less well-qualified Tibetans preference for jobs in government offices. But since getting things done in China depends to a large extent on friendship and contacts (the so-called back door), many of the incoming Chinese have been able to secure all sorts of government permits and opportunities because they are relatives or friends of Han cadres and army officers.

Thus, from the perspective of the Tibetans' confidence in the government and the reform policy, the crash development program for the TAR was a serious miscalculation with unintended negative consequences. By creating forces that exacerbated existing local feelings of anger and bitterness over harms done to Tibet during the Cultural Revolution, it worked to undermine the positive impact of the new reforms on Tibetans' attitudes and feelings. Moreover, it focused Tibetans' attention precisely on the volatile ethnic or national issue—too many Han in Tibet and too many benefits for them. In turn, this fueled the Tibetans' feeling of powerlessness and abuse at the hands of the dominant Han.

Another important problem area was Beijing's reluctance to permit as full an expression of cultural and religious freedom as Tibetans wanted. Continuing restrictions on the monasteries angered the monks and many laymen. For most Tibetans, the three great monasteries of Lhasa symbolized the essence of Tibetan culture, and the refusal of the new policy to let them flourish to their former level of greatness served to highlight Tibet's subordination to an alien, Chinese value system. The monks had other grievances, to be sure, but in 1987 the main problem was Beijing's unwillingness to give the monasteries complete internal autonomy and the right to grow to the extent to which they could be supported by the masses—whether this resulted in 1,000 or 10,000 monks in a monastery.

The government also appeared to be dragging its feet on language reform. Since full implementation of a policy that made Tibetan the official working language of the TAR would mean that virtually all Han cadres and clerks would have to leave, this proposed reform had much deeper connotations than language per se. Beijing's failure to quickly approve and begin the long phase-in period signaled a reluctance to institute the additional reforms that most Tibetans wanted: those that would truly "Tibetanize" the Tibet Autonomous Region.

And last but not least, one cannot underestimate the strong historical sense of Tibet as the exclusive homeland of Tibetans. Many Tibetans felt that the Chinese had taken their country and transformed it into just another part of China, and in the process destroyed Tibetan institutions and attacked core values. While Tibetans clearly did not want to return to "feudalism" and "serfdom," they believed that Tibet should be a country (whether independent or not) that is run by Tibetans, uses the Tibetan language, and follows Tibetan laws and customs. For most Tibetans, the new reforms had made progress toward that end, but it was not enough to be allowed to turn prayer wheels and burn butter lamps if Tibet were not a homogeneous entity.

The October 1, 1987, riot, therefore, was the product of emotion and anger. It was primarily an unplanned response to a situation that Tibetans felt symbolized the loss of their nationhood and the denigration of their culture since 1959 by a dominant and alien group, rather than a rejection of the reform policy since 1980. Building one more arena, road, factory, or apartment building would not address the sources of the discontent.

The Tibet Question after the 1987 Riot

The 1987 riot presented Dharamsala with a tremendous propaganda victory. Not only had the Dalai Lama's visit to Washington, D.C., produced major support from the Congressional Human Rights Caucus and influential senators on the Foreign Relations Committee, but it had also precipitated dramatic civil disobedience and a bloody riot in Lhasa that were perceived in the West as confirmation of current unbearable oppression. Moreover, Tibetans in Lhasa had been diverted from their consumerism and materialism to the issue of their ethnicity—the struggle to regain a cultural and political homeland.

The immediate response of Tibetans in Lhasa, both the masses and the cadres, was interesting. People were not fearful of the consequences of the riot nor even doubtful of its wisdom. Rather, they were elated. Although it had not accomplished anything concrete, it had given them something to be proud of as Tibetans. No one talked of anything else for weeks on end. Even dedicated Tibetan cadres and party members thought the impact of the riot was positive since they believed it would shock Beijing into seeing the real problems in Tibet and prompt the leaders of the CCP to take decisive action to rectify these by accelerating the reform program.

Beijing's initial reaction to the riot, however, exacerbated the situation. For two months it stubbornly blamed a few people manipulated by Dharamsala and did not criticize the police or admit that the police had shot a number of demonstrators. To understand this decision, it is important to realize that the cadres running the government of the TAR were no more homogeneous than was the exile community.

There were actually four factions pulling and tugging against each other in Tibet (as well as differences of opinion among the leadership in Beijing). One faction was the older Han officials (including military leaders), who tended to be more conservative and more leftist (Maoist) in their thinking. They saw Beijing's concession to Tibetan religion and language as unwise and the new economic freedoms as undesirable, and tended to drag their feet in implementing them. Another faction was composed of the older Tibetan cadres. They exhibited a similar conservatism, favoring a policy of trying to integrate Tibet more closely with China, and thus not reinforcing Tibet's cultural, linguistic, and demographic distinctions. The third faction, composed of the younger and middle-aged Tibetan cadres, was generally better educated and supportive of Beijing's new policies. They were also, however, strongly pro-nationalistic, believing that they could secure a better Tibet, run by Tibetans, in the Tibetan language, and for Tibetans, within the context of the PRC. Surprisingly, they found their greatest support among the fourth faction, the younger Han cadres, who also tended to be better educated and more liberal than the older Han and Tibetan cadres. But there was a clear cleavage along ethnic lines between all Han cadres and all Tibetan cadres. Han and Tibetan cadres rarely socialized except at office functions, and a typical complaint of Han officials in Lhasa was that while a Tibetan would invite a foreigner he had just met on the street to his house for dinner, he would not do the same for a Chinese colleague he had worked with for years.

Thus, in the discussions among cadres as to what to advise Beijing about the riot, the younger Tibetan cadres argued for an even-handed approach. The police as well as the monks should be censured and punished. They conceded that the demonstrators were wrong and had broken the law but believed that they should have been arrested and sent to prison, not beaten. Beating them was against Chinese law and an affront to Tibetans. The more conservative Han and Tibetan cadres, however, were not enthusiastic about this line. When the word finally came down from Beijing, it said that the police were not to be accused of wrongdoing. This decision infuriated the ethnically sensitive Tibetans, to whom it seemed that Han did not have to abide by the law in their dealings with Tibetans.

Nevertheless, life in Lhasa for most people went back to normal quickly. The tea shops and beer halls were full a week after the riot, and the Chinese reappeared hawking their wares in the market area. The people of Lhasa appeared unwilling to risk losing what they had gained in the 1980s by initiating their own mass demonstrations, regardless of their feelings.

The same was not true of the monks and secular nationalists. They had learned how to keep world attention focused on the independence issue. A few monks willing to risk imprisonment or death could challenge the entire People's Republic of China, simultaneously supporting the Dalai Lama and radicalizing Tibetans in Tibet. The impressive support given the Dalai Lama by the U.S. Congress reinforced the monks' initial perception of events abroad and provided new motivation for them to continue their program of demonstrations for independence. The Dalai Lama's public support for civil disobedience further energized the dissidents.

The role of the U.S. Congress was critical here. Despite the efforts of the State Department to provide a balanced perspective on what was going on in Tibet, Congress adopted a strongly pro-Tibetan position. On June 18, 1987, the House of Representatives unanimously adopted legislation on the Tibet question condemning China for its human rights violations in Tibet. On September 27, 1987, Claiborne

Pell, the chairman of the Senate Foreign Relations Committee, and seven other congresspeople sent a letter to Premier Zhao Ziyang expressing grave concern over the current situation in Tibet and stating that they completely supported the Dalai Lama's proposal, which they called a historic step toward resolving the Tibet question. And on October 6, the U.S. Senate unanimously adopted a strong resolution paralleling the House's June legislation as an amendment to the State Department Authorization Act. The resolution linked U.S. sale or transfer of defense articles to China's treatment of Tibet, authorized scholarships and other aid for Tibetan refugees, and indicated that it was the sense of the Congress that the United States should make the treatment of the Tibetan people an important factor in U.S.-China relations. On December 22, 1987, President Reagan signed this bill. This was all known in Lhasa, and on a number of occasions Tibetans I did not know came up to me on the street and expressed their thanks for the U.S. government's support of the Tibetan cause.

As 1988 began, attention in Lhasa turned to the coming Great Prayer Festival, scheduled to begin on February 17, when almost 2,000 monks would come to the central temple in Lhasa for three weeks of joint prayers. This was a major event with all the high government officials of the TAR attending and thousands of pilgrims flocking to Lhasa from the hinterland. The question on everyone's mind was whether the prayer festival would go on as planned, and if so, whether the monks would try to use it to launch a major demonstration.

Beijing now made a decision that, in retrospect, was a disaster. On the defensive internationally, the Chinese leadership apparently felt it was important to show the world that its liberal Tibetan religious policy was working, so it pushed ahead with holding the prayer festival.

To facilitate this, Beijing shifted policy, suddenly admitting that the October 1, 1987, riot was caused in part by "remnant leftist thought," that is, by serious deficiencies in the manner in which the reform policy had been carried out in the TAR. On the face of it, this was almost as striking an admission as had been Hu Yaobang's comments in 1980. This turnabout buoyed the optimistic hopes of many young Tibetan cadres and gratified people, who felt vindicated by Beijing's acceptance of their complaints. To many, it seemed as if this might at last produce the additional cultural, linguistic, and religious reforms that were desired and needed.

Beijing also tried to ameliorate the tense situation by offering new concessions to the monks. The Lhasa monks had been complaining about all the books, paintings, statues, and land that had been confiscated from the monasteries since 1959, and Beijing now authorized property restitution and monetary compensation for that which no longer existed. Then the Panchen Lama, Tibet's number-two lama after the Dalai Lama, arrived in Lhasa to try to calm the monks and ensure the success of the prayer festival. The monks had insisted that they would not attend the festival unless their fellow monks were released from jail, and on January 26, 1988, after intervention by the Panchen Lama, the TAR government released about 59 monks, leaving only about 15 in custody. All but one of these were in fact released two weeks before the festival started. The Panchen Lama also indicated publicly that the government was going to continue to make restitutions to monks and monasteries for past abuses. For example, on January 27 he announced at Drepung Monastery that the government was going to give the three great Lhasa monasteries about 2 million yuan (US$500,000) as partial compensation.

But once again, as with the development program, Beijing misjudged the situation and tried to treat the Tibet problem as economic and financial rather than as nationalistic and emotional. The anger of most of the monks was now too great to be assuaged simply with money, particularly since they felt that the Chinese were trying to turn their revered religious event into a propaganda stunt. Thus, while the Panchen Lama was announcing the payments at Drepung Monastery, one of the monks actually stood up and interrupted him, saying, "Don't expect us to show gratitude. The Chinese destroyed so much of our things that this [grant] is nothing." Interestingly, he was not arrested.

During this tense period, many of the older monks advised the government against holding the prayer festival, saying that they could not guarantee what the younger monks would do. With so many people and monks massed in the narrow and cramped temple area, they warned that the result could be a disaster and suggested that it would be better if the monks conducted the prayer festival that year at their own monasteries. In retrospect, that would have been the prudent decision.

But the government now dug in its heels and insisted that the prayer festival had to go on. Foreign journalists had been invited, so it cajoled, threatened, and pleaded with the monks to appear. Although many monks boycotted the opening, the prayer festival began on schedule. All went well until March 5, 1988, the last day. As the monks completed a traditional procession, one or more of them suddenly shouted at the ranking TAR officials seated in the temple, demanding that the remaining monk in custody be released from prison. A Tibetan official apparently yelled at them to "shut up," and the monks responded angrily with political slogans, such as "Tibet is an independent country." Just when everyone thought that the ceremony had passed without disaster, the situation disintegrated. The police intervened with excessive force and the latent anger again exploded, producing the second bloody riot in Lhasa. Arrests and a clampdown in Tibet followed, only serving to further alienate the mass of moderates.

The Dalai Lama's 1988 Campaign

Meanwhile, outside of Tibet, the Dalai Lama continued his campaign to get Western parliaments and congresses to actively intervene in the Tibet question. In April 1988 he responded to a new Chinese announcement that he could live in Tibet (rather than Beijing) provided he publicly gave up the goal of an independent Tibet by saying that within 12 months he would make public proposals to Beijing with a view to securing "proper" autonomy for Tibet. He took a very moderate line, saying only that a "middle way" had to be found. Apparently Dharamsala felt that its new offensive and the riots had so successfully demonstrated its clout that Beijing would now be ready to accept new terms.

Soon afterward, in his second major political address in the West, the Dalai Lama made the first detailed statement of his conditions for a political settlement of the Tibet question. On June 15, 1988, at the European Parliament at Strasbourg, he gave the main points. Tibet and the ethnic Tibetan areas in Qinghai, Gansu, Sichuan, and Yunnan provinces should become a self-governing democratic political entity, founded on a constitution granting democratic rights. An enlarged Tibet would operate under a democratic system of government (i.e., one different than that under which the rest of China operated) and would have the right to decide all matters relating to Tibet and Tibetans. China would remain responsible for Tibet's foreign policy, although Tibet would develop and maintain relations through its own foreign affairs bureau in nonpolitical fields like commerce, sports, and education. China could maintain a limited number of troops in Tibet until a regional peace conference was convened and Tibet was made a demilitarized zone. Finally, all of this would have to be ratified by a nationwide referendum of Tibetans. The Dalai Lama indicated that he was ready to talk with the Chinese about this proposal and that he had already selected a negotiating team.

Although these terms represented a compromise within the exile community, they did not go over well in China, which saw them as a disguised form of "independence." Again the Dalai Lama and his advisers seemed to be playing primarily to the Western audience, not

Beijing. On September 23, 1988, China responded. Taking a hard line, Beijing indicated that while it hoped to have direct talks with the Dalai Lama, this was possible only under certain conditions: the talks must be with the Dalai Lama himself, not members of a delegation chosen by the government-in-exile; there could be no foreigners involved; and the unacceptable Strasbourg proposal could not be considered as the basis for talks because "it has not at all relinquished the concept of the independence of Tibet."

The Dalai Lama's new initiative also ran into opposition within the exile community, where it was sharply criticized by many segments, including the large Tibetan Youth Congress, the Tibetan Youth Association in Europe, and an elder brother of the Dalai Lama living in the United States (who sent a letter to Tibetans throughout the world attacking his brother's decision to relinquish the goal of independence). For the remainder of 1988 there was intense debate among the exiles over whether to support this proposal, and although most of them apparently ended up hesitantly backing the Dalai Lama's initiative, there was little enthusiasm for it, and the extent of the hostility among the younger and better-educated exiles led the Dalai Lama to state publicly soon after the Strasbourg announcement that he would make no further concessions.

The possibility of fruitful negotiations now seemed remote. The Dalai Lama went through the motions of proposing that talks be held in Geneva in January 1989 but refused to meet personally with the Chinese, refused to discard the foreigner acting as his legal adviser, and indicated that the Strasbourg statement provided the only reasonable basis for solving the Tibet question. Although the Dalai Lama's brother in Hong Kong appears to have visited Beijing several times in 1988 in an attempt to keep communications open, as the year drew to a close, movement toward beginning direct talks was stalled.

Dharamsala now concentrated on dramatizing its version of the Tibetans' plight in Tibet, working to persuade members of Western parliaments and congresses (and the Western media) to support its cause and act on its behalf. At the same time, it encouraged the monks, nuns, and other nationalistic elements in Tibet to engage in civil disobedience, since each such incident held the potential for becoming a riot or mass demonstration. In a sense, a kind of monk-driven *intifada* was fostered.

Tibet in 1988 and 1989

The March 5, 1988, riot forced a major reassessment of China's policy in Tibet. The prospect of rapprochement with the Dalai Lama was now remote, and the policy of reform had not kept Tibetans from joining the dissidents and rioting against the government. Beijing had several options. One was to implement quickly more radical reforms in order to win the loyalty of the 2 million Tibetans in Tibet. However, given the presence of the exiles and the die-hard nationalist monks, granting substantially more autonomy and freedom to Tibetans (including, of course, the monasteries) and withdrawing Han from Tibet could lead to even worse trouble there. Another option was to "close the door" in Tibet, end tourism, decrease support for Tibetan culture, and foster assimilation using the threat of force to control the population. A third course fell between these. Beijing could take a hard line with respect to demonstrators and nationalists and go neither backward nor forward with regard to cultural reforms.

In the summer of 1988 Qiao Shi, Politburo member and head of China's security apparatus, was sent to Tibet and apparently called together a number of Han cadres who had been leading officials in the prereform days to advise him. A version of the third option was chosen. It was publicly announced that dissenters would now be treated severely, and behind closed doors it was decided that there would be no further attempt to win the support of the monasteries by making major restitutions for past confiscations and losses. At the same time, the plan to make Tibetan the working language of the TAR was shelved, and tourism was sharply curtailed. However, existing cultural and religious freedoms were not rescinded, and the push to develop Tibet economically was supported.

In the meantime, the nationalists in Tibet continued to engage in civil disobedience, and five months later, on December 10, 1988, a demonstration of monks to commemorate the 40th anniversary of the UN Declaration of Human Rights precipitated the third major riot. Three months later, on March 5, 1989, monk demonstrations produced a fourth riot which resulted in much loss of life. This time Beijing arrested many Tibetans and declared martial law, which remains in effect in early 1990.

Nevertheless, despite the martial law, current Chinese policy in Tibet has not shifted to the "closed door" alternative. As 1989 came to a close, Beijing appeared unwilling to discard its reform policy in Tibet, yet was also unwilling to make a dramatic leap forward that might undermine the exiles and win the goodwill and confidence of the mass of Lhasans. For example, a modified version of the new Tibetan-language policy has been announced. This new language policy makes Tibetan the medium for all education, not just primary school (as it had been). It requires all teaching in the junior middle school to be conducted in Tibetan by 1993 and in the senior middle school by

1997. By the year 2000, most subjects in colleges are to be taught in Tibetan. The regulation also states that in all judicial and public security issues Tibetans can use either Tibetan or Chinese and that by the end of 1990 all official communications should be written primarily in the Tibetan language. Yet it stops short of fulfilling the hopes of many Tibetans by making Tibetan the official working language of the TAR.

Beijing did not deal with the problem of too many Han in Tibet, however, and the monastic situation has deteriorated, with the government now talking of imposing a nontraditional format guaranteed to infuriate even the monks who have not demonstrated. Official rhetoric in Lhasa stressed law and order and economic development and ignored the other, more critical, issues.

The end of 1989 brought another issue to the forefront—the situation in Tibet's villages and nomad areas. The original reform package exempted villagers and nomads from having to pay taxes or make quota sales, and was extremely popular. It is due to expire in 1990, and there has been no word about whether it will be extended. Failure to renew it will certainly anger the rural Tibetans who, interestingly enough, have been largely mute during the two years of civil disobedience in Lhasa and some of Tibet's other towns.

There is a marked attitudinal difference between Tibetans in Lhasa and those in the nomad areas I studied between 1986 and 1988. Although the nomads are as bitter as Lhasans about tne suffering and humiliations they experienced during the Cultural Revolution, they are much more positive about the new reforms than Lhasans and less angry and resentful about the present. This may be because of a key difference in the way the reforms played out in their areas. Unlike in Lhasa, there were no Han anywhere. All cadres were Tibetans, and all official correspondence was conducted in Tibetan. The nomads, therefore, never experienced condescending slights or slurs and did not feel swamped by a flood of alien Han. Once the new reforms were instituted, the flavor of life reverted quickly to something akin to what it had been traditionally. There were still problems, to be sure, but there was also satisfaction at having regained the right to behave in accordance with traditional values and norms.

Events outside Tibet in 1989

Outside Tibet, 1989 saw Beijing for the first time come face-to-face with a serious mass demonstration of Han, the results of which are well known. Just as Beijing had opted for coercive force to quell the riots and maintain law and order in Tibet, it ultimately did the same in Beijing and the other involved cities. With the exception of Tibet University in Lhasa, where there was a brief strike and a demonstration to show sympathy with the Beijing students, these events had no direct impact in Tibet. Many Tibetans, I am told, actually considered it fitting that Han demonstrators were shot just as Tibetans had been in the previous riots. Indirectly, however, the more conservative stance of the post-Tiananmen Beijing leadership certainly has reduced the likelihood of a major new policy in Tibet aimed at satisfying the grievances of Tibetans there.

Another important event in 1989 was the decision of the Norwegian Nobel Commission to award the 1989 Nobel Peace Prize to the 14th Dalai Lama. This represented a major international victory for the exile community, adding to the prestige of His Holiness and at the same time making a powerful, albeit indirect, statement that the proposals he made in the United States and at Strasbourg are valid and proper. Subsequent events in Eastern Europe and Mongolia have even further energized Tibetan exiles, since they believe that the day when China will become part of this syndrome is but around the corner. These events appear to have hardened opinion in Dharamsala and reduced the likelihood that the Dalai Lama will be willing to accept a substantial compromise to achieve a negotiated settlement to the Tibet question in the next year or so. In a recent speech, for example, the Dalai Lama told the exile community that the current state of affairs represents a great opportunity for Tibetans and that within five to ten years there will definitely be a major change in China. The message is that if Tibetans hold tight and continue to dramatize their case, they will prevail. Thus, it is likely that the exiles will continue to work energetically to present their views in the West and wait for events in China to solve the Tibetan question. However, it is also possible that elements in the exile community will try to escalate their leverage by encouraging the underground nationalistic groups in Lhasa to launch a larger-scale program of civil disobedience, or even to begin a campaign of anti-Han terrorism. Events external to Tibet in 1989 have, therefore, produced more hard-line policy orientations in both Beijing and Dharamsala.

Are There Solutions?

As 1989 ended, the Tibet question remained one of the world's most intractable disputes. The current situation suggests that the political offensive the exiles launched several years ago has been a tactical victory. The Tibetans' cause is acclaimed throughout the West, and the Dalai Lama was awarded the Nobel Peace Prize. Human rights groups have focused on Tibet and denounced Beijing for alleged violations against specific individuals and the entire Tibetan race. The U.S. Congress has adopted an activist, pro-Tibetan policy, passing legislation to provide funds for Tibetan refugees, create Tibetan-language Voice of America broadcasts, and take account of Tibet in its dealings with Beijing. Underlying this is the almost universal acceptance in the West of the exiles' cultural and political construction of modern history and the contemporary situation in Tibet. U.S. congressional leaders, for example, now talk of the ethnic Tibetan borderlands as if they were part of political Tibet, following the line taken by the Dalai Lama. And on the Tibetan side, the persistent nationalistic demonstrations and periodic riots have pushed Beijing to impose martial law and place a brake on the forward momentum of the reform policy, these actions in turn helping to radicalize the mass of Tibetans and inflame ethnic tensions. In this sense, Beijing has inadvertently played into the hands of the exile government.

But despite the exiles' successes, the peaceful solution to the Tibet question that the Dalai Lama and the exiles apparently desire seems farther away than at any other time since 1979. Tibet is firmly a part of the People's Republic of China, and the key international players still do not support the exiles' claims that Tibet was and should be independent. Time, moreover, does not appear to be on the exiles' side, since unlike the situation in South Africa or even Israel where the demographic reality does not favor the politically dominant group, China could easily swamp Tibet with large numbers of permanent Han settlers. The histories of Sikkim and Ladakh (absorbed by India) reveal with clarity the political vulnerability of sparse Tibetan populations vis-à-vis their more numerous ethnic neighbors.

Have Dharamsala and the Dalai Lama, therefore, really won a meaningful victory? If China disintegrates politically in the near future and, in the ensuing chaos, if Tibet gains its independence, then Dharamsala will, with justification, declare its strategy to have been successful. But short of this, even a major change in Beijing is unlikely to significantly affect the Tibetan question in the manner the exiles hope. The Tibetan exiles' interaction with the post-Tiananmen Chinese dissident community in the West, for example, has revealed that while these dissidents would like the Dalai Lama to join their ranks in opposing Beijing, they do not agree that Tibetans should have the right to self-determination. Like Beijing, they see Tibet as an inseparable part of China. This is also the policy of Taiwan, which firmly considers Tibet an integral part of China even though it is said to have clandestinely poured enormous sums of money into the exile community. The ethnic and territorial basis of the Tibet question transcends a particular form of government or a particular set of leaders.

It appears, therefore, that Dharamsala's strategy has really won only a Pyrrhic victory. It has secured large-scale sympathy and support in the West, but has not succeeded in protecting and fostering Tibetan culture in Tibet. Ironically, it has created a set of conditions under which the aspirations of Tibetans in Tibet will probably not be met. It may even result in Beijing deciding to marginalize Tibetan culture and promote the permanent immigration of Han settlers to the TAR. From this point of view, the 2 million Tibetans in Tibet are the losers of the confrontation between the Dalai Lama and Beijing during the 1980s. The lives of the Tibetan exiles have stayed constant or improved during this period, with some now coming to the United States on scholarships mandated by Congress, but Tibetans in Lhasa live under martial law and there is a danger that the important gains they recently won will be lost.

What of the future? The fate of Tibet and Tibetans appears now to be at a turning point. Whether Tibet will join Northern Ireland, Israel, and Lebanon as a region where unending reciprocal conflict and hatred consume the inhabitants is clearly the question for the 1990s.

Solving the Tibet question in the 1990s on one level requires terms that would be acceptable both to the Dalai Lama and the exiles and to Beijing. For the former, at the very least a workable compromise would require a substantial degree of political independence—a "one country, two systems" solution. This, however, is unlikely to be acceptable to Beijing, so barring the disintegration of the rule of the CCP in a manner analogous to recent events in Eastern Europe, it is implausible to expect a "political" solution to make meaningful progress in the near future. Thus, it is certain that the exiles will strive to keep their version of the Tibet question alive using the techniques they have successfully honed in the 1980s, or will even escalate their attack through more violent forms of protest.

However, although the prospect for rapprochement between the exiles and Beijing seems bleak, there is another solution advocated by many thoughtful people in Tibet that is worthy of serious consideration. This solution to the Tibet question involves conditions that would be acceptable, I think, to most Tibetans living in the TAR, but not necessarily to the exiles. It would create not a different political system, but rather considerably more cultural and ethnic autonomy—a TAR that is *homogeneous in population, language, and culture*. It is difficult to spell out precisely the form of such a solution, but clearly the changes required to produce it could not all be accomplished overnight. Generally speaking, it would require that within some fixed period of time Beijing withdraw from Tibet all Han engaged in administration and trade except those with special skills, such as doctors, engineers, and teachers. The Tibetan language would at the same time become the basic medium of communication in government, although Tibetan schools would continue to teach Chinese, and all higher-level cadres would have to be bilingual. This "ethnic" solution is not incongruent with the goals of Beijing's 1980 reform policy and would offer it a viable alternative to risking indefinite perpetuation (or escalation) of the current violence and unrest in Tibet.

Many Tibetans in Tibet believe such a program would gradually win the approval of the people in Tibet. In fact, this solution is not very radical, for in essence what would be required is to create an urban situation analogous to that extant in remote rural areas such as those of the nomads in Western Tibet. There would certainly be risks in this policy, but the present alternative of halfway measures seems even more fraught with risk. Such an "ethnic" solution might ultimately even be acceptable to the Dalai Lama, who, at 55 years of age, must worry about the future of his people after his death. He may himself not wish to return to Tibet without a "political" solution, but he might give his tacit blessing to such an "ethnic" policy as an interim measure while he and the exiles wait for that shift in the tide of history that will provide them the solution they really desire.

One key issue, however, is whether the West would support such a move. It is difficult to see how China could take the risk of enacting such dramatic reforms if they felt that influential Westerners would ignore this and continue to talk about a Tibetan "holocaust." Ironically, although China is insistent that Tibet is an internal issue and not the business of the United States or other countries, a key element in solving the Tibet question at this level appears to be the willingness of influential Westerners vigorously and publicly to support such a solution.

Only time will tell if China's leaders have the vision and energy to launch such a move, and, critically, whether Western scholars, politicians, and media leaders are willing to take a fresh and objective look at China's policy in Tibet and provide encouragement for Beijing to move in this direction. There is no simple answer to the Tibet question or questions, but it is clear that the level of debate in the West must go beyond the current partisan accounts to examine more thoroughly the world of the grays.

1989: A Chronology

January

11 To encourage elderly officials to retire, the Central Standing Committee of the Kuomintang (KMT) on Taiwan approves a plan to give members of the National Assembly and the Legislative Parliament a bonus if they agree to step down.

28 Panchen Lama, the second-ranking Tibetan religious leader, dies. He was the only ranking lama to accept Chinese sovereignty over Tibet and hold office in the Chinese government.

February

8 President George Bush makes a state visit to China. Chinese officials prevent Fang Lizhi from attending a dinner hosted by the president.

23 China's official news agency attacks a petition drive by dissidents seeking amnesty for China's political prisoners. The organizers hold a news conference to respond to the government charges. A four-member working group, "Amnesty 1989," is established, with a telephone number billed as a "hotline for democracy."

March

5 Intense rioting by pro-independence groups begins in Lhasa, Tibet.

6 Taiwan President Lee Teng-hui makes the first state visit to Singapore in 12 years.

8 Martial law is declared in Tibet. At least 12 persons have been killed and more than 100 wounded since the unrest began.

20 The Second Session of the Seventh National Party Congress meets in Beijing. Premier Li Peng tells the Chinese people to be "mentally prepared for a few years of austerity" amid rumors that he has displaced Zhao Ziyang as China's number-two leader.

21 Chinese leaders announce new restrictions on business including cutting investment loans to rein in growth and closing poor-quality production plants.

29 Tenth anniversary of imprisonment for political prisoner Wei Jingsheng. Chinese officials rule out the possibility of amnesty for political prisoners.

April

8 Yang Jing, a well-known pro-democracy campaigner who was sentenced to eight years in prison in 1981, is released.

15 Hu Yaobang, ousted Chinese Communist Party (CCP) general secretary and a leading advocate of change, dies. Within hours of the news, mourning wreaths and posters appear on several university campuses and at the Monument to the People's Heroes in Tiananmen Square. Students at Beijing University praise him and indirectly criticize his opponents who forced his resignation after student demonstrations in 1986–87.

16 Protesters mourning Hu Yaobang continue to appear and wreaths are again placed at the Monument to the People's Heroes in Tiananmen Square.

17 In support of Hu Yaobang and democracy, thousands of students march in Beijing and Shanghai

shouting slogans such as: Long Live Hu Yaobang! Long Live Democracy!

The focus of the demonstrations begins to shift to include calls for greater democracy, freedom of the press, and the open election of delegates to the National People's Congress (NPC). Students also request dialogue with government officials.

18 More than 10,000 people march to Tiananmen Square in a rally for democracy. Thousands of students stage a sit-in at the Great Hall of the People demanding repudiation of past official campaigns against liberalism, as well as freedom of the press, more money for education, and the abolition of regulations banning demonstrations. They also want leaders to reveal their incomes and reassess the career of Hu Yaobang.

Several thousand students then march to CCP headquarters and try to force their way in to see the nation's leaders. The area is cleared in the early morning hours by 1,000 police officers.

Minor demonstrations are reported in Shanghai.

19 Tens of thousands of people gather in Tiananmen Square. More than 10,000 march for the second time on the party headquarters, this time staging a sit-in demonstration. Police break up the protests.

20 China's government-controlled news agency sharply criticizes pro-democracy demonstrators and hints at a crackdown. Protests spread to Shanghai, Nanjing, and other cities.

21 After a government announcement closing Tiananmen Square to Hu Yaobang's memorial service, scheduled for the following day, more than 100,000 people pour into the square and camp overnight to prevent the government from sealing off the area.

22 Tens of thousands join the students while official memorial ceremonies for Hu Yaobang are held in the

Great Hall of the People. Chinese leaders observe the demonstrations from behind a wall of soldiers.

Demonstrations in Xian and Changsha turn violent as rioters attack and burn several vehicles and buildings.

23 Independent student councils are established and plans for the next round of protests are made. Students gain support from university professors and lecturers who sign letters that are sent to government officials.

Zhao Ziyang departs for a one-week official visit to North Korea.

24 Students at Beijing universities begin a class boycott, demanding dialogue with the government.

The CCP bans an issue of China's most independent newspaper, Shanghai's *World Economic Herald,* for unauthorized coverage of the protest movement and articles praising Hu Yaobang.

25 A secret Politburo meeting is called to discuss an editorial for the *People's Daily* and a possible crackdown on student demonstrations. Zhao Ziyang is absent from the meeting.

26 The *People's Daily* newspaper publishes an editorial that says the students are involved in a "planned conspiracy" and warns demonstrators to stop their protests. Fears of a crackdown are renewed.

Qin Benli, editor of the independent *World Economic Herald* in Shanghai, is suspended and the paper put under control of a CCP work team.

27 In response to the *People's Daily* editorial, more than 150,000 students, with wide support from people on the street, surge past police lines and fill Tiananmen Square chanting slogans calling for democracy.

28 Senior Politburo member Hu Qili tells major newspapers that they may report "the actual state of affairs." Li Peng urges students to return to class.

29 Senior Chinese officials meet with hand-picked university students and broadcast portions of the meetings on national television. Student protest leaders reject the meeting because the students were chosen by the official student union and not the Autonomous Students Union of Beijing Universities (ASUBU).

30 Zhao Ziyang returns to Beijing from North Korea.

May

2 Student leaders present the government with 11 conditions for talks, including demands that the dialogue be open to the press and public. A response is demanded by noon the following day.

Recent protests in several other cities, including Tianjin, Wuhan, Xian, Changsha, and Chengdu, are reported.

3 The government rejects the students' demands for talks.

4 The meeting of the Asian Development Bank (ADB) opens at the Great Hall of the People. Zhao Ziyang speaks positively about the student demonstrations with governors of ADB. Shirley Kuo, Taiwan's finance minister, attends the meeting, becoming the first Republic of China official to visit the Peoples's Republic of China since the Nationalists fled 40 years ago.

More than 300 journalists representing all of China's major official media demonstrate. They demand freedom of the press and the reinstallation of Qin Benli as editor of the *World Economic Herald*.

100,000 pro-democracy demonstrators force their way through police lines into Tiananmen Square on the 70th anniversary of the May Fourth Movement. Worker participation in the demonstrations grows, fueled in part by inflation and corruption.

Major demonstrations are reported in provincial cities across the country.

5 CCP chief Zhao Ziyang calls for dialogue. In response, classes resume at some Beijing universities. A minority of students resists the decision to return to class and calls for a continuation of the boycott.

6 Zhao Ziyang says that there is no need to fear reporting of student demonstrations by the press.

Another student petition demanding dialogue is issued.

9 More than 1,000 Chinese journalists from 30 news organizations sign a petition calling for greater freedom of the press and protesting the dismissal of Qin Benli.

11 In support of journalists' demands for greater freedom of the press, 5,000 students bicycle around Beijing. Overall, the Democracy Movement is slowing down.

13 More than 1,000 university students begin a hunger strike and set up an encampment in Tiananmen Square to press their demand for direct talks with government leaders. A new demand includes the retraction of the April 26 *People's Daily* editorial condemning the demonstrations.

14 Thousands of students continue to occupy Tiananmen Square through the night, blocking government plans to seal off the area before the arrival of Mikhail Gorbachev the following day. The hunger strikers, who now number 3,000, draw a crowd of 80,000 supporters.

15 Approximately 1,200 foreign journalists are in Beijing to cover the Sino-Soviet Summit.

The Sino-Soviet Summit commences, the first meeting between Chinese and Soviet leaders in 30 years.

A welcoming ceremony near Tiananmen Square for Soviet leader Mikhail Gorbachev is moved to the airport as crowds at the square swell and the government appears increasingly paralyzed by the demonstrations.

Yan Mingfu meets with student leaders for three hours; a possible reevaluation of the student-led movement is hinted at.

16 At the Sino-Soviet Summit, Gorbachev yields ground on key issues, agreeing to a pullback of Soviet forces deployed opposite China, steps toward a border settlement, and modest adjustment of political support for Vietnam. Discussions cover five areas: military pullbacks and reduction of tensions; enhanced economic and technical cooperation; pooling of information and experience on political and economic reform; upgrading of cultural, scientific, and intellectual contact; and foreign policy collaboration in East Asia.

Soviet and Chinese leaders formally announce the normalization of relations between their two nations.

Leading intellectuals issue a six-point manifesto with more than 1,000 signatures, supporting the students and advising the government to adopt democratic measures to cope with the political crisis.

More than 200,000 workers, students, and onlookers rally in and around Tiananmen Square.

Large-scale demonstrations are reported in Shanghai, Wuhan, Nanjing, and Guangzhou.

17 The students receive a predawn plea to leave the square from Zhao Ziyang, who says the April 26 editorial was too harsh. Students reject his appeal and hold mass marches that generate one million supporters in Beijing, including soldiers, police, and government workers. Demands increase for the resignations of Deng Xiaoping and Li Peng.

Gorbachev praises the students in Tiananmen Square, saying that the process of socialist reform is both painful and necessary.

Planned visits to the Beijing Opera and the Forbidden City by Gorbachev have to be canceled because of the continuing unrest.

18 One million people again take to the streets, ignoring the government's call for restraint.

Zhao Ziyang, Li Peng, and other government officials visit hospitalized hunger strikers in the early morning. Later in the day Li Peng issues a stern lecture to student leaders at a nationally televised meeting in the Great Hall of the People.

In Shanghai, Gorbachev ends his official four-day visit to China and returns to the Soviet Union.

19 A tearful Zhao Ziyang makes a predawn visit to Tiananmen Square urging the weakened hunger strikers to end their strike. Li Peng also visits the students briefly. The students agree to end the hunger strike. Rumors of military action are heard throughout the city.

20 The students change their minds about ending the hunger strike when Li Peng and President Yang Shangkun announce that the military will be deployed to end the student demonstrations and declare martial law. Troops attempt to enter the city but are blocked by thousands of defiant citizens who urge the troops not to use force and to join the movement themselves. Zhao Ziyang reportedly resigns.

Chinese authorities order foreign television news agencies to cut transmission of live news broadcasts. The military takes control of key newspaper offices and radio and television stations.

Deng Xiaoping travels to Wuhan for a special meeting of military leaders.

The U.S. Department of State issues a statement of regret that China ordered military action.

21 Nearly a half-million Hong Kong residents supporting the Democracy Movement in China protest in the streets.

Tens of thousands of people, defying martial law, stage a sit-in in Tiananmen Square. Residents occupy large areas of Beijing and prevent further troop movements in or out of the city. Protesters plead with the army not to use force on the people and hand out food and drink to the stranded soldiers.

The government on Taiwan openly condemns China's imposition of martial law.

Taiwan President Lee Teng-hui accepts the resignation of Prime Minister Yu Kuo-hwa, considered by many to be a political liability for the KMT in the coming December elections. Moderate Lee Huan is named as prime minister.

22 Subway and bus service in Beijing is suspended because of crowds in the streets.

Workers and students block advances by the army. It is rumored that the military is reluctant to enforce martial law. Intellectuals march in Beijing protesting the governments declaration of martial law.

Wan Li, chairman of the NPC, meets with Vice President Dan Quayle and Secretary of State James Baker and states that there will be no bloodshed in Beijing if demonstrators continue to exercise restraint.

Taiwan calls for economic sanctions against China. The Democratic Progressive Party (DPP) issues a statement supporting the students on the mainland and opposing the crackdown attempts.

23 Zhao Ziyang states that the April 26 *People's Daily* editorial should be retracted and that open dialogue between student demonstrators and leaders must occur on equal footing.

Seven former military commanders reportedly issue a letter objecting to the government's plan to move troops into the capital to suppress the Democracy Movement. The government's ability to implement the martial law order and to control the situation comes increasingly into question.

Satellite transmission of television news reports resumes for the first time since the declaration of martial law.

The portrait of Mao Zedong that hangs in Tiananmen Square is defaced by three men in the midafternoon. They are turned over to the police by angry students.

Wuer Kaixi is voted out as leader of the ASUBU after urging the students to withdraw from the square.

One million protesters again take to the streets.

24 About 70,000 military troops surround Beijing.

Wan Li cuts short his trip to the United States after meeting with President Bush.

The number of protesters in Tiananmen Square begins to dwindle. Many bus routes and subway lines reopen.

At midnight authorities once again halt foreign television transmissions.

25 Li Peng appears on national television, the first public appearance by any senior official since the declaration of martial law. He delivers a message that suggests that he and his allies are in complete charge of the government. The People's Liberation Army (PLA) confirms its support for Li Peng and martial law.

Some 10,000 Chinese journalists march in Beijing in support of the demonstrations.

26 Attacks on Zhao Ziyang intensify as he is accused of forming an anti-party clique. He is reportedly placed under house arrest.

Chen Yun delivers a speech indicating his support for Li Peng and Yang Shangkung.

27 At a press conference student leaders Wuer Kaixi, Chai Ling, and Wang Dan announce that the occupation of Tiananmen Square will end on May 30. Some students disagree, pledging to continue with large-scale demonstrations until Li Peng resigns. The number of students in the square drops significantly.

Wan Li speaks out in support of Li Peng, Yang Shangkung, and martial law.

28 After three somewhat quiet days in Tiananmen Square, 80,000 demonstrators march to the square. In a student vote, over half of the voters decide to continue the protests until June 20 when the NPC is scheduled to convene.

The Soviet Union announces that it will withdraw 50,000 troops from Mongolia over the next year and a half.

29 The Goddess of Democracy and Freedom, a 33-foot statue resembling the Statue of Liberty, is assembled by the students in Tiananmen Square. The statue draws large numbers to the square, restoring some of the movement's momentum.

30 About 2,000 students and workers protest in front of the Public Security Ministry.

The first arrests since the movement began include three workers' union leaders. They are released after two days of interrogation.

June

1 Student crowds in Tiananmen Square continue to shrink, with the majority of the remaining students from areas outside Beijing. Dissension within the student ranks becomes apparent and the movement appears on the verge of collapse.

2 One thousand unarmed troops march into Beijing, the largest military presence since the declaration of martial law.

3 In the pre-dawn hours, up to 5,000 unarmed troops try to reach Tiananmen Square on foot in an effort to end the student occupation but are turned back by huge numbers of students and citizens. Tensions rise in Beijing, and a number of confrontations between soldiers and civilians are reported. At 2:10 P.M. security forces fire tear-gas canisters in an effort to disperse crowds.

4 Chinese troops move in shortly after midnight to retake the center of the capital. At least several hundred people are killed as soldiers fire on the crowds and armed personnel carriers break through barricades erected by civilians. Many resist the occupation, attacking soldiers with metal and wooden poles, stones, and Molotov cocktails. Several trucks and personnel carriers are set ablaze, and a number of soldiers are reported killed. Students in Tiananmen Square itself are reportedly allowed to leave peacefully several hours after the fighting in the area around the square had begun. Sporadic gunfire continues throughout the day as enraged citizens taunt soldiers and the PLA tightens its grip on Beijing.

Violent clashes between demonstrators and police also erupt in Chengdu, where several hundred deaths are reported. Additional demonstrations are reported in Wuhan, Shanghai, and Shenyang as well as in Hong Kong and Macau.

President Bush, along with many European countries, publicly deplores the Chinese government's decision to use force to end the demonstrations in Beijing.

Fang Lizhi and his wife, Li Shuxian, take refuge in the U.S. Embassy in Beijing.

5 Periodic clashes are reported between civilians and soldiers. A second violent confrontation between police and civilians in Chengdu is reported.

Asian Development Bank president announces that the bank will stop lending to China until the situation returns to normal.

The Hong Kong stock market loses about 22 percent of its value, or $16.6 billion in U.S. currency, in the territory's biggest stock plunge since October 1987.

President Bush halts US$600 million worth of U.S. arms sales to China, suspends contact between the two nations' military forces, and orders a review of all requests for aid.

6 Amid rumors of a rift between army units, soldiers of the 27th Army take up what appear to be defensive positions in areas of the capital. Reports of confrontations between army units on the outskirts of Beijing are confirmed by Bush administration officials in Washington.

In Shanghai, several protesters blocking a main rail line are run down and killed. Angry demonstrators set fire to the train and beat the conductor and engineer. Continued demonstrations are reported in Wuhan.

7 Chinese troops fire on Jianguomenwei diplomatic compound. The United States orders the dependents of U.S. officials to leave China and urges all other Americans to do so as well. European nations follow suit.

Taiwan reopens telecommunication links with China for the first time in 40 years in order to combat China's news blackout.

8 Talk of civil war recedes as units of the 27th Army pull back from visible spots in the city and large numbers of trucks and troops enter the capital unobstructed.

In reference to U.S. sanctions, the Chinese government accuses the United States of meddling in internal affairs.

9 Li Peng appears on state television to praise soldiers who carried out the weekend crackdown, the first such appearance by a top leader since May 25.

Beijing University ends the school year one month early.

10 Chinese government announces the arrest of over 400 participants in the Democracy Movement, including student and labor organization leaders.

In Shanghai more than 100,000 people march in a tribute to those killed in Beijing on June 4.

11 A warrant is issued for the arrest of Fang Lizhi and Li Shuxian.

12 New regulations are announced banning unofficial pro-democracy and independent organizations.

BBC crews are arrested in Beijing.

13 China's state television broadcasts a list of 21 most-wanted student leaders who are reported to have gone into hiding following the June 4 crackdown.

Tiananmen Square reopens to traffic.

14 China expels two American journalists, Voice of America's Beijing bureau chief, Alan W. Pessin, and Associated Press's John E. Pomfret, accusing them of violating martial law.

A warrant is issued for the arrest of three leaders of the Beijing Autonomous Workers Union.

Ma Shaofang, Beijing student leader on the government's 21-most-wanted list, surrenders to police in Guangzhou.

Mass ceremonies in Taiwan publicly mourn those killed in Tiananmen Square.

15 Three Shanghai workers are sentenced to death for their involvement in a June 6 protest.

16 Two Chinese officials in the United States seek asylum.

Another student leader on the 21-most-wanted list, Yang Tai, is arrested in Gansu.

17 Eight workers and peasants are sentenced to death in Beijing for participating in the "counterrevolutionary riot" in the capital. Two men are arrested after firing on two soldiers, wounding one, at a military check point in Beijing.

Beijing issues new regulations for obtaining exit visas, making it more difficult for Chinese to travel abroad.

19 Beijing student leader Liu Gang is arrested in Hebei.

An opinion poll released in Hong Kong concludes that one out of every six Hong Kong Chinese plans to leave the colony by 1997. Less than half of those polled are content to stay in Hong Kong.

20 President Bush suspends high-level contacts between U.S. and Chinese government officials. The United States will take steps to postpone consideration of loan applications by China to international financial institutions. Chinese authorities announce the arrest of a sixth student leader.

21 Of 45 "common criminals" sentenced in Jinan, the capital of Shandong, 17 are believed to have been executed. No names are released.

Three workers convicted in Shanghai are executed. Secretary of State James Baker, Prime Minister Margaret Thatcher, and Australian Prime Minister Robert Hawke denounce China's execution of the three men from Shanghai.

22 Twenty-four people are reportedly executed, seven for their role in the "anti-government" protests, bringing the nationwide total since the June 4 crackdown to 27.

The U.S. House of Representatives votes unanimously to back President Bush's call for clemency for pro-democracy demonstrators and for an end to executions of those arrested.

Prime Minister Thatcher rules out trade sanctions against China.

23 The U.S. Congress introduces legislation to curtail sales of computers, weapons, and satellites to Beijing.

24 At the Fourth Plenum of the Thirteenth CCP Central Committee, Zhao Ziyang is stripped of all his posts, including that of general secretary of the Central Committee and first vice chairman of the Central Committee Military Commission. Jiang Zemin is elected general secretary and member of the Standing Committee of the Politburo. Song Ping and Li Ruihuan are also elected to the Standing Committee. Hu Qili is removed from all his posts with the exception of his seat on the Central Committee.

Italy and Belgium announce economic penalties against China.

25 The CCP calls for a purge of party members active in the Democracy Movement. Yan Mingfu is released from his job in the Secretariat, but remains on the Central Committee. Rui Xingwen, a close ally of Zhao Ziyang, also loses his job in the Secretariat.

29 U.S. House of Representatives votes 418–0 in favor of sanctions against China.

July

1 West Germany freezes more than US$110 million in development aid to China.

3 British Foreign Secretary Sir Geoffrey Howe, in an address to 250 Hong Kong officials, states that the British government will not give Hong Kong nationals the right to live in the United Kingdom.

8 U.S. Department of State waives sanctions against China in order to allow Boeing to sell four commercial jetliners to China; the decision was made by Secretary of State James Baker.

14 U.S. Senate votes 81–10 in favor of additional sanctions that include suspension for six months of

arms sales, high-level official visits, exports of sensitive equipment, and insurance and financing of American business in China by the U.S. Government's Overseas Private Investment Corp.

23 KMT and DPP primaries are held on Taiwan for the upcoming December 2 national election.

31 Zhou Yang, a leading literary arbiter in the CCP and former culture "czar," dies.

August

23 Ding Shisun is replaced by Wu Shuqing as head of Beijing University.

September

2 China announces that it will restrict the number of graduate students it sends to the United States.

13 Chinese courts sentence ten Tibetans to prison terms ranging from three years to life on charges of rioting and spying during pro-independence unrest in March.

14 General Agreement on Tariffs and Trade (GATT) resumes consideration of China's request to join.

Liang Xiang is dismissed as governor of Hainan province after being accused of using his power for personal gain.

18 Su Xiaokang, author of "River Elegy," is expelled from the CCP.

19 Four of Beijing University's departments considered too liberal for the communist orthodoxy—history, philosophy, administration, and international politics—are closed to new students.

October

2 Hsu Hsin-liang, an activist for Taiwan independence, is held in a detention center after illegally reentering Taiwan on September 27. Chen Wan-jen leads protest for amnesty for Hsu Hsin-liang.

5 The Dalai Lama, exiled Tibetan leader, wins the Nobel Peace Prize.

8 Hong Kong allows Yang Yang, a top Chinese swimmer who sought political asylum in Hong Kong, to leave for the United States. In reaction, China refuses to take back any of the illegal immigrants who left China for Hong Kong.

9 Taiwan and Liberia establish diplomatic relations.

10 China suspends formal relations with Liberia.

14 In protest against repatriation to Vietnam, 11,000 Vietnamese boat people in Hong Kong detention centers stage a hunger strike.

18 A series of major earthquakes rocks northern China. Twenty-nine people are reported killed and between 5,000 and 8,000 homes destroyed.

24 China agrees to resume normal border routines with Hong Kong.

28 China announces new regulations that would encourage the unemployed to establish private and collective enterprises in Beijing.

Richard Nixon visits China on a private fact-finding mission. Over the course of the next few days Nixon meets with Li Peng, Deng Xiaoping, and other top officials.

30 The Chinese government announces that martial law troops in Tiananmen Square will be replaced by armed police officers.

31 Beijing expels two Hong Kong members of the Basic Law Drafting Committee, Szeto Wah and Martin Lee, from the committee for their "antagonistic stand" against the Chinese government. Both are outspoken supporters of the Democracy Movement.

November

7 China reveals that it has shut down more than 1 million rural industrial collectives and forced the demise of 2.2 million private enterprises.

9 Deng Xiaoping resigns as chairman of the Central Military Commission, his last formal post in the CCP. Jiang Zemin is appointed to succeed him.

26 In an attempt to restore "a glow of revolutionary virtue to the national complexion," China starts a new campaign against the "six evils": prostitution, pornography, sale of women and children, narcotics, gambling, and profiteering from superstition.

30 President Bush vetoes legislation that would have allowed Chinese students to stay in the United States after the expiration of their visas.

Police are called into Hong Kong refugee camps to break up fighting between rival Vietnamese groups.

December

2 For the first time in 40 years, opposition parties can legally run for office in Taiwan elections. While the KMT maintains a clear majority, the opposition DPP wins top positions in 6 of the island's 21 counties and cities.

Nanchang motorcycle factory in Jiangxi Province becomes the first state-owned enterprise to go bankrupt.

10 Brent Scowcroft, National Security Adviser, and Lawrence S. Eagleburger, Deputy Secretary of State, visit Beijing, breaking the ban on high-level

exchanges with the Chinese. Their trip, not made public until after their arrival in China, was the second such trip this year. In July, shortly after a ban on high-level exchanges was issued, Scowcroft and Eagleburger secretly visited Beijing.

15 China devaluates its currency by 21.2 percent against the dollar, the first such action since 1986.

Glossary

Common Abbreviations.
ADB: Asian Development Bank
CCP: Chinese Communist Party
KMT: Kuomintang
NPC: National People's Congress
PLA: People's Liberation Army
PRC: People's Republic of China
ROC: Republic of China

Anti-Rightist Campaign. A campaign begun in 1957 aimed at suppressing "poisonous weeds" of dissent which had grown in response to the party's earlier call to "let a hundred flowers bloom."

Asian Development Bank (ADB). A multilateral financial institution based in Manila. Founded in 1966, it aims to raise funds from private and public sources for development purposes and to give technical assistance in development projects.

Chen Yun. Chairman of the Central Advisory Commission. Active in the CCP since the 1920s, Chen was an architect of the PRC's first Five-Year Plan and was influential in restoring order to the economy after the Great Leap Forward (1958–60). Although a close associate of Deng Xiaoping, he has been a critic of radical economic reform and political liberalization.

Cultural Revolution. A decade of turmoil and intraparty struggle initiated by Mao Zedong in 1966 and terminated by his death in 1976.

Democracy Wall. A wall near Beijing University where hundreds of posters were pasted in 1978 and 1979 calling for more freedom and democracy in China.

Democratic Progressive Party (DPP). The leading opposition party in Taiwan.

Deng Xiaoping. China's senior leader, who won international respect for achieving market-oriented reforms after the end of the Cultural Revolution. An old-time revolutionary, Deng was himself purged, first in 1966 and again in 1976, but returned to lead China's recovery in the 1980s. He retired in November from his last post as chairman of the Central Military Commission.

Dual Price System. A mixed pricing system in which certain goods are sold at two different prices: one a fixed price set by the state, the other determined by the market.

Fang Lizhi. Prominent PRC astrophysicist and the former vice-president of the University of Science and Technology in Anhui province. He was purged from the CCP in January 1987 for his outspoken views on democracy but continued to be an influential voice among Chinese intellectuals. He took refuge in the U.S. Embassy in Beijing following the spring 1989 crackdown.

Five Principles of Peaceful Coexistence. Intended to encourage peaceful relations between China and its neighbors. The principles are: respect for the sovereignty and territorial integrity of all states, nonaggression against other states, noninterference in internal affairs of other states, equality of relationships and benefits, and peaceful coexistence.

Four Basic Principles. Outlined in China's state constitution and used to distinguish between permissible and impermissible dissent. The principles are: adherence to socialism, the dictatorship of the proletariat, rule by the CCP, and Marxism-Leninism-Mao Zedong Thought.

Four Little Dragons/Four Tigers. Terms used to describe the four major newly industrialized economies in the Pacific region: Hong Kong, Taiwan, South Korea, and Singapore.

Four Modernizations. A development program first advocated by Zhou Enlai and finally implemented by Deng Xiaoping following the death of Mao and the fall of the Gang of Four in 1976. The term refers to the modernization of agriculture, industry, national defense, and science and technology.

Gang of Four. The ultra-left faction accused of exploiting power in the Cultural Revolution. In constant struggle with Deng Xiaoping and his reform-oriented supporters, the Gang was arrested and purged after Mao's death in 1976. The four are Jiang Qing (Mao

Zedong's widow), Wang Hongwen, Zhang Chunqiao, and Yao Wenyuan.

Hu Qili. CCP Politburo member from 1985 and Standing Committee member since the Thirteenth Party Congress in October 1987. He was in charge of party propaganda until 1989, when he was dismissed for showing sympathy toward the student Democracy Movement.

Hu Yaobang (1915–1989). General Secretary of the CCP from 1981–87. He was forced to resign in the wake of widespread student demonstrations demanding greater democratic freedoms. However, Hu was able to retain his seat in the Politburo. His death on April 15 sparked the demonstrations that eventually led to the June 1989 crackdown.

Iron Ricebowl. Term referring to the tradition of lifetime guaranteed employment at a fixed wage in the PRC.

Jiang Zemin. Former mayor and party secretary of Shanghai. He encouraged economic relations with the West but remained tough on dissent, firing *World Economic Herald* editor Qin Benli in April. In June he became general secretary of the Central Committee of the CCP and chairman of the Central Military Commission, replacing Deng Xiaoping in both positions.

Kuo, Shirley. Taiwan's finance minister and the first woman in the cabinet. She became the first Taiwan government official to visit the mainland when she attended the April ADB meeting in Beijing.

Kuomintang (Guomindang, Nationalist Party, KMT). The governing party in Taiwan. Organized in 1912 by Sun Yat-sen, the KMT became a major political force in China during the first half of the 20th century. In 1928 Chiang Kai-shek became chairman of the KMT and head of the ROC government in Nanjing, and he remained the leader throughout the civil war. In 1949 the KMT government on the mainland collapsed; Chiang and his followers retreated to Taiwan.

Lee Teng-hui. The first native Taiwanese to become president of the ROC and chairman of the KMT. Lee is an agricultural economist and former university professor with a Ph.D. from Cornell University. He was mayor of Taipei from 1978–81 and governor of Taiwan from 1981–84. He was vice president from 1984 until President Chiang Ching-kuo's death in 1988.

Li Peng. Member of the Standing Committee of the Politburo. At the Seventh National People's Congress in 1988 Li succeeded Zhao Ziyang as premier of the State Council. His study at the Moscow Power Institute, where he trained for a career as a hydroelectric engineer, has made him a key player in relations with the Soviet Union and Eastern Europe. Li played a crucial role in the economic retrenchment introduced in September 1988 and eventually became the chief spokesperson for conservatives in the government.

Li Ruihuan. Former carpenter and mayor of Tianjin, now a member of the Standing Committee of the Politburo. He is considered a hard-liner toward political dissent and a moderate in economic matters.

Liu Binyan. An investigative reporter and activist who was purged from the CCP in 1987 for his exposure of corruption in the Chinese political system.

May Fourth Movement. A political and cultural movement that gave birth to Chinese Marxism-Leninism, the CCP, and anti-imperialist nationalism. It was named for an outburst of patriotic fervor on May 4, 1919, against the Versailles Treaty, which granted Japan sections of Shandong province formerly controlled by the Germans.

National People's Congress (NPC). The supreme state legislative body in the PRC. The NPC consists of 2,700 delegates nominated by senior party leaders and elected for five-year terms by local people's congresses. It elects the president and vice president of the PRC, the State Council, Central Military Commission, and Supreme People's Court.

New Authoritarianism. Theory introduced by Chinese reformers which states that strong, nondemocratic authority is necessary to overcome the enormous obstacles to economic reform.

One Country, Two Systems. The PRC's proposal for reunification of Hong Kong and Taiwan with the mainland. As Special Administrative Regions, each would maintain its current system under the administration of the Beijing government.

Open Policy. A development strategy adopted in 1978 by the Chinese government based on active participation in the world market. Under this policy, the government has sought to increase technology transfer and foreign direct investment, become more active in international organizations, and encourage study and training abroad.

Politburo. The Political Bureau of the CCP. Elected by the Central Committee, it handles the daily running of the CCP as well as the major policy decisions of the party. Greatest power is embodied in its six-member Standing Committee.

Qiao Shi. Member of the Politburo Standing Committee since 1987. He has been a full member of the Central Committee since 1985 and was appointed vice premier of the State Council in 1986. In this capacity he oversaw the Departments of Public and State Security, Justice, and Civil Affairs. Qiao has a history of work in security matters and rarely lets his political views be known. According to Chinese officials, he did not advocate the use of force in dealing with the student demonstrations.

Qin Benli. Editor of the *World Economic Herald,* a Shanghai-based weekly newspaper that became known for its courageous defence of economic reform. He was removed in April 1989 for supporting the Democracy Movement.

Renminbi. The official Chinese currency.

"River Elegy" (*He shang*). A six-part Chinese television miniseries aired during the summer of 1988. Because it advocated the need for radical cultural change in order for China to compete with Western societies, it became a focus of official controversy and intellectual debate.

Special Administrative Regions (SARs). Areas allowed to maintain their own systems of government under the administration of the PRC.

Special Economic Zones (SEZs). Established in 1979 as part of an effort to attract direct foreign investment to the PRC and to test new economic policies. They enjoy economic freedoms not allowed in other parts of China.

Spratly (Nansha) Islands. A group of small islands in the South China Sea. Their ownership has been the focus of controversy and military conflict since the 1970s among the contending governments of Taiwan, the Philippines, Vietnam, Malaysia, and the PRC.

State Council. The executive arm of the PRC government, headed by the premier and composed of numerous ministries, commissions, and subordinate organizations.

Three Obstacles. The three primary impediments to normalization of Sino-Soviet relations according to Chinese policy. They were: Soviet support for Vietnam's occupation of Cambodia, the Soviet occupation of Afghanistan, and the presence of large Soviet troop concentrations along the Sino-Soviet border.

Tiananmen Square. The central square in Beijing and the largest public square in the world.

Township enterprises. Rural, nonagricultural enterprises owned by the township and operated outside the realm of central planning.

Wan Li. Chairman of the NPC. A solid proponent of reform, he is an old friend of Deng Xiaoping and apparently refused to oppose him in the wake of the crackdown.

Wuer Kaixi. A 21-year-old student from Xinjiang province who played a major role in the student demonstrations. He claimed he was not against the party itself but against the government's corruption and inefficiency. He is now in exile.

Xinhua (New China News Agency). The PRC's official domestic and international news agency.

Yang Shangkun. President of the PRC and vice-chairman of the Central Military Commission since November 1987. Yang has devoted much time to reform of the armed forces and modernization of China's national defense. However, it was he who announced that troops would be brought into Beijing, and he appears to be firmly behind Li Peng.

Yao Yilin. Member of the Standing Committee of the Politboro. Regarded as a competent technocrat and economist, Yao is credited with having implemented a number of significant economic reforms aimed at increasing efficiency of individual enterprises and stimulating new technological developments. However, he is still considered to favor central planning.

Yuan. Standard unit of currency in the PRC.

Zhao Ziyang. Premier of the State Council from 1980 until his appointment in 1987 as general secretary of the CCP and first vice chairman of the Military Affairs Commission. A trusted colleague of Deng Xiaoping, Zhao built a reputation at home and abroad as a reformist technocratic leader and a chief architect of the post-Mao reform program. He fell from power during the student demonstrations for being too sympathetic toward the students and disagreeing with the use of force in suppressing the demonstrations. He is reportedly under house arrest.

Appendix A: Leadership of the Chinese Communist Party as Elected at the 1st Plenum of the 13th Party Congress, November 2, 1987

General Secretary: Zhao Ziyang

Standing Committee of the Politboro (order as listed in official documents):
Zhao Ziyang, Li Peng, Qiao Shi, Hu Qili, Yao Yilin

Politboro of the Central Committee (by Chinese stroke order):

Wan Li
Jiang Zemin
Li Ruihuan
Yang Shangkun
Zhao Ziyang
Yao Yilin
Tian Jiyan
Li Peng
Li Ximing
Wu Xueqian
Hu Qili
Qin Jiwei
Qiao Shi
Li Tieying
Yang Rudai
Song Ping
Hu Yaobang
Alternate:
Ding Guangen

Secretariat of the Central Committee:
Hu Qili, Qiao Shi, Rui Xintgwen, Yan Mingfu; Alternate: Wan Jiabao

Central Military Commission of the Central Committee:
Chairman: Deng Xiaoping
First Vice Chairman: Zhao Ziyang
Permanent Vice Chairman: Yang Shangkun

New Leadership Determined at the 4th Plenum of the 13th Party Congress, June 24, 1989

General Secretary: Jiang Zemin

Standing Committee of the Politboro: Jiang Zemin, Li Peng, Song Ping, Yao Yilin, Qiao Shi, Li Ruihuan

Politboro of the Central Committee:

Wan Li	Tian Jiyun	Qiao Shi
Jiang Zemin	Li Peng	Li Tieying
Li Ruihuan	Li Ximing	Yang Rudai
Yang Shangkun	Wu Xueqian	Song Ping
Yao Yilin	Qin Jiwei	Alternate: Ding Guangen

Secretariat of the Central Committee:
Qiao Shi, Li Ruihuan, Yang Baibing, Ding Guangen; Alternate: Wan Jiabao

Central Military Commission of the Central Committee:
Chairman: Jiang Zemin
First Vice Chairman : Yang Shangkun
Vice Chairman: Liu Huaqing
Secretary General: Yang Baibing

Appendix B: Book and Articles on Tiananmen

Books

Cheng Chu-yuan, *Behind the Tiananmen Massacre* (Boulder, CO: Westview Press, May 1990).

Han Minzhu, ed., *Cries for Democracy* (Princeton: Princeton University Press, May 1990).

Fathers, Michael and Andrew Higgins, *Tiananmen: The Rape of Peking* (London: Independent, 1989).

Liu Binyan, with Ruan Ming and Xu Gang, *Tell The World* (New York: Pantheon, 1990).

Nathan, Andrew, *China's Crisis: Dilemmas of Reform and Prospects for Democracy* (New York: Columbia University Press, 1990).

Oksenberg, Michel and Marc Lambert, eds., *Beijing Spring, 1989* (Armonk, NY: M. E. Sharpe, 1990).

Roderick, John, ed., *China: From the Long March to Tiananmen Square* (New York: Henry Holt, 1990).

Saich, Tony, ed., *Perspectives on the Chinese People's Movement, Spring 1989* (Armonk, NY: M. E. Sharpe, 1990).

Salisbury, Harrison E., *Tiananmen Diary* (Boston: Little, Brown, 1989).

Simmie, Scott, and Bob Nixon, *Tiananmen Square* (Seattle: University of Washington Press, 1990).

Time magazine, ed, *Massacre in Beijing: China's Struggle for Democracy* (New York: Warner Books, 1989).

Turnley, D. and P. Turnley, *Beijing Spring* (New York: Stewart, Tabori, and Chang, 1989).

Yi Mu and Mark V. Thompson, *Crisis at Tiananmen* (San Francisco: China Books and Periodicals, 1989).

Yu Mok Chiu and J. Fran Harrison, *Voices from Tiananmen Square: Beijing Spring and the Democracy Movement* (Montreal: Black Rose Books, 1990).

Articles

Ching, Frank, "Red Star over Hong Kong," *World Policy Journal* (Fall 1989), pp. 657–66.

Dreyer, June Teufel, "The Role of the Military," *World Policy Journal* (Fall 1989), pp. 647–56.

Gottschalk, Marie, "The Failure of American Policy," *World Policy Journal* (Fall 1989), pp. 667–84.

Huan Guocang, "The Roots of the Political Crisis," *World Policy Journal* (Fall 1989), pp. 609–20.

MacFarquar, Roderick, "The End of the Chinese Revolution," *New York Review of Books*, July 20, 1989, pp. 8–10.

Solinger, Dorothy J., "Democracy with Chinese Characteristics," *World Policy Journal* (Fall 1989), pp. 621–32.

Zweig, David, "Peasants and Politics," *World Policy Journal* (Fall 1989), pp. 633–46.

Suggestions for Further Reading

Books

Byrd, William and Lin Qing Song, eds., *China's Rural Industry: Structure, Development, and Reform* (New York: Oxford University Press, 1990).

Ching, Frank, *Hong Kong and China: For Better or For Worse* (New York: The Asia Society and the Foreign Policy Association, 1985).

Dreyer, June, ed., *Chinese Foreign and Defense Policy* (New York: Paragon House, 1989).

Goldstein, Melvyn C., *A History of Modern Tibet, 1913–51: The Demise of the Lamaist State* (Berkeley: University of California Press, 1989).

Goldstein, Melvyn C., *Nomads of Western Tibet: The Survival of a Way of Life* (Berkeley: University of California Press, 1990).

Harding, Harry, *China's Second Revolution* (Washington, DC: Brookings Institute, 1987).

Harding, Harry, ed., *Chinese Foreign Relations in the 1980s* (New Haven: Yale University Press, 1984).

Kim, Samuel S., ed., *China and the World: New Directions in Chinese Foreign Relations*, 2nd ed. (Boulder, CO: Westview Press, 1989).

Lieberthal, Kenneth and Michel Oksenberg, *Policy Making in China: Leaders, Structures, and Processes* (Princeton: Princeton University Press, 1988).

Liu, Binyan, *People or Monsters?*, edited by Perry Link (Bloomington, IN: Indiana University Press, 1983).

McGurn, William, ed., *Basic Law, Basic Questions* (Hong Kong: Review Publishing, 1989).

Nathan, Andrew, *Chinese Democracy* (New York: Alfred G. Knopf, 1985; paperback, Berkeley: University of California Press, 1986).

Perkins, Dwight, *China: Asia's Next Economic Giant* (Seattle: University of Washington Press, 1986).

Rafferty, Kevin, *City on the Rocks: Hong Kong's Uncertain Future* (New York: Viking Press, 1989).

Richardson, Hugh E., *Tibet and its History*, 2nd ed. (Boston: Shambhala Press, 1984).

Schell, Orville, *Discos and Democracy: China in the Throes of Reform* (New York: Pantheon, 1988).

Spence, Jonathan, *The Search for Modern China* (New York: W. W. Norton, 1990).

Tai, Jeanne, tr. and ed., *Spring Bamboo: A Collection of Contemporary Chinese Short Stories* (New York: Random House, 1989).

Wesley-Smith, Peter and Albert Chin, eds., *The Basic Law and Hong Kong's Future* (Stoneham, MA: Butterworth Legal Publications, 1988).

Articles

Calhoun, Craig, "Beijing Spring: An Eyewitness Account," *Dissent* (Fall 1989).

Calhoun, Craig, "Revolution and Repression in Tiananmen Square," *Society*, Vol. 26, no. 6 (1989), pp. 21–38.

Chan, Anita, "The Challenge to the Social Fabric," *The Pacific Review*, Vol. 2, no. 2 (1989), pp. 121–131.

Chan, Anita, "China's Long Winter," *Monthly Review*, Vol. 41 (1990).

Dittmer, Lowell, "China in 1989," *Asian Survey* (January 1990), pp. 25–41.

Goldman, Merle, "Vengeance in China," *New York Review of Books* (November 9, 1989), pp. 5–9.

Lee, Benjamin and Leo Ou-fan Lee, "The Goddess of Democracy Deconstructed," *New Perspectives Quarterly* (Fall 1989), pp. 58–61.

Liu, Zaifu, "Chinese Literature in the Past Ten Years: Spirit and Direction," *Chinese Literature* (Autumn 1989).

Nathan, Andrew, "Politics: Reform at the Crossroad," in Anthony Kane, ed., *China Briefing, 1988* (Boulder, CO: Westview Press, 1989), pp. 7–26.

Rosen, Stanley, "The Chinese Communist Party and Chinese Society: Popular Attitudes toward Party Membership and the Party's Image," *Australian Journal of Chinese Affairs*, forthcoming.

Rosen, Stanley, "Public Opinion and Reform in the People's Republic of China," *Studies in Comparative Communism*, Vol. 22 (1989), pp. 153–70.

"Tiananmen 1989: A Symposium," *Problems of Communism*, Vol. 38 (1989), pp. 1–71 (contributions by Lowell Dittmer, Andrew Nathan, Andrew Walder, and June Dreyer).

Wakeman, Frederic Jr., "All the Rage in China," *New York Review of Books* (March 2, 1989), pp. 19–21.

Zha, Jianying, "Notes on the Emergence of a Counter-Public in China," unpublished paper (January 1990), Center for Psycological Studies, Chicago.

About the Contributors

Frank Ching is a freelance writer whose weekly column on Hong Kong politics appears in the *South China Morning Post*. He is the author of *Ancestors: 900 Years in the Life of a Chinese Family* (New York: William Morrow, 1988).

Melvyn C. Goldstein is Chairman of the Department of Anthropology and Director of the Center for Research on Tibet at Case Western Reserve University in Cleveland, Ohio. He is the author of *A History of Modern Tibet, 1913–51: The Demise of the Lamaist State* (Berkeley: University of California Press, 1989), and his articles have appeared in *National Geographic* and *National History*.

Leo Ou-fan Lee is Professor of Modern Chinese Literature in the Department of East Asian Languages and Cultures at the University of California, Los Angeles. His publications include *Land Without Ghosts: Chinese Impressions of America from the Mid-19th Century to the Present*, coauthored with R. David Arkush (Berkeley: University of California Press, 1989) and *Voices from the Iron House: A Study of Lu Xun* (Bloomington, IN: Indiana University Press, 1981), and he is the editor of *Lu Xun and His Legacy* (Berkeley: University of California Press, 1985)

Kenneth Lieberthal is Professor of Political Science and Associate of the Center for Chinese Studies at the University of Michigan. His most recent publication is *Policy Making in China: Leaders, Structures, and Processes*, coauthored with Michel Oksenberg (Princeton: Princeton University Press, 1988). He is currently a consultant to the U.S. Department of State and the World Bank.

Dwight H. Perkins is Director of the Harvard Institute for International Development and H. H. Burbank Professor of Political Economy at Harvard University. He is the author or coauthor of numerous books and articles on the economies of China, Korea, and East Asia and on general issues of economic development. He has served as a consultant to various governments in Asia, to the World Bank, and to the Ford Foundation.

Martin King Whyte is Professor of Sociology and Associate of the Center for Chinese Studies at the University of Michigan. He is the author of several works on grass-roots social organization in the People's Republic of China, including *Village and Family in Contemporary China* and *Urban Life in Contemporary China* (both coauthored with William Parish and published by the University of Chicago Press). His current research is based upon a survey of the mate choice process and marriage relations conducted in Chengdu in 1987.

Allen S. Whiting is Professor of Political Science at the University of Arizona in Tucson. Formerly he worked at the Rand Corporation and the U.S. Department of State. He is the author or coauthor of ten books, including *China Eyes Japan* (Berkeley: University of California Press, 1989).

Index

Academy of Chinese Culture, 90, 102
ADB. *See* Asian Development Bank
Africa, 79
Agricultural Bank, 12
Agriculture
  outputs, 28–29, 30(n4), 31, 32, 32n, 43
  reform, 10, 11, 27, 33(n9)
  See also Rural sector
Akihito, Emperor, 76
Anti-Rightist Campaign, 86, 104, 189
Arafat, Yasser, 80
Asian Development Bank (ADB), 173, 180, 189

Ba Jin, 94
Baker, James, 73, 177, 183, 184
Bankruptcy, 38–39, 53
Basic Law, 107, 108, 112–114, 117, 118, 121–123
Basic Law Drafting Committee (BLDC), 107, 111–114, 121–123
Bei Dao, 100
Birth control, 56, 75, 146n
BLDC. *See* Basic Law Drafting Committee
Borders
  Sino-Indian, 66
  Sino-Soviet, 65, 70, 175
  Sino-Tibetan, 130, 134
Bo Yibo, 20
Buddhism
  dissident monks, 157, 158–160, 163
  in Tibet, 134, 138, 143–144, 147, 155
Bureaucrats. *See* Chinese Communist Party
Bush, George, 2, 6, 8, 72–73, 169, 180, 181, 183, 187
Bush administration, 74, 187–188

Cambodia, 70, 78
Can Xue, 99
Carter, Jimmy, 149
CASS. *See* Chinese Academy of Social Sciences
CCP. *See* Chinese Communist Party
Ceausescu, Nicolae, 67
Chai Ling, 179
Change, 2–3, 7–8, 23, 47–49, 101–102. *See also* Culture; Foreign influence; Reform
Chen Xitong, 118–119
Chen Yong, 93
Chen Yun, 13, 20, 28, 32, 178, 189
Chiang Ching-kuo, 68
China International Trust and Investment Corporation, 16
Chinese Academy of Social Sciences (CASS), 92, 93, 96, 100, 104
Chinese Communist Party (CCP), 5, 65, 89, 195–196
  bureaucrats and reform, 54–55, 57
  political dominance of, 15, 19, 21, 86, 87, 94

in Tibet, 137, 139–141, 154, 156–157. *See also* Politics, Tibetan policy
See also Leadership; Political power
Cold war, 65
Communications. *See* Journals; Media
Competition, 35, 39–40, 57. *See aso* Market economy
Confucianism, 83–84, 90–91
Corruption, 4, 11–12, 13, 15, 16, 41, 57, 60, 86, 87
and dual-pricing, 37–38
Cradock, Sir Percy, 122
Credit, 12–13, 25, 42–43
Cultural Revolution, 1, 5, 9, 18, 27, 65, 189
and Chinese culture, 83, 85, 86, 87, 94
and Hong Kong, 108
in Tibet, 6, 139, 153
Culture
and change, 4–5, 47–48, 52, 55, 56
in Hong Kong, 116–117
self-reflection movement, 83, 85–105
Tibetan, 139, 143–144, 155, 166
See also Values
Curzon, Lord, 131

Dai Qing, 97
Dalai Lama, 13th, 132–134
Dalai Lama, 14th, 6
in exile, 138, 145–148, 150–151, 152, 157, 160–161, 167. *See also* Dharamsala
and Nobel Peace Prize, 68, 77, 129, 164, 186
and 17-Point Agreement, 136
Democracy Movement, 8, 9–10, 14–15, 84, 189. *See also* Demonstrations, 1989 spring; Tiananmen Square
Democratization, 59n, 109–114, 116–123
Demography
emigration, 108, 114–115, 126, 149
urbanization, 11
Demonstrations, 41, 83
in Hong Kong, 107, 116
1989 spring, vii, 1, 14–15, 49, 59–61, 84, 100–101, 163–164, 170–181, 182
Tibetan riots, 6, 129, 151–160, 162, 165, 169, 170
Deng Xiaoping, 108, 187, 198
and foreign relations, 76, 77, 80
and reform, 13, 15–16, 19–20, 22, 28, 49–50, 50n, 86
Tiananmen Square, 5, 14, 49, 62, 66, 84, 85, 176
and United States, 2, 7, 74
Dharamsala, 130, 140–142, 144–148, 150–151, 161, 164, 165–166
and Tibetan riots, 152, 156, 164
Donald, Sir Alan, 122
Dissent, 58–59, 60n, 62–63, 67, 165, 169. *See also* Buddhism, dissident monks; Instability; Intellectuals
Double Hundreds policy, 86
Dule Bookshop, 97
Du Rensheng, 34
Dushu (journal), 96, 102

Eastern Europe, 29, 45, 46, 47, 59n, 66–67, 72, 78, 164
Eastern Record (journal), 96–97
Economic growth, 10, 23, 27–28, 30, 30(n3), 43, 63n
decline in, 25, 170
in Tibet, 142
See also Economic reform; Economy
Economic reform, 1, 4, 10, 26–30, 71, 192
future of, 25–26, 44–46
results of, 2–3, 10–11, 40–44, 67–68
in rural sector, 31–34
social groups on, 50, 55–56
in Tibet, 153–154
in urban sector, 11, 34–40, 53(n5), 186
See also Reform

Economic sanctions, 44, 67–68, 73, 177, 183, 184–185
Economy
administrative controls, 16, 34, 35–36, 37–38, 44–46
Hong Kong, 115, 126–127
See also Economic growth; Economic reform
Education, 50, 125, 126, 162–163
Ehrman, William, 123–124
Emigration. *See* Demography
Employment, 39, 42, 53(n5), 126
security, 52–53, 62–63, 191
Energy, 27, 36
Ethnic conflict, 137, 153–155, 157, 163, 165
European Community, 66, 77
Exports, 29, 33, 33–34(n10), 34, 43

Fang Lizhi, 2, 12, 51–52, 72–73, 75, 97, 100, 169, 180, 182, 190
First Congress of the Federation for a Democratic China, 77, 103
First Five-Year Plan, 9, 18
Five Principles of Peaceful Coexistence, 69, 190
Ford, Sir David, 115
Foreign aid, 76, 80. *See also* Economic sanctions; Investment, foreign
Foreign exchange, 27, 32, 33, 34, 43, 43(n18)
Foreign influence
fear of, 5–6, 7–8, 21–22, 55, 68, 69, 82
on intellectuals, 86, 95–96, 101–102
reform and, 10–11, 22–23, 40–41, 47, 67, 167
See also Foreign relations
Foreign policy. *See* Foreign relations; Politics
Foreign relations, 5, 65–69, 75–80, 120, 121, 186
with Hong Kong, 80–81, 118–120, 186
and Open Policy, 10, 17, 21–23, 22(n8), 68–69, 82, 192
Sino-American, 2, 6–7, 65, 66, 72–75, 150, 158, 187–188
Sino-Soviet, 1–2, 22(n8), 65, 69–72, 193–194
with Taiwan, 68, 81–82, 186
See also Politics
Four Basic Principles, 190

Gandhi, Rajiv, 78
Gang of Four, 84, 86, 153, 190
Gan Yang, 93–94, 96, 100
GNP. *See* Gross national product
Gorbachev, Mikhail
1989 Sino-Soviet summit meeting, 1, 2, 13, 14, 66, 69–70, 174–176
and reform, 66–67, 72
Grain, 29, 31–34, 32n, 33(n8), 33–34(n10), 43
Great Britain
Basic Law, 114, 120–123
Hong Kong nationalities issue, 114–115, 118, 120, 121
Joint Declaration, 108–111, 149
and Tibet, 131–132, 133–135, 150
and Vietnamese refugees, 124
Great Leap Forward, 9, 18
Gross national product (GNP), 25, 30, 30(n3), 43
Group of Seven, 76, 77
Guo Fengmin, 126
Gyalo Thundrup, 140

Hainan Reportage, The (journal), 97
Hangzhou writers conference, 98
Han Shaogong, 99
Havel, Vaclav, 85
He Jingzhi, 104
He Xin, 104
Hong Kong
autonomy, 107–109, 112, 114, 126–127, 192
culture, 116–117
economy, 115, 126–127
infrastructure, 125–126

nationalities issue, 114–115, 118, 120, 121, 184
political structure, 109–114, 117–118, 120–123
repatriation issue, 123–124
and Tiananmen Square, viii, 5–6, 80–81, 107, 116, 117–120, 127, 177, 181, 183
and Vietnamese refugees, 124–125, 186, 187
Hong Kong Alliance in Support of the Patriotic Democratic Movement in China, 117, 118, 119
Hong Kong People Saving Hong Kong, 118
Howe, Sir Geoffrey, 109, 115, 120–121, 184
Hsu Hsin-liang, 186
Human rights, 72, 75, 113
in Tibet, 129, 138, 146, 146n, 148, 150, 151, 157, 164–165
Hu Qili, 172, 184, 191
Hurd, Douglas, 121, 122, 123
Hu Yaobang, 2, 4, 14, 60, 84, 141, 170, 191

Ideology, 5, 85–96, 98–100, 103–104
Income, 10, 26, 27, 33(n8)
and reform, 54, 56
rural, 28, 42, 56
India, 66, 78–79, 150
Indonesia, 78
Industry, 27–28, 35
output, 25, 30, 30(n5), 43
See also Urban sector
Inflation, 16, 25, 26, 36, 37, 42, 56
and unrest, 11–13, 15, 41, 60
See also Prices
Infrastructure, 125–126, 142–143
Instability, 9, 12–13, 33, 62–63
and reform, 40–42, 58–59, 138
See also Demonstrations; Ethnic conflict; Reform, popular support for
Intellectuals, 4–5
and cultural self-reflection, 85–102
in exile, 103–105
and unrest, 12, 50–52, 83–84, 102–103, 175, 177
Investment, 11, 31, 33, 34, 42
foreign, 33, 34, 43, 44, 67–68, 69, 76, 126–127
in Tibet, 143
Ito, Masayoshi, 76–77

Japan, 66, 75–77
Jiang Zemin, 4, 16, 61, 76, 119, 184, 187, 191
Jia Pingwa, 99
Jin Guantao, 88, 96
JLG. *See* Sino-British Joint Liaison Group
Journals, 96–98, 101. *See also* Media

Kim Il-Song, 78
Kissinger, Henry, 74
Kohl, Helmut, 149
Kuo, Shirley, 173, 191

Labor, 31, 31n, 42, 45
Language, 94–95, 99
Tibetan, 144, 155, 162–163, 167
Laos, 78
Leadership, 195–196
and change, 2–4, 5
divisiveness within, 13, 15, 59, 61, 82, 102
popular support for, 13, 48–49, 57, 57n, 62–63, 88. *See also* Reform, popular support for
succession, 19, 20–21
See also Chinese Communist Party; Political power
Lee, Martin, 119, 121–122, 127, 187
Lee Huan, 177
Lee Teng-hui, 68, 177, 191
Lhasa, 6, 140, 149, 163, 164
riots in, 129, 151–160
Lhasa Convention of 1904, 132
Liang Xiang, 185
Liberation Army Daily (journal), 69

Liberia, 186
Lin Yü-sheng, 90–91
Li Peng, 170, 172, 176, 178, 181, 192
and foreign relations, 71, 72, 76, 79, 80, 82
and Hong Kong, 119
and reform, 4, 13, 15
Li Ruihuan, 16, 192
Li Shuxian, 182
Literature, 92–93, 95–96, 98–100
Tibetan, 143
Li Tieying, 79
Li Tse-chung, 120
Li Tuo, 98, 99
Li Zehou, 91, 93, 104
Liu Binyan, 86, 87, 104, 192
Liu Gang, 183
Liu Xiaobo, 95
Liu Zaifu, 91–93, 92(n3), 94, 95, 104
Lukyanov, Anatoly, 70

MacLehose, Sir Murray, 108
Mao Zedong, 1, 5, 41, 54, 86, 138
and foreign relations, 65, 82
and political power, 18, 18(n5), 19
Market economy, 30, 34–35, 38, 40, 44–46, 142
and management goals, 38–39
Markets, 28, 32, 33, 142
May Fourth Movement, 4, 52, 192
and Democracy Movement, 83, 84, 88, 90
and literary revolution, 85–86, 91
Media, 118, 143, 151, 173, 174, 176, 178
foreign, 67, 174, 178, 181, 182. *See also* Voice of America
See also Journals; New China News Agency; "River Elegy"
Middle East, 80
Military
on reform, 52, 54
and Tiananmen Square, 176, 177–178, 179–180, 181
See also People's Liberation Army
Modernization, 4, 65–66, 88, 90
Four Modernizations, 190
and Tibet, 134, 137
See also Reform
Mongolia, 164, 179
Mo Yan, 99

Nationalism, Tibetan, 148, 149, 151–153, 154–155, 157, 159, 162, 164, 165
National People's Congress (NPC), 192
National security, 66, 67
NCNA. *See* New China News Agency
New China News Agency (NCNA), 120, 123, 126, 194
New Enlightenment (journal), 97
New Hong Kong Alliance, 122
Nixon, Richard, 7, 74, 186
North Korea, 77–78
NPC. *See* National People's Congress

Panchen Lama, 159, 169
Peasantry. *See* Rural sector
Peng Zhen, 20
People's Daily (newspaper), 67, 79, 87, 93n, 119, 121
April 26 editorial, 2, 14, 172
People's Liberation Army (PLA), 66, 178
in Tibet, 135–136, 137, 138
See also Military
PLA. *See* People's Liberation Army
Police, 52, 54
Politburo, 16, 193. *See also* Leadership
Political power
experts versus bureaucrats, 51–52, 54–55
individuals versus institutions, 10, 17–21, 23
See also Chinese Communist Party; Leadership
Political reform
Deng and, 19–20, 50n

pressures for, 51–52, 59, 72, 86. *See also* Demonstrations
realities of, 2, 5, 49–50, 58–59, 70, 71
See also Reform
Politics
and culture, 83–90, 94, 99–105
and foreign relations, 65, 66–69, 75
Hong Kong, 5–6, 118–120, 126–127, 192
Tibetan policy, 130–131, 132–146, 149–150, 153–155, 158–159, 161–163, 164, 167
See also Foreign relations
Population growth, 11, 32n. *See also* Demography
Prices, 4, 11(n2), 25–26, 42, 42(n15)
dual-price system, 36–37, 190
market-controlled, 35, 41
See also Inflation
Privatization, 31, 39, 53–54. *See also* Economic reform

Qian Qichen, 70–71, 79
Qiao Shi, 67, 162, 193
Qin Benli, 172, 173, 174, 193
Quayle, Dan, 177

Reagan administration, 148
Reform
future of, vii, 1, 15–16, 62–63
goals of, 7–8, 10
popular support for, 3–4, 12, 49–57
results of, 9, 17, 47–49, 58–59
in Tibet, 137–139, 141–145, 149–150, 154–155
See also Economic reform; Political reform
Religion, 48
Tibetan, 137, 139, 143–144, 155
See also Buddhism; Confucianism
Ren Rong, 139, 140, 141
Repression, 8
on Hong Kong, 107, 118
in Mao period, 53(n4), 138–139
relaxation of, 48, 56, 58
and Tiananmen Square, vii, 2, 15, 16–17, 61–62, 74, 104–105, 165, 182–183, 185, 187
Resources, 35, 38
Riots. *See* Demonstrations
"River Elegy" (mini-series), 88–90, 91, 94, 185, 193
Rural sector
reform in, 28, 29, 30(n4), 31–34, 42, 54, 194
support for reform, 56–57, 57n, 93
Tibetan, 138, 139, 142, 163

Saudi Arabia, 80
Seventeen-Point Agreement for the Peaceful Liberation of Tibet, 135–136, 137, 138
Shi Tiesheng, 99
Simla Compromise, 133–134, 135
Sino-British Joint Declaration on the Question of Hong Kong, 107, 109–111, 114, 115
Sino-British Joint Liaison Group (JLG), 120
Social groups
and demonstrations, 59–61, 60n
and reform, 49–57, 49n, 63
See also Intellectuals
South Asia, 78–79
South Korea, 45
Soviet Union, 179
relations with, 1–2, 22(n8), 65, 69–72, 78, 193–194
See also Gorbachev, Mikhail
Special Economic Zones, 34, 76, 193
Spratly Islands, 66, 193
Standards of living, 11, 46, 142
Su Xiaokang, 185
Szeto Wah, 119, 121–122, 127, 187

Taiwan, 165–166, 169, 177, 181, 185, 187, 191
relations with, 68, 79–80, 81–82, 186

Takeshita, Noboru, 75, 76
Tang Yijie, 90
Taxes, 38, 142
Technology, 7, 21–22, 27
Thailand, 78
Thatcher, Margaret, 109, 121, 183
Third Plenum of the Twelfth Central Committee, 29
Third World, 68, 77–80
Tiananmen Square, 1, 194
  demonstration in, vii, 1, 2, 5, 14–15, 60, 61, 66, 83, 84, 85, 102–103, 116, 170–180, 182. *See also* Demonstrations, 1989 spring
Tian Jiyun, 13
Tibet
  instability in, 129, 151–160, 162, 163, 166, 169, 170
  political status of, 130–138, 139–141, 145–151, 160–161, 164–167
  post-Mao reforms, 141–145, 149–150, 161–163
  relations with, viii, 6, 66, 75
  socialist reforms, 137–139
Tibetan exiles. *See* Dharamsala
Tibetan Youth Association, 147, 161
Tibetan Youth Congress, 161
Tibet Autonomous Region (TAR), 130, 138, 166–167. *See also* Tibet
Today (journal), 98, 100
Tourism, 33, 43, 48, 126
  in Tibet, 143, 154, 162
Trade, 10, 30, 43–44, 69, 81, 131
Transportation, 36, 177
Tu Wei-ming, 90

Unemployment, 13, 39, 45. *See also* Employment, security
United Democrats of Hong Kong, 127
United Nations, 149
United States, 176, 181
  and Hong Kong, 124, 125
  relations with, 2, 6–7, 65, 66, 72–75, 150, 183, 187–188
  and Taiwan, 68
  and Tibet, 148, 150–151, 152, 156, 157–158, 165, 167
  See also Bush, George
Unrest. *See* Demonstrations; Instability
Urban sector
  reform in, 29–30, 34–40, 52–56
  in Tibet, 142

Values, 41, 52
  Sino-American collision of, 73, 75
  Tibetan, 134, 139, 143–144, 155
  and Westernization, 21–22, 23, 55
  See also Culture
Vietnam refugees, 124–125, 186, 187
Voice of America, 67, 73–74, 151, 165, 182

Wang Dan, 102, 179
Wang Meng, 87, 104
Wang Zengqi, 87
Wan Li, 28, 141, 177, 178, 179, 194
Wan Runnan, 103
Wei Jingsheng, 100, 170
Westernization, 8, 52, 55, 84, 90. *See also* Foreign influence; Values
Wilson, Sir David, 115, 125
Women, 53, 53(n5)
Women's Federation, 53
World Bank, 73, 77
World Economic Herald (newspaper), 172, 173
Writers, 85, 86–88, 92–96, 97–100, 101
Wuer Kaixi, 77, 118, 178, 179, 194

Xinhua. *See* New China News Agency
Xu Jiatun, 111, 120

Yan Jiaqi, 77, 84, 118
Yan Mingfu, 175, 184
Yang Jing, 170
Yang Shangkun, 80, 81, 176, 194
Yang Tai, 182
Yang Yang, 123, 186

Yao Xueying, 93
Yao Yilin, 13, 194
Youde, Sir Edward, 110
Yu Hua, 99
Yu Kuo-hwa, 177

Zhao Ziyang, 194
  and foreign relations, 72, 77–78, 110
  house arrest of, 15, 20, 61, 103, 107, 178, 184
  and 1989 spring demonstrations, 172, 173, 174, 175, 176, 177
  and reform, vii, 3, 4, 13, 29, 34, 59, 93, 93n
Zhaxi, Dawa, 99
Zheng Tuobin, 76
Zheng Wanlong, 99
Zhou Enlai, 1, 84
Zhou Nan, 116, 120
Zhou Yang, 185
Zhuozhou conference, 93, 93n